2016
中国金融市场发展报告

CHINA FINANCIAL MARKET DEVELOPMENT REPORT

中国人民银行上海总部
《中国金融市场发展报告》编写组

中国金融出版社

责任编辑：童祎薇
责任校对：孙　蕊
责任印制：裴　刚

图书在版编目(CIP)数据

2016中国金融市场发展报告（2016 Zhongguo Jinrong Shichang Fazhan Baogao）/中国人民银行上海总部《中国金融市场发展报告》编写组编.—北京：中国金融出版社，2017. 5

ISBN 978-7-5049-8888-1

Ⅰ.①2… Ⅱ.①中… Ⅲ.①金融市场—研究报告—中国—2016 Ⅳ.①F832.5

中国版本图书馆CIP数据核字（2017）第108130号

出版
发行 中国金融出版社

社址 北京市丰台区益泽路2号

市场开发部 (010)63266347，63805472，63439533 (传真)

网上书店 http://www.chinafph.com (010)63286832，63365686 (传真)

读者服务部 (010)66070833，62568380

邮编 100071

经销 新华书店

印刷 北京市侨友印刷有限公司

装订 平阳装订厂

尺寸 210毫米×285毫米

印张 11. 25

字数 214千

版次 2017年5月第1版

印次 2017年5月第1次印刷

定价 120.00元

ISBN 978-7-5049-8888-1

Committee 编写委员会

主　任：孙　辉　纪志宏

副主任：吴水平

成　员（按姓氏笔画排序）：

马贱阳　王红霞　王振营　冯润祥　匡小红　杜要忠
邹　澜　沈　伟　宋钰勤　张晓刚　张翠微　陈刚明
陈建平　陈晓升　荣艺华　徐晓岚　谢　多

执笔并统稿：

陈晓虹　朱永行　杨　婕　叶可松

其他执笔人（按姓氏笔画排序）：

王　莹　王　然　王永涛　王丽洁　王雯珠　边宇卒
邢莹莹　向祥华　刘　胤　刘　彦　刘华伟　闫丽娟
闫晓梅　孙　钰　孙　凌　李　霖　李良松　李冀申
邹　江　邹　琼　邹春昊　汪办兴　张　璨　陆媛媛
陈光新　周永坤　郑凌云　胡迎春　祝　佳　袁沁敔
徐　浒　高　飞　郭　芳　唐　烈　黄　伟　曹媛媛
龚　芳　常鑫鑫　董　明　蒋健蓉　程南雁　焦　琳
曾令美　曾梓梁　谢国晨　戴　赜　蹇　娜

英文翻译：

王丽洁　叶可松　王　莹　徐　浒　江　舟

Contents 目 录

2016 中 国 金 融 市 场 发 展 报 告
CHINA FINANCIAL MARKET DEVELOPMENT REPORT 2016

第一章 总 论

2016年，在全球经济复苏势头趋缓、国内经济发展面临改革艰巨任务的内外环境下，国民经济在稳定运行的基础上呈现出积极向好的势头。中国金融市场加快完善制度建设、拓展市场深度和广度、加强风险防控管理、推动市场开放创新，在推进供给侧结构性改革、优化资源配置、提升经济发展实效等方面发挥了积极作用。

一、2016年中国金融市场发展的宏观环境分析

（一）国际经济与金融形势

2016年，全球经济增速有所下滑，多数经济体经济活动在下半年开始增强。国际金融市场经历年初大幅下跌、“黑天鹅”事件频发后，市场信心逐渐恢复，总体保持上行态势；伴随着世界经济运行中的积极因素增多，原油等国际大宗商品价格全面反弹。

1. 2016年全球经济复苏势头趋缓

（1）发达经济体经济复苏动力整体有所下降，新兴市场经济体经济企稳回升。

美国经济增长动力明显下降。初步数据显示，2016年，美国经季节调整的实际GDP平均增长1.6%，大幅低于上年的2.6%，但下半年经济增速反弹至1.8%。上半年，欧元区经济下行压力继续增大，下半年经济逐步企稳，全年增长1.7%，略低于上年的1.9%。上半年，日本经济增速明显下滑，同比增长0.6%，第三季度实际GDP同比增长1%。英国2016年下半年GDP同比增长2.2%，超出市场预期。多数新兴市场经济体经济下行压力依然较大但触底回升势头比较明显。前三个季度，巴西和俄罗斯经济萎缩程度由5.8%和3.8%分别缩小至2.9%和0.4%。南非经济从第二季度开始由负转正，第三季度同比增长1.1%。印度经济继续保持较快增长，前三个季度实现增长7.4%。

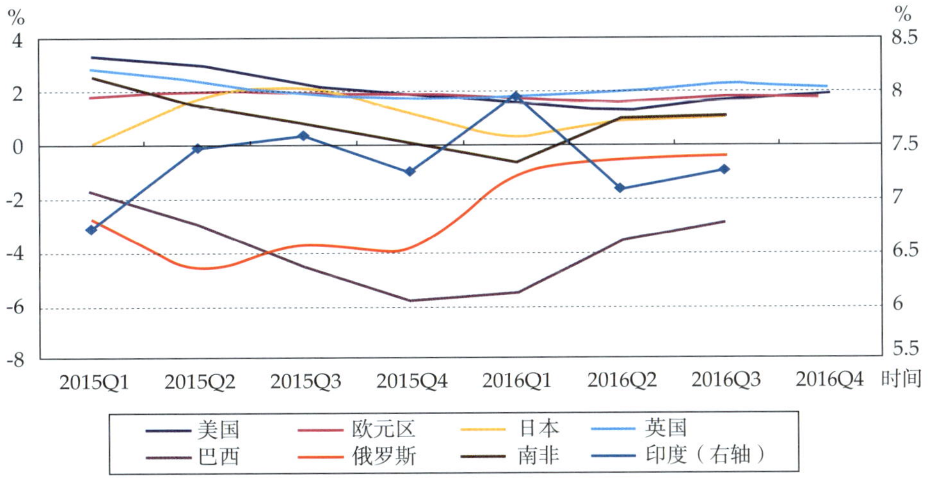

注：俄罗斯、印度、巴西实际GDP增长率未经季节调整。

资料来源：路透DATASTREAM。

图1-1　2015—2016年主要经济体经济增速

（2）全球贸易增长乏力，直接投资明显下滑。

2016年，全球经济增长乏力，尤其是主要新兴市场经济体经济下行压力依然较大，显著影响全球贸易。世界贸易组织（WTO）下调全球贸易增长预测值至1.7%，成为2009年以来的最低增速。第一季度全球贸易活跃程度的领先指标波罗的海干散货指数（BDI）延续跌势至290，下半年开始逐渐反弹，全年平均值为676，较上年下降约6%。2016年上半年，全球对外直接投资（FDI）仅7 930亿美元，环比下降5%。流入经济合作与发展组织（OECD）的FDI环比增长14%至5 680亿美元，而OECD对外直接投资则环比下降16%；发达经济体成为FDI主要接受国，但对外直接投资明显下降。多数国家FDI流入均大幅下跌，其中巴西环比下降20%至290亿美元，印度环比下降20%至173亿美元，南非环比下降45%至13亿美元，印度尼西亚环比下降28%至63亿美元。

（3）国际原油和大宗商品价格全面反弹。

虽然全球经济增长依然乏力，但由于前期下跌较多，2016年，大宗商品价格全面反弹。以美国西得克萨斯轻质原油（WTI）衡量的国际原油价格在2016年初一度跌破27美元/桶，自2月中旬起原油价格开始反弹，11月美国大选后美元走强，带动原油价格一度小幅下跌；2016年底，产油国最终达成为期半年的减产协议，原油价格应声大涨；截至2016年底，WTI收报53.72美元/桶，全年上涨44%。伦敦市场黄金、白银、铂金价格全年分别上涨9%、16%和3.5%；伦敦市场铝、铜、镍价格分别上涨13.6%、17.4%和13.5%。农产品价格多数涨幅较大，与年初相比，棉花价格上涨12.7%，糖价格上涨28.6%。彭博大宗商品价格指数较年初上涨11.8%，升至177。

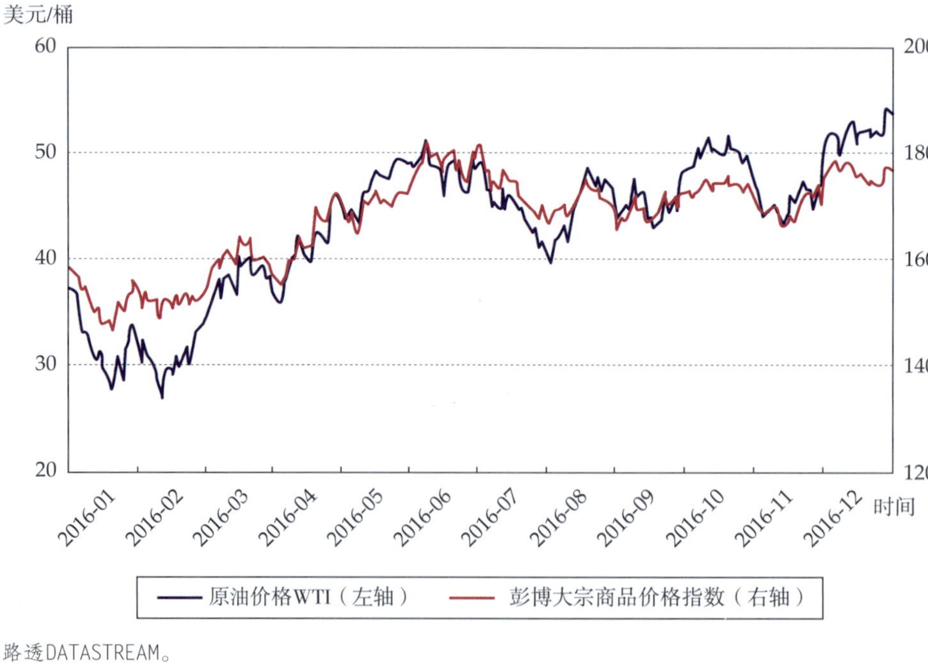

资料来源：路透DATASTREAM。

图1-2 2016年原油和大宗商品价格走势

2. 国际金融市场延续波动行情

（1）主要经济体货币政策以宽松为主，但分化更加明显。

2016年，美国经济保持温和复苏，劳动力市场和通胀状况继续改善，美联储全年仅在12月加息一次，加息幅度为25个基点，同时维持了本金再投资政策，显示对加息保持谨慎态度。欧洲中央银行和英格兰银行则加大了货币政策宽松力度。欧洲中央银行将存款便利利率由-0.3%下调至-0.4%，两次延长购债时间，保持资产购买规模在600亿欧元以上。为应对“脱欧”可能造成的负面影响，英格兰银行下调基准利率25个基点，并将资产购买计划存量增加600亿英镑至4 350亿英镑。包括引入负利率政策、扩大基金购买规模、采用“附加收益率曲线控制的量化和质化宽松政策（QQE）”的货币政策新框架、通胀超调承诺等措施在内，日本货币政策宽松度接近极限。新兴市场经济体经济下行压力有所增大，多数国家保持宽松的货币政策格局。

（2）全球股市先抑后扬，外部冲击频现。

年初，全球金融市场风险急剧上升，各国股市普遍下跌，跌幅在10%左右，部分国家接近20%，自3月开始，市场投资者信心有所恢复，全球股市逐步触底反弹。其间，英国“脱欧”公投和美国大选事件多次冲击全球金融市场，全球主要股指均反应激烈，多次经历短暂大幅震荡行情。主要新兴市场方面，俄罗斯MICEX指数、印尼IDX指数、印度IBOMESE指数2016年分别上涨27%、15.3%和3.2%，南非JSE指数微跌0.08%。拉美主要国家经济金融状况改善，股市大幅上涨，阿根廷MERVAL指数全年上涨45%，秘鲁利马股票综合指数全年上涨58%。

注：以2016年年初为基准。

资料来源：路透DATASTREAM。

图1–3 2016年主要经济体股票指数涨幅走势

（3）多数经济体利率水平总体下行，年末发达经济体国债收益率走高。

多数经济体复苏进程缓慢，利率水平总体下行。日本10年期国债收益率于2月底正式进入负利率区间并维持9个月，最低达到-0.295%。3月，欧央行进一步下调政策利率，在6月底英国公投“脱欧”后，投资者避险情绪上升，德国10年期国债收益率也进入负利率区间并维持了近4个月。11月初，美国国债收益率飙升，带动发达经济体国债收益率显著走高。以10年期国债收益率为例，12月末，美国为2.4467%，英国为1.2403%，日本为0.0481%，德国为0.1084%，法国为0.6853%；与2015年底相比，除美国上升18个基点外，其他发达经济体分别下降72个、23个、53个和30个基点。

资料来源：路透DATASTREAM。

图1-4 2016年主要发达经济体10年期国债收益率走势

（4）主要经济体货币汇率以周期性调整为主，外部事件影响显著。

年初，除日元成为国际金融市场主要避险资金外，多数货币兑美元汇率出现贬值，随着市场出现积极信号，全球外汇市场逐步趋于稳定。全年来看，主要经济体货币兑美元汇率以周期性调整为主基调，前期贬值较大的货币以升值为主，前期升值较大或对美元币值稳定的货币以贬值为主。英国公投“脱欧”事件超出市场预期，英镑大幅贬值，截至2016年末，英镑兑美元汇率贬值16%。美国大选改变了日元汇率上升走势，日元基本回吐了前期的升值幅度，截至2016年末，日元兑美元汇率由最高的升值20%回落至升值3%。前10个月，欧元对美元升值幅度在3%左右，美国大选后，欧元显著贬值，全年贬值3%。

巴西、俄罗斯、南非等三国货币汇率在

上年大幅贬值的基础上，2016年对美元显著走强，全年分别升值22%、20%和13%；印度卢比对美元全年贬值约2.5%，小于上年贬值幅度。在东盟主要新兴市场经济体中，前期印尼卢比、马来西亚林吉特对美元由上年的大幅贬值逐渐走强，最高分别升值5%和10%，年末受美元走强影响有所回落，全年印尼卢比对美元升值2.3%，马来西亚林吉特对美元则贬值4.3%。

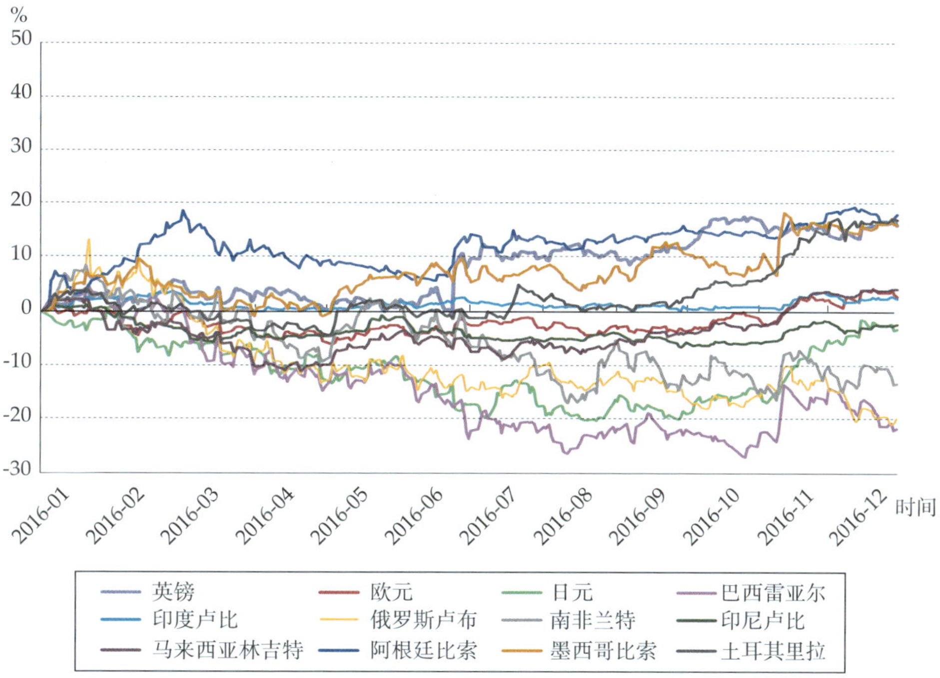

资料来源：路透DATASTREAM和工作人员计算。

图1-5 2016年主要货币汇率走势

（二）国内经济与金融环境

2016年，我国深入实施和推进了供给侧结构性改革，国民经济运行缓中趋稳、稳中向好，实现了“十三五”良好开局。在新的经济形势下，金融业不断推动机构改革、深化行业创新，以服务实体经济为大局，配合各项改革取得积极进展，实现了金融行业整体稳健发展。

1. 国民经济运行稳中向好

（1）经济运行缓中趋稳，总量增速保持稳定。

2016年，国内生产总值为74.4万亿元，同比增长6.7%。分季度看，第一季度同比增长6.7%，第二季度同比增长6.7%，第三季度同比增长6.7%，第四季度同比增长6.8%。全年来看，国民经济运行趋于平稳，积极信号显示经济发展向好势头。

（2）需求结构继续改善，固定资产投资缓中趋稳。

2016年，社会消费品零售总额突破33万亿元，同比增长10.4%，其中最终消费支出对经济增长的贡献率为64.6%，比上年高出4.9个百分点，消费对经济增长的贡献不断提高。进出口总额24.3万亿元，同比下降0.9%，降幅比上年收窄6.1个百分点。其中，出口总额13.8万亿元，同比下降2.0%；进口总额10.5万亿元，同比增长0.6%，进出口降幅明显收窄。全年固定资产投资59.7万亿元，同比增长8.1%，增速比上年回落1.9个百分点，比前三季度回落0.1个百分点。其中第一产业全年投资同比增长21.1%，第二产业投资同比同比增长3.5%，第三产业投资同比增长10.9%，投资总量缓中趋稳。

（3）消费价格温和上涨，居民收入稳定增长。

2016年，居民消费价格同比上涨2.0%，涨幅比上年提高0.6个百分点。其中，食品烟酒价格上涨3.8%，医疗保健价格上涨3.8%，成为居民消费价格上涨的主要因素。工业生产者出厂价格由降转升，全年工业生产者出厂价格下降1.4%，自9月起结束连续54个月同比下降后，同比涨幅不断扩大，12月同比上涨5.5%。全国居民人均可支配收入为23 821元，实际增长6.3%。其中，城镇居民人均可支配收入实际增长5.6%，农村居民人均可支配收入实际增长6.2%，居民收入实现稳定增长。

（4）产业结构持续优化，供给侧结构性改革取得积极进展。

2016年，全国服务业增加值为38.4万亿元，同比增长7.8%，继续领跑三次产业运行，服务业占国内生产总值的比重和对国民经济增长的贡献率持续增加。全国规模以上工业增加值同比增长6.0%，企稳态势明显。其中，高新技术产业增加值比上年增长10.8%，占规模以上工业增加值比重继续提高。2016年钢铁煤炭行业完成全年去产能任务，全年原煤产量比上年下降9.4%。商品房库存水平持续下降，工业企业资产负债率及成本均有所下降。全年生态保护和环境治理、水利管理业、农林牧渔业投资分别比上年增长39.9%、20.4%和19.5%，分别快于全部投资31.8个百分点、12.3个百分点和11.4个百分点，短板领域投资加快。

2. 金融环境保持平稳

（1）货币运行环境总体适度。

12月末，广义货币供应量M2余额为155.0万亿元，同比增长11.3%，增速比上年同期低2个百分点，货币总量保持平稳增长。人民币各项存款余额为150.6万亿元，同比增长11%，增速比上年同期低1.4个百分点，金融机构存款增长有所放缓。人民币各项贷款余额为106.6万亿元，同比增长13.5%，增速比上年同期低0.8个百分点，金融机构贷款增速保持平稳。社会融资规模全年增量为17.8万亿元，比上年增加2.4万亿元。其中，对实体经济发放的人民币贷款增加12.4万亿元，同比多增1.2万亿元，占同期社会融资规模的69.9%；企业债券净融资3万亿元，同比增加605亿元，占同期社会融资规模的16.8%；非金融企业境内股票融资1.2万亿元，同比增加4 826亿元，占同期社会融资规模的7%。社会融资规模适度增长的同时，企业债券和股票融资等直接融资占比进一步提高。金融机构存贷款利率稳中小幅下行，非金融企业及其他部门贷款12月加权平均利率为5.27%，与上年同期持平，个人住房贷款加权平均利率为4.52%，比上年同期下降0.18个百分点。

（2）金融业发展总体稳健。

一是银行业金融机构资产和负债规模稳步增长，信贷资产质量总体平稳，风险抵御能力较强，流动性水平稳健。截至2016年末，我国银行业金融机构本外币资产总额为232万亿元，同比增长15.8%；本外币负债总额为215万亿元，同比增长16.0%。商业银行不良贷款余额为15 123亿元，不良贷款率1.74%，全年不良贷款率基本保持稳定。商业银行实现净利润16 490亿元，同比增长3.54%；平均资产利润率为0.98%，平均资本利润率为13.38%，盈利能力较强。商业银行贷款损失准备金余额为26 676亿元，拨备覆盖率为176.40%，贷款拨备率为3.08%，资本充足率为13.28%，处于国际同业良好水平。

二是证券业资产规模和盈利能力有所下降。截至2016年末，129家证券公司总资产为5.79万亿元，净资产为1.64万亿元，净资本为1.47万亿元，全年共实现营业收入3 279.94亿元，实现净利润1 234.45亿元，124家公司实现盈利。

三是保险业保费收入稳步增长，资产规模继续扩大。截至2016年末，保险业累计实现原保险保费收入3.1万亿元，同比增长27.5%，增速比上年高7.5个百分点；赔款和给付支出1.1万亿元，同比增长21.2%；总资产15.1万亿元，同比增长22.3%，增速比上年高0.6个百分点。

二、2016年中国金融市场运行的主要特点

2016年，中国金融市场整体规模继续壮大，传统业务和创新业务的快速发展，不断拓展了金融市场的深度和广度；在双向融合进一步深入的同时，市场制度建设日益完善；市场化监管力度持续加强，激发和强化了市场自身风险防范能力；在实现金融市场稳定发展的前提下，优化服务实体经济成为驱动市场不断创新和改革的动力。

（一）金融市场传统业务与创新业务协同发展

2016年金融市场整体运行平稳，市场规模继续壮大。同业拆借全年累计成交逾95万亿元，债券回购总额近600万亿元，同比分别大幅增长48.48%和36.84%；债券市场发行总量达36万亿元，增速超过50%，二级市场现券交易累计达132.2万亿元，同比增长46.6%，债券市场增量和存量规模平稳增长；股票市场融资规模明显增加，全年募集资金1.8万亿元，同比增长12.54%，A股日均交易额达5 677亿元，日均成交量处于历史第二高的水平；银行间外汇市场全年成交金额约124万亿元，同比增长44%；上海黄金交易所黄金产品、上海期货交易所黄金期货交易量同比分别增长42.88%和37.30%，国内黄金市场发展增速领先国际主要黄金市场；商品期货成交金额创出历史新高，国债期货成交893.40万手，成交金额8.90万亿元，同比分别增长48.09%和46.76%。

金融市场传统业务保持较快增长速度的同时，2016年各市场创新产品和创新业务发展迅速，市场广度不断扩展。同业存单发行和交易大幅增加，全年累计发行金额13.04万亿元，二级市场成交金额70万亿元，同比分别大幅增长144%和262%；电子票据市场大幅增长，前三个季度，电子商业汇票出票金额和承兑金额同比分别增长55.2%和53.9%，电子票据规模在整个票据市场的比重显著增加；各类绿色债券累计发行超过1 700亿元，我国成为全球最大的绿色债券市场；

可交换债发行总金额890.56亿元，同比增长207.32%；银行间外汇市场挂牌交易的货币对总数扩展至近30对，涵盖国际主要储备货币、新兴市场货币以及“一带一路”沿线货币。外汇远期衍生品交易量爆发式增长，同比大幅增长逾3倍，其中中央对手清算业务量同比增长6倍多。

（二）金融市场体系建设与开放战略不断深化

2016年金融市场在发行机制、交易制度、市场结构等方面不断完善，强化自身建设，积极适应日益开放融合的新型市场体系建设。货币市场方面，全国银行间同业拆借市场准入管理改革推进，市场化监管进一步提升了同业拆借市场运行效率；大额存单发行和投资者主体扩容；上海票据交易所成立，票据市场发展进入新阶段。债券市场方面，债券预发行机制和国债做市支持机制正式推出，发行和交易机制进一步完善；银行间市场非金融企业债券投融资行为进一步规范；个人投资者被引入银行间债券市场债券柜台市场；地方债纳入国库现金管理质押品范围；国债收益率曲线进一步完善，绿色债券相关指数随着市场发展应运而生。股票市场方面，《上市公司筹划重大事项停复牌业务指引》正式出台，停复牌管理制度进一步确立；新三板分层制度正式推出，场外市场多层次建设持续推进，资本市场资源配置效率不断提升。外汇市场方面，外汇交易确认和交易获取报文正式注册发布，银行间外汇市场建立了从交易执行、交易获取、交易确认到资金支付的直通式处理机制。期货市场方面，白糖、豆粕期权上市获批，商品期货市场将步入期权时代。衍生品市场方面，外汇期权中央对手清算业务批准开展，非法人产品进入利率互换市场，衍生品投资者结构显现多元化格局。

2016年金融市场结合自身发展实际，适时稳步推进和实施各项对外开放战略。市场主体方面，世界银行在银行间债券市场成功发行首期SDR计价债券；熊猫债市场发行主体和发行规模大幅增加；更多符合条件的境外机构成为银行间债券市场的参与主体，同时取消了境外机构的额度限制，简化相关管理流程；随着人民币购售业务境外参加行的进入，银行间外汇市场的各个子市场、各类产品都已向境外机构开放，境外机构总数占比已达10%；深港通的正式启动，吸引了更多境外长期资金进入A股市场，国内股票市场投资者结构、流动性进一步改善和丰富。市场制度方面，QFII、RQFII管理制度得以完善，管理方式进一步优化统一；外汇交易时间实现覆盖欧洲交易时段，便利境外机构更好地参与银行间外汇市场。此外，中国（上海）自由贸易试验区各项金融市场开放措施得以全面展开，多项自贸区金融业务指引和规则条例陆续出台，市场服务平台对接顺利完成，包括柜台债券业务、地方政府债发行、利率互换交易等在内的金融基础产品和衍生产品业务全面展开。

（三）金融市场规范管理与风险防控持续推进

2016年，金融市场不断发展壮大的同时市场化监管力度持续加大。票据业务监管进一步规范了同业账户管理，积极防范和控制了票据业务风险。《银行业金融机构全面风险管理指引》发布，对提升银行业金融机构全面风险管理水平提出了新的要求。《上市公司重大资产重组管理办法》修订发布，明确了并购重组的监管方向，私募机构管理推进去伪存真，同业业务加速去通道和去杠杆过程，证券期货经营机构私募资产管理业务监管明确负面清单和“八条底线”，杠杆并购监管更趋严格规范，同时明确金融资产管理公司处置不良资产通道限制，进一步清理和规范了保险资产管理公司银行存款通道，严防“资金池”和“嵌套”性质的组合类保险资产管理产品；《债券质押式回购交易结算风险控制指引》发布，进一步明确了投资者准入、标准券使用率、回购质押杠杆、入库集中度等风控指标要求。交易手续费、保证金标准和涨跌停板幅度调整等一系列及时有效的市场监管措施出台，抑制了部分大宗商品过度投机，维护了商品期货市场的平稳运行。

2016年金融市场深化风险防范、保障金融安全、稳定运行等多项措施有序推出，各项市场化风险管理机制激发和强化了金融市场自身风险防范能力。银行间债券市场《投资人保护条款范例》正式出台，以法治化、市场化理念积极推进和维护债券市场健康稳定发展；新修订的《银行间市场信用风险缓释工具试点业务规则》以及相关产品指引的发布，为市场参与者提供了信用风险保护和对冲工具，银行间市场信用风险分散分担机制逐步建立。信贷资产支持证券信息披露强化“事中事后”管理，进一步维护了投资者合法权益。全国外汇市场自律机制的成立，有利于维护外汇市场正当竞争和健康有序运作。金融期货市场实现跨市场账户连通，联动监管、跨市场监管有效推进。互联网金融风险专项整治工作开展的同时，全国性互联网金融行业自律组织和互联网金融监管长效机制得以建立，为互联网金融长期稳定发展打下坚实基础。

（四）金融市场服务经济与优化配置功能有效发挥

2016年，金融市场适应实体经济发展新需要，落实国家“三去一降一补”五大任务，积极引导供给侧结构性改革方向。适应新的经济形势和市场环境的债转股指导意见正式出台，以市场化、法治化为方向，以稳妥降低企业债务风险、增强经济中长期发展韧性为目标的新一轮债转股充分发挥金融市场在化解过剩产能、企业兼并重组、降低实体经济企业成本、深化企业改革中的决定性作用。对房地产、产能过剩行业公司债券发行审核试行分类监管的同时强化了相关行业公司债券募集资金用途的监管要求。在资产支持票据（ABN）交易结构中引入特定目的载体（SPV），实现“真实出售”和“破产隔离”，推进信托型ABN创新产品落地。首单社会效应债券成功发行，开启了债券市场资金直接解决社会问题的新模式，进一步补足了实体经济融资薄弱环节的“短板”。

2016年金融市场服务实体经济更加注重实效，不断提升资源配置效率，有力支持了实体经济转型和发展。创新创业公司债、可续期公司债、“小公募”公司债等相继成功发行，进一步优化了中小企业资本形成机制，切实支持各类科技型、小微型企业的创业创新；资产证券化产品发行日趋常态化，基础资产类型进一步丰富，参与主体更加多样，持续发挥了在盘活资产存量、优化资源配置、服务实体经济中的作用；期货交易所、保险机构、期货经营机构以及涉农企业扩大了“保险+期货”试点力度，服务“三农”工作得到进一步深化。易地扶贫搬迁专项金融债券发挥了债券市场支持精准扶贫、精准脱贫的作用。一系列关于绿色债券发展的政策出台，全面覆盖绿色金融的纲领性指导文件《关于构建绿色金融体系的指导意见》颁布，我国建立了比较完整的绿色金融政策体系。与此同时，绿色债券市场以及碳金融衍生品等多样化绿色金融产品发展迅速，发行人类型不断丰富，产品种类不断增加，上市交易市场不断扩充，呈现出强大的发展潜力。

三、2017年中国金融市场发展展望

2017年是党的十九大召开之年，也是实施“十三五”规划的重要一年和推进供给侧结构性改革的深化之年。我国金融市场发展将紧紧围绕国家“五位一体”总体布局和“四个全面”战略布局，坚持稳中求进工作总基调，牢固树立和贯彻落实新发展理念，适应把握引领经济发展新常态，坚持以提高发展质量和效益为中心，坚持以推进供给侧结构性改革为主线，进一步推动创新开放和规范运行，保持金融市场健康平稳发展。

（一）金融市场改革开放与制度建设将继续深化

中央经济工作会议将2017年宏观政策的目标定位于“稳增长、促改革、调结构、惠民生、防风险”。对于我国金融市场而言，发展仍是第一要务，但要实现更有质量、更高层次的发展，不仅要做大金融市场的量，更要提升金融市场的质。2017年，我国金融市场将着力于进一步推进以市场为导向的体制和机制改革，尤其是重点领域和关键环节的金融改革。一是深入推进利率市场化改革。不断健全市场化的利率形成、调控和传导机制，增强中央银行利率调控能力。提高常备借贷便利（SLF）、中期借贷便利（MLF）和央行逆回购等操作效率，有效发挥利率走廊上限作用。二是进一步完善人民币汇率市场化形成机制。加大市场决定汇率的力度，增强人民币兑美元汇率弹性。积极引导和稳定市场预期，平衡跨境资本流动，保持人民币汇率在合理均衡水平上的基本稳定。三是持续推动金融市场规范管理和平稳健康运行。推动建立债券标准委员会，统一公司信用债信息披露和准入标准。推进资产证券化市场规范健康发展，稳步扩大不良资产证券化试点范围。推动股票市场体制机制改革，进一步发展和健全多层次股权市场。进一步稳妥推进期货及衍生品市场发展。加强黄金市场制度建设。继续推动票据市场建设和规范治理。进一步推动金融市场对外开放。四是进一步推进自由贸易试验区金融开放创新试点，推进绿色金融体系构建的落实，稳妥推动市场化、法治化债转股等。

（二）金融风险防范与控制将被放到更加重要的位置

中央经济工作会议提出，2017年要把防控金融风险放到更加重要的位置，下决心处置一批风险点，着力防控资产泡沫，提高和改进监管能力，确保不发生系统性金融风险。因此，2017年我国金融市场工作也将不断加强监管，把防控金融风险作为重中之重，切实防范化解金融风险，守住不发生系统性金融风险底线。一是加强宏观审慎管理，有效防范各类资产泡沫化。加强金融风险研判和预警，重点关注产能过剩行业、

银行业资产质量、资本市场、地方各类交易场所、交叉性金融业务及非法集资等领域风险。尊重市场规律，及时应对化解风险隐患，在复杂多变的环境下，使市场实现平稳健康发展。二要着力推动金融监管协调机制建设，深入研究并积极稳妥推进金融监管体制改革。加快构建适应现代金融市场发展和业务需要的监管体系。强化金融监管协调和跨部门监管协作。强化金融管理业务的功能化、穿透式监管。建立健全适应互联网金融特征的监管体系。三要致力于提升金融机构稳健性，稳妥处置一批高风险金融机构。研究制定系统重要性金融机构风险评估和处置的监管标准和政策。探索金融机构风险市场化处置机制。深入推进互联网金融风险专项整治，开展长效机制建设。四要依法从严监管，严厉打击各种违法违规行为。落实“依法、从严、全面”的监管要求，维护资本市场稳定。

（三）金融市场服务实体经济的宗旨和功能将进一步凸显

中央经济工作会议指出，2017年我国经济工作将坚持稳中求进总基调，坚持以推进供给侧结构性改革为主线。供给侧结构性改革的根本途径是深化改革，完善市场在资源配置中起决定作用的体制机制。要提升供给体系质量和效率，增强经济持续增长动力，需要更有效地配置和使用金融资源，提升金融供给效率。这就要求全面深化金融体制改革，增加金融供给，提升金融效率，使市场在资源配置中起决定性作用。2017年，我国金融市场发展将坚持服务实体经济的根本宗旨，进一步发挥金融市场在优化资源配置、服务经济结构转型升级、支持促进供给侧结构性改革等方面的作用。一是金融市场将适应和引领经济发展新常态，树立并贯彻新的发展理念，引导经济朝着更高质量、更有效率、更加公平、更可持续的方向发展。二是金融市场将不断深化体制机制改革，夯实市场基础，强化激励约束，提升运行效率和服务效能，从而切实发挥优化资源配置、引导要素流动、管理风险和财富的作用，为实体经济的振兴提供源源不断的支持。三是金融市场将配合供给侧结构性改革，在深入推进“三去一降一补”战略任务中发挥更大作用。资本市场将进一步深化多层次市场体系改革，不断优化融资结构，加大股权融资力度等，为实体经济提供多样化的金融服务，切实降低企业杠杆率和融资成本。资本市场并购重组机制和市场化改革也将进一步深入推进，更好地支持经济结构转型和产业升级。四是在支持服务实体经济过程中，金融市场尤其是资本市场必须要维持其自身的稳定发展。金融市场的平稳运行，是服务好实体经济的首要前提和决定因素，是未来改革发展的基础。

Part I Overview

In 2016, despite of the slowdown of global economic recovery and the arduous tasks faced by domestic economic development and reform, China's economy witnessed sound operation with good momentum for growth. China's financial market accelerated institutional construction, deepened market depth and breadth, strengthened risk management, and pushed forward opening-up and market innovation,and thus played a positive role in promoting supply-side structural reform, optimizing resource allocation, and enhancing the effectiveness of economic development.

I. Analysis of the macro environment for China's financial market development in 2016

1.1 International economic and financial conditions

In 2016, global economic growth slowed down, yet economic activities in most economies began to strengthen in the second half. After a sharp decline early in the year, and a series of "Black Swan" events, market confidence had been gradually restored, and the international financial market maintained an overall upward trend. With increasingly positive factors in the world economy, commodity prices such as price of crude oil rebounded comprehensively.

1.1.1 Global economic recovery slowed down in 2016

1.1.1.1 Recovery in advanced economies slowed down, while growth in emerging economies resumed.

The growth momentum of the U.S. economy witnessed significant decline. Preliminary data shows that, in 2016, the average real gross domestic product (GDP) grew by 1.6% on a seasonally-adjusted basis, significantly lower than the growth rate of 2.6% in 2015. In the second half of the year, GDP growth rebounded to 1.8%. Downward pressure on the euro zone economy continued to increase in the first half, while the economy gradually stabilized in the second half, with GDP growth of 1.7% for the year, slightly lower than 1.9% in 2015. Japanese economy recorded a significant slowdown in the first half of the year, which grew by 0.6% year on year, and the real GDP in the third quarter grew by 1% compared to the same period in 2015. The British economy expanded by 2.2% in the second half compared to the same period in 2015, which was beyond market expectation. Despite of the downward pressure on most emerging economies, there were clear signs of bottoming out and edging up. In the first three quarters, the economy of Brazil and Russia contracted by 2.9% and 0.4% respectively, compared with 5.8% and 3.8%. The growth in South Africa turned positive starting from the second quarter, and posted 1.1% in the third quarter. Indian economy maintained rapid growth, expanding by 7.4% in the first three quarters.

1.1.1.2 Global trade growth was sluggish, and direct investment declined significantly.

In 2016, the weak growth of global economy, particularly the downward pressure on major emerging economies, weighed on global trade significantly. The World Trade Organization (WTO) had reduced its forecast of global trade

Figure 1-1 Economic Growth Rates of Major Economies, 2015–2016

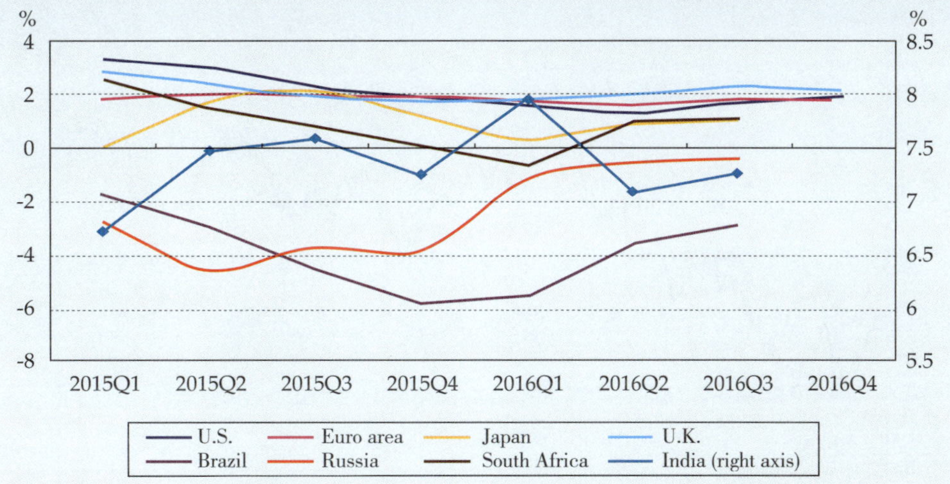

Note: The real GDP growth rates for Russia, India and Brazil were not seasonally adjusted.

Source: Reuters DATASTREAM.

growth to 1.7%, the slowest growth since 2009. In the first quarter, the Baltic Dry Index (BDI), a leading indicator of global trade activities, continued decreasing to 290, although it started to recover in the second half. The year's average was 676, decreasing by around 6% from 2015. In the first half of 2016, foreign direct investment (FDI) was merely $793 billion, decreasing by 5% month on month. The FDI inflows to OECD countries rose by 14% month on month, to $568 billion, while the FDI outflows of OECD countries fell by 16% month on month. Advanced economies had become major recipients of FDI, while their direct investment to other countries declined sharply. The FDI inflows in most countries dropped significantly, among which, the inflows to Brazil, India, South Africa and Indonesia fell by 20%, 20%, 45% and 28% to $29 billion, $17.3 billion, $1.3 billion, and $6.3 billion respectively.

1.1.1.3 Crude oil and commodity prices rebounded.

In spite of the sluggish global economy, commodity prices rebounded in 2016 due to marked decline in the early period. International oil price measured by the WTI declined to $27 per barrel at the beginning of 2016, and edged up from Mid February. It fell slightly when the U.S. Dollar strengthened after the president election in November, and rose significantly after the oil producing nations finally reached a half-year agreement to limit the oil production. At the end of 2016, the WTI registered $53.72 per barrel, growing by 44% in the year. Gold, silver and platinum prices in London market increased by 9%, 16% and 3.5% respectively, and aluminum, copper and nickel prices rose by 13.6%, 17.4% and 13.5% respectively in the year. Prices of most agricultural products experienced large increases. Compared with the beginning of the year, cotton price increased by 12.7%, and sugar price by 28.6%. Bloomberg Commodity Index stood at 117, up by 11.8% compared to the beginning of the year.

Figure 1-2 Movements of Crude Oil and Commodity Prices in 2016

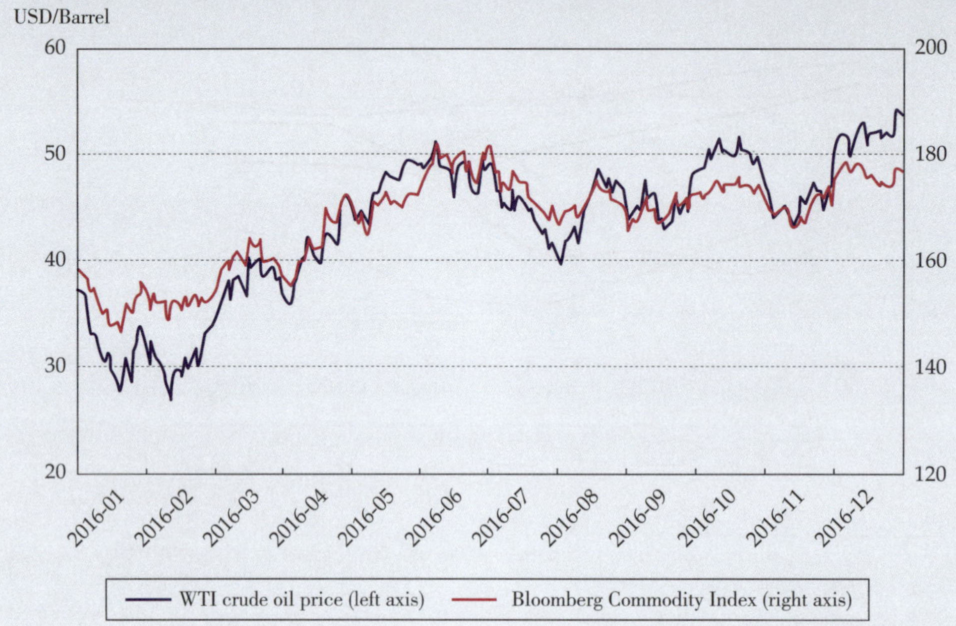

Source: Reuters DATASTREAM.

1.1.2 Volatility continued in international financial markets

1.1.2.1 Monetary policies of major economies remained accommodative but diverged further.

In 2016, the U.S. economy maintained moderate recovery, labor market and inflation kept improving. The Fed raised the federal funds rate only once by 25 bps in December, and maintained the existing policy of reinvesting principal payments, showing prudential attitude on raising the rate. The European Central Bank (ECB) and the Bank of England (BOE) strengthened accommodative monetary policies. The ECB cut the interest rate on the deposit facility from -0.3% to -0.4%, extended twice the asset purchase program, with the amount of asset above 60 billion euro. In order to cope with potential negative impact of Brexit, the BOE cut the benchmark interest rate by 25 bps, and increased the stock of asset purchase program to 435 billion pounds by adding 60 billion pounds. Japan's accommodative monetary policy was approaching the limit, which included introduction of negative interest rate policy, an increase in purchases of ETFs, the new policy framework of "Quantitative and Qualitative Easing with Yield Curve Control", and inflation overshooting commitment etc. Downward pressure faced by emerging economies heightened and most countries maintained accommodative monetary policy.

1.1.2.2 Global stock market dropped first and then rose, with frequent external shocks.

At the beginning of the year, risks in global financial market rose sharply, stock markets dropped around 10% in general, nearly 20% in some countries. From March, investors' confidence had been restored, and global stock market hit the bottom and edged up. The Brexit vote and the US presidential election shocked global financial markets repeatedly, which caused intense reaction of major stock indexes with temporary turbulence. In major emerging economies, Russia's MICEX, Indonesia's IDX and India's IBOMESE went up by 27%, 15.3% and 3.2% respectively in 2016, while JSE of South Africa dropped slightly by 0.08%. The economic and financial situation of major countries in Latin America improved, stock markets rose significantly. Argentina's MERVAL jumped by 45% in the year, and Peru Lima Stock Composite Index surged by 58%.

Figure 1-3 Movements of Stock Indices in Major Economies in 2016

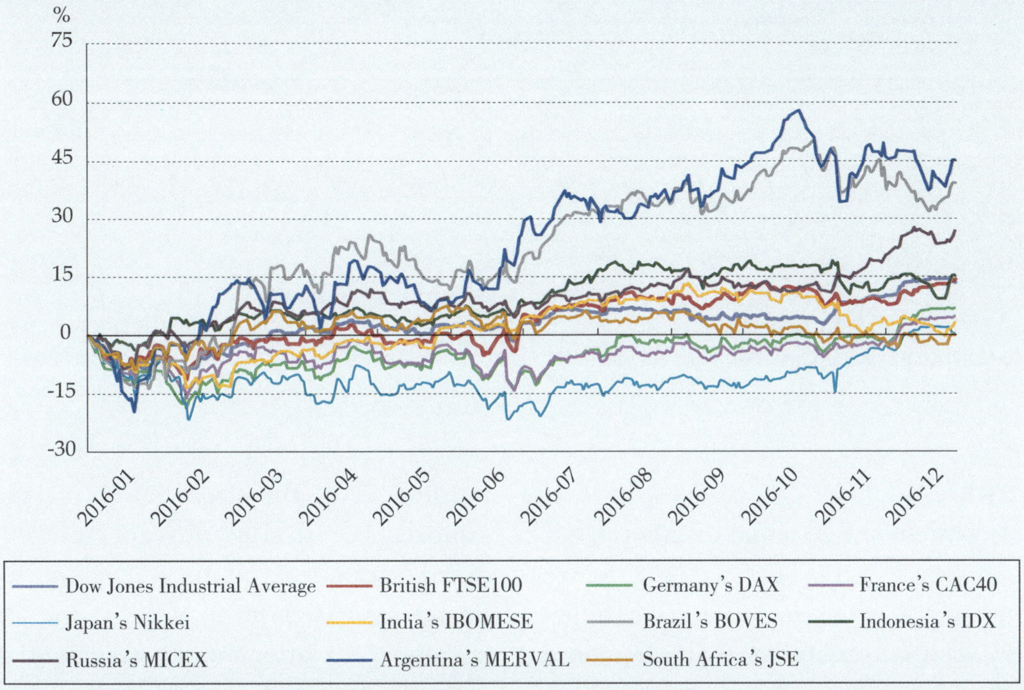

Source: Reuters DATASTREAM.

1.1.2.3 Interest rates in most economies moved down, the government bond yields in advanced economies moved up at the end of the year.

Most economies witnessed slow recovery and the interest rates moved down in general. The yield of Japan 10-year treasury bonds became negative from February and it lasted for 9 months, with the lowest level recording -0.295%. In March, the ECB lowered policy rates further. After Brexit vote in the end of June, the yield of Germany 10-year treasury bonds turned to negative as well and it lasted for nearly 4 months. In early November, the yield of U.S. treasury bonds surged greatly, driving the upward movement of those in other advanced economies. At end-December, the yield of U.S. 10-year treasury bonds was 2.4467%, and that in the U.K., Japan, Germany and France was 1.2403%, 0.0481%, 0.1084% and 0.6853% respectively. Compared to those at end 2015, the yield of U.S. 10-year treasury bonds went up by 18 bps, while that of other advanced economies down by 72, 23, 53 and 30 bps respectively.

Figure 1-4 Movements of 10-year Treasury Bond Yields in Major Advanced Economies in 2016

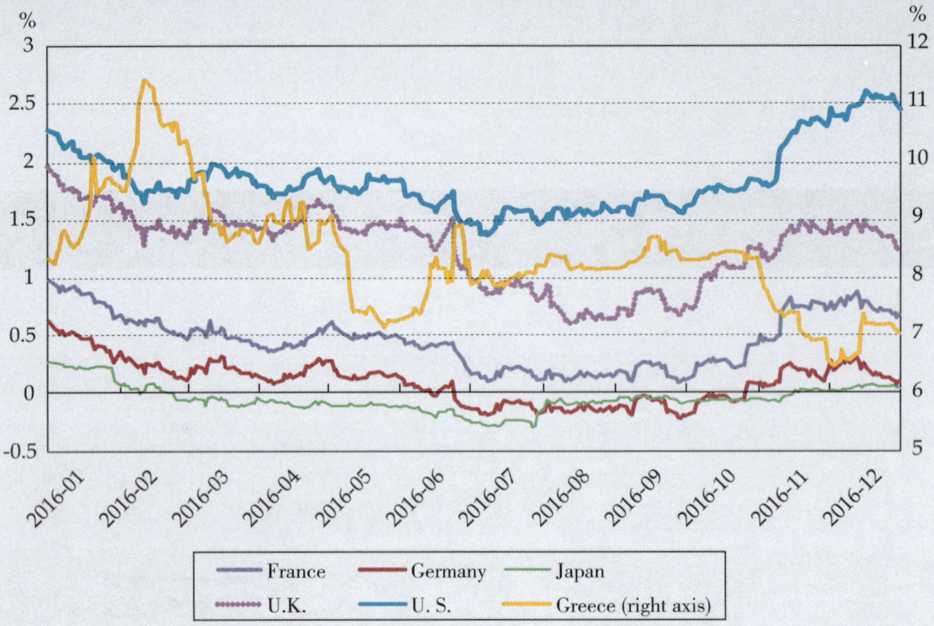

Source: Reuters DATASTREAM.

1.1.2.4 Currencies in major economies witnessed periodic adjustment and external events proved significant impacts.

At the beginning of 2016, most currencies depreciated against U.S. dollar, while Japanese Yen became a safe-haven currency. With emerging positive signs, global foreign exchange markets gradually stabilized. In the whole year, currencies in major economies witnessed periodic adjustment. Currencies recorded substantial depreciation earlier appreciated in general, while currencies recorded appreciation or remained stable against U.S. dollar earlier depreciated in general. As the Brexit vote exceeded market expectations, British Pound Sterling depreciated substantially. At end-2016, GBP depreciated by 16% against U.S. dollar. US presidential election ended the upward movement of Japanese Yen, which almost returned to the level before appreciation. The appreciation of Japanese Yen against U.S. dollar moved from 20% to 3%. Euro appreciated about 3% against U.S. dollar in the first 10 months of 2016, and depreciated substantially after the US presidential election, posted a depreciation of 3% for the whole year.

After significant depreciation in 2015, currencies of Brazil, Russia and South Africa strengthened sharply against U.S. dollar, which appreciated by 22%, 20% and 13% respectively in 2016. Indian rupee weakened by about 2.5% against U.S. dollar, less than the depreciation of 2015. Among major ASEAN economies, Indonesian rupiah and Malaysian ringgit stopped the downward trend in 2015 and went up gradually against U.S. dollar in early 2016, with the highest appreciation recording 5% and 10% respectively. During the year of 2016, Indonesian rupiah appreciated by

2.3% against U.S. dollar, while Malaysian ringgit depreciated by 4.3% due to the stronger U.S. dollar at the end of 2016.

Figure 1-5 Movements of Major Currencies in 2016

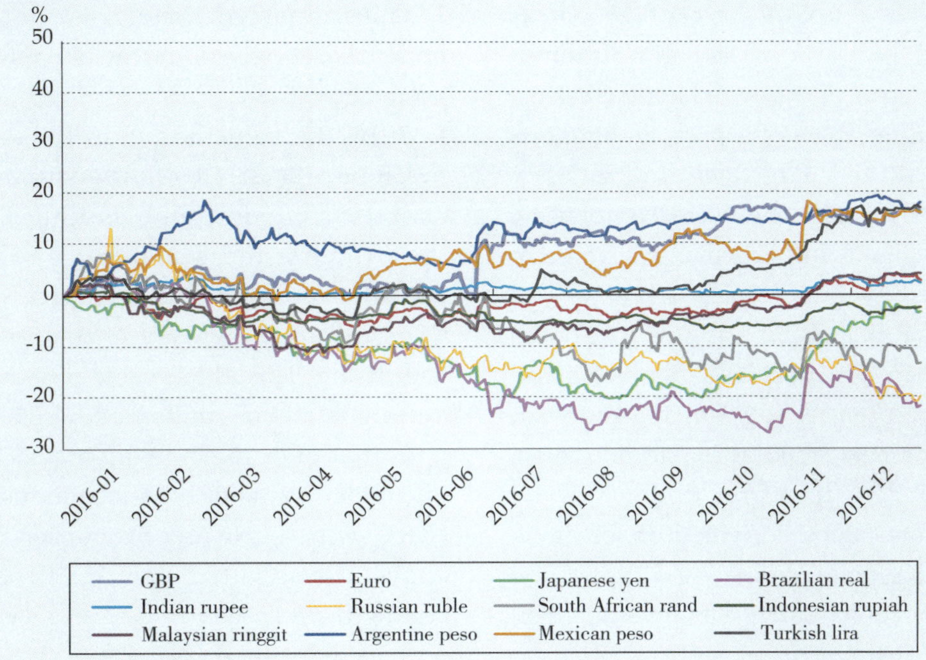

Source: Reuters DATASTREAM and staff calculations.

1.2 Domestic economic and financial conditions

In 2016, China vigorously implemented supply-side structural reform. National economy registered a slower but stable performance with good momentum for growth, and got the 13th Five-Year Plan off to a great start. Under current economic conditions, financial sector reform was advanced steadily, and innovation was deepened, to serve the development of the real economy. Reforms had made positive progress, and the financial sector achieved overall stability and development.

1.2.1 The national economy grew steadily with good momentum

1.2.1.1 The development of national economy was slower but stable, GDP and its growth remained stable.

In 2016, GDP reached 74.4 trillion yuan, representing a growth of 6.7 percent, with the year-on-year growth of 6.7 percent, 6.7 percent, 6.7 percent and 6.8 percent in four quarters respectively. The performance of the national economy was stable, and positive signals showed the economic development was picking up.

1.2.1.2 The composition of demand continued to improve, and fixed asset investment growth was slower but stable.

In 2016, total retail sales of consumer goods increased by 10.4% year on year, hitting 33 trillion yuan, among which the contribution of final consumption expenditure to the economic growth was 64.6%, up 4.9 percentage points compared to a year earlier. The contribution of consumption to economic growth kept increasing. During the year, the value of exports and imports totaled 24.3 trillion yuan, declining by 0.9% from a year earlier, with the decrease down by 6.1 percentage points. In particular, the value of exports reduced by 2.0% from last year to 13.8 trillion yuan, and that of imports rose by 0.6% to 10.5 trillion yuan. The decrease of exports and imports dropped remarkably. During the year, fixed asset investment stood at 59.7 trillion yuan, increasing by 8.1%, with a growth down by 1.9 percentage points compared with 2015, or down by 0.1 percentage point compared with the first three quarters of 2016. In particular, investment on the primary industry increased by 21.1% year on year, and investment on the secondary industry and tertiary industry increased by 3.5% and 10.9% respectively. The fixed asset investment registered a slower but stable growth.

1.2.1.3 Consumer price rose moderately, resident income grew steadily.

During the year, the CPI rose by 2.0%, up 0.6 percentage points compared with the growth in 2015. Among it, the price of food, liquor and cigarette rose by 3.8 percent, while the price of health care rose by 3.8 percent, both contributed mainly to the CPI growth. The producer price index (PPI) declined first and increased then. During the year, the PPI lost 1.4% year on year. The PPI started to pick up in September of 2016, ending a continuous year-on-year decline of 54 months, and the PPI growth kept enlarging and registered 5.5% year on year in December. The per capita disposable income of Chinese residents was 23,821 yuan, a year-on-year increase of 6.3% in real terms. Among it, the per capita disposable income of urban residents rose by 5.6% and that of rural residents by 6.2%, both in real terms.

1.2.1.4 Industrial structures continued to be optimized, supply-side structural reform achieved positive progress.

In 2016, the value added of the service sector in China was 38.4 trillion yuan, increasing by 7.8% year on year, and continued to outgrow the primary and secondary industries. The contribution ratio of the service sector to the GDP and to the growth of national economy kept rising. The added value of industries above a designated size increased by 6.0% compared with that of 2015, showing a stabilizing trend. The added value of high-tech industries rose by 10.8%, with a growing proportion in industries above a designated size. In 2016, the task of cutting overcapacity in coal and steer industries was accomplished, and the output of raw coal declined by 9.4% from that of 2015. The inventory of commercial housing was declining, and both the debt-to-asset ratio and the cost of industrial enterprises declined. During the year, investment on ecological conservation and environmental management, water conservancy, as well as agriculture, forestry, farming and fishery increased by 39.9%, 20.4% and 19.5% respectively, 31.8, 12.3 and 11.4 percentage points faster than the overall investment growth rate, showing that investment on areas of weakness gained speed.

1.2.2 Financial environment was stable in general

1.2.2.1 Monetary environment was appropriately accommodative.

At end-December, M2 posted 155.0 trillion yuan, rising by 11.3%, 2 percentage points lower than the growth in the same period of the previous year, monetary aggregate increased steadily. Outstanding RMB deposits stood at 150.6 trillion yuan, rising by 11%, 1.4 percentage points lower than the growth in 2015. Outstanding RMB loans grew by 13.5% over last year to 106.6 trillion yuan, 0.8 percentage points lower compared to the growth in 2015. In 2016, all-system financing aggregates increased 17.8 trillion yuan, up 2.4 trillion yuan compared with that in 2015. In particular, RMB loans to the real economy increased 12.4 trillion yuan, accounting for 69.9% of the total, and up 1.2 trillion yuan on a year-on-year basis. Net financing by enterprise bonds registered 3 trillion yuan, increased 60.5 billion yuan on a year-on-year basis, accounting for 16.8% of the total. The domestic equity financing by non-financial enterprises posted 1.2 trillion yuan, increasing 482.6 billion yuan on a year-on-year basis, accounting for 7% of the total. As the all-system financing aggregates increased moderately, the percentage of direct financing such as enterprise bonds and stocks picked up. Deposit and loan rates of financial institutions fell slightly. In December 2016, the weighted average rate on loans to non-financial enterprises and other sectors was 5.27%, which was even with the same period of 2015. Besides, the weighted average rate on housing mortgage loans was 4.52%, down by 0.18 percentage points from the same period of 2015.

1.2.2.2 Overall performance of the financial sector was sound.

First, assets and liabilities of banking financial institutions continued to grow, quality of credit assets was stable, risk prevention ability was strong, and liquidity remained adequate. As of end-2016, domestic and foreign currency assets of China's banking financial institutions totaled 232 trillion yuan, up by 15.8% year on year, and total domestic and foreign currency liabilities jumped by 16.0% to 215 trillion yuan. Outstanding non-performing loans (NPLs) posted 1.5123 trillion yuan, and the NPL ratio was 1.74%, which kept basically stable throughout the year. Net profit of commercial banks stood at 1,649 billion yuan, increasing by 3.54% year on year. The average return on assets (ROA) was 0.98%, and the average return on equity (ROE) was 13.38%. Thus, the profitability remained strong. Outstanding balance of loan loss provisions stood at 2,667.6 billion yuan, with a provision coverage of 176.40%, provision coverage for loans was 3.08%, and the capital adequacy ratio was 13.28%. The performance was at a good level among international counterparts.

Second, overall size and profitability of securities sector declined slightly. As of end-2016, total assets of 129 securities companies stood at 5.79 trillion yuan, with the net assets of 1.64 trillion yuan and the net capital of 1.47 trillion yuan. During the year, total operating revenues posted 327.994 billion yuan, cumulative net profits reached 123.445 billion yuan, and 124 firms made a profit.

Third, premium income of the insurance sector grew steadily, and overall asset continued to expand. As of end-2016, premium income of the insurance sector reached 3.1 trillion yuan cumulatively, a year-on-year increase of 27.5%, up by 7.5 percentage points than the growth of the previous year. Cumulative payments on claims rose by 21.2% year on year to 1.1 trillion yuan. Total assets of the insurance sector hit 15.1 trillion yuan, surging by 22.3% year on year, up by 0.6 percentage points compared with the growth of the previous year.

2. Main features of China's financial market performance in 2016

In 2016, China's financial market continued to grow, rapid development of traditional and innovative businesses kept expanding the depth and scope of the financial market. With the further deepening of two-way integration, the construction of market institution was improving. Market-based regulation was enhanced, which stimulated and strengthened the risk prevention ability of financial institutions. On the premise of its sound development, the financial market optimized its way of serving the real economy, which became the driving force of innovation and reform.

2.1 Traditional businesses and innovative businesses developed coordinately

In 2016, China's financial market operated steadily, and the size of deals concluded in financial markets continued to grow. Turnover of interbank funding amounted to 95 trillion yuan, and turnover of bond repurchases (repos) reached 600 trillion yuan, incresing by 48.48% and 36.84% year on year respectively. Bond issuance totaled 36 trillion yuan, with a year-on-year increase of over 50%. Trading of spot bonds on secondary market amounted to 132.2 trillion yuan, growing by 46.6% year on year. Both stock and increment of bond market increased steadily. Financing from the stock market increased significantly to 1.8 trillion yuan in 2016, a year-on-year increase of 12.54%. Daily average trading value of the A-share market hit 567.7 billion yuan, the second highest level on record. The turnover of jnter-bank foreign exchange market reached 124 trillion yuan, up by 44% from the previous year. Trading volume of gold-based products traded in Shanghai Gold Exchange and gold futures traded in Shanghai Futures Exchange increased by 42.88% and 37.30% year on year respectively. China's gold market outperformed other main gold markets in the world in terms of growth rate. Turnover of commodity futures posted a record high. Trading of treasury bond futures stood at 8.9340 million lots, or 8.90 trillion yuan in total, increasing by 48.09% or 46.76% year on year respectively.

While traditional businesses in the financial market kept a relatively high pace of development, innovative products and businesses grew rapidly, with market breadth expanding in 2016. Issuance and trading of certificate of deposits increased sharply , the cumulative issuance value amounted to 13.04 trillion yuan, and its trading in secondary market reached 70 trillion yuan, a year-on-year increase of 144% and 262% respectively. The market of electronic bills expanded greatly, for the first three quarters of 2016, the drawing and accepting value of electronic commercial drafts increased by 55.2% and 53.9% respectively, and the proportion of electronic bills in the bill market rose remarkably. Cumulative issuance value of green bonds was more than 170 billion yuan, and China had become the world's biggest green bond market. The issuance value of exchangeable bonds was 89.056 billion yuan, surging by 207.32% year on year. Number of foreign currency pairs listed on the interbank foreign exchange market increased to almost 30, covering main international reserve currencies, emerging market currencies and currencies used by countries along the Belt and Road. Turnover of foreign exchange forward derivatives witnessed exponential growth, more than 4 times as much as the level of the previous year, among which, turnover of central counterparty clearing grew by more than 6 times year on year.

2.2 Financial market construction and opening-up strategy continued to deepen

In 2016, improvements were made on the

issuance mechanism, trading system, and market structure of China's financial market. It strengthened self-construction to adapt to the increasingly open and harmonized new market system. On money market, reform of market access management and market-based regulation had further improved the operation efficiency of China's interbank funding market. The scope of issuer and investor of certificates of deposits was further broadened. Shanghai Commercial Paper Exchange Corporation Ltd. was established, and the development of China's bill market entered a new stage. On bond market, bond pre-issue mechanism and treasury bond market making support mechanism were launched. The issuance and trading mechanism was further improved. Investment and financing activities of non-financial enterprises bonds in the interbank market were further regulated. Individual investors gained access to interbank OTC bond market. Local government bonds were included as collaterals in treasury cash management. The treasury bond yield curve was further improved, and the green bond-related indexes emerged during the market development. On stock market, *Guidelines of Shanghai Stock Exchange on Stock Suspension and Resumption of Trading for Listed Companies Planning for Material Events* was released, regulations on stock suspension and resumption of trading were further established. A structured system of National Equities Exchange and Quotations was officially launched, construction of a multi-layered OTC market was pushed forward, and the resource allocation efficiency of capital market was promoted constantly. On foreign exchange market, messages of foreign exchange transactions confirmation and acquisition were officially registered and launched, and the Straight Through Processing (STP) mechanism was established covering the process of conducting, acquisition, confirmation and payment of transactions in the interbank foreign exchange market. On futures market, white sugar options and soybean meal options got the approval for trading, and the commodity futures market would enter an era of options. On derivatives market, the business of central counter party clearing for foreign exchange options was approved, and non-incorporated products entered the interest rate swap market, presenting a pattern of diversified investors.

Combined with its development situation, the financial market timely and steadily pushed forward and implemented opening-up strategy in 2016. On market participants, the World Bank successfully issued bonds denominated in Special Drawing Rights (SDR) in the interbank bond market. The amount of issuers and issuance in Panda Bond market increased significantly. There were more qualified overseas institutional investors participating in the interbank bond market. Quota limits for overseas institutional investors were removed, and relevant administration process was streamlined. With the opening up of RMB purchases and sales business for overseas participating banks, each sub markets and all kinds of products in the interbank foreign exchange market had been opened to overseas institutions, which accounted for 10 percent of all market participants. Operation of the Shenzhen-Hong Kong Stock Connect attracted more long-term foreign capital into the A-share market. Investor structure and liquidity of China's stock market was further improved and enriched. On market institutions, the administration institutions of QFII and RQFII were improved, and administration methods were further optimized and unified. Operating hour of the foreign exchange market trading system was extended to cover European trading sessions, which benefited overseas institutions to better participate in the interbank foreign exchange market. In addition, financial market opening-up procedures in the

China (Shanghai) Free Trade Zone was unfolded comprehensively, a number of guidelines and rules for free trade zone financial businesses were introduced, and market service platform completed connection. Business of underlying financial products and derivatives were proceeded in full swing, including exchange-traded bond business, issuance of local government bonds, as well as interest rate swap.

2.3 Regulation and risk control of the financial market made progress

In 2016, the financial market continued to grow, and market-based regulation continued to strengthen. Regulation on bill businesses further standardized the interbank account management, prevented and controlled the risks in bill businesses. *Guidelines on Managing Comprehensive Risks of Banking Institutions* was issued, which brought forward new requirements on promoting comprehensive risk management capacity of banking institutions. The revised *Administrative Rules on Major Asset Restructuring of Listed Companies* was released, clearly identifying the direction of regulation on mergers and acquisitions. Administration on private equity firms was developed to separate that valuable from what is worthless. De-channelization or deleveraging process of interbank businesses gained speed. Negative list and eight bottom lines were specified in the regulation of private placement asset management business of securities and futures business institutions. Regulation on levered mergers and acquisitions became more and more strict. Limitation was made clear for financial asset management companies in the channel of disposing non-performing assets. Bank deposit channel for insurance asset management companies was further cleaned up and regulated, to prevent composite insurance asset management products involving "pool of funds" or "embedded funds". *Guidance for Risk Control on Trading and Settlement in Collateralized Repo of Bonds on Exchange-traded Market* was released, further defining requirements on risk control indicators such as entry of investors and use rate of standard bonds, repo lever and concentration degree of in-storage etc. A series of market regulatory measures were launched on trading fees, margin standard and daily limit range adjustment and etc. to restrain excessive speculation of some commodities and to maintain the smooth operation of commodity futures market in a timely and effective manner.

In 2016, measures were introduced in financial market in an orderly manner, to deepen risk prevention, safeguard financial security and smooth market operation. Those market-based risk management mechanisms stimulated and strengthened risk prevention capability of the financial market. *The Investor Protection Clauses Paradigm* of the interbank bond market was released to push forward and maintain the healthy and steady development of bond market on a legal and market-oriented footing. The revised *Regulations on Pilot Business of Credit Risk Mitigation Instruments in the Interbank Market* and related products guidance were released, which provided market participants with credit risk protection and hedging tools. The credit risk diversification and sharing mechanism was gradually established in the interbank market. Concurrent and ex post management was strengthened in the information disclosure of asset-backed securities, further safeguarding the legitimate rights and interests of investors. The establishment of the self-discipline mechanism in foreign exchange market would help maintain the fair-play competition, promoting the orderly operation and healthy development of the foreign exchange market. Cross-market accounts connect was realized in financial futures market, effectively promoting joint regulation and cross-market regulation. Rectification of risks in internet finance was carried out, at the same time, self-discipline organization and long-term mechanism for internet finance regulation was established, laying a solid foundation for the steady growth of internet finance in the long run.

2.4 Financial market played an effective role in support of the economy and optimizing resource allocation

In 2016, the financial market made efforts to cater to the new demands arising from the development of the real economy, implemented China's five priority tasks, including cutting overcapacity, reducing excess inventory, deleveraging, lowering costs and strengthening areas of weakness, and actively steered supply-side structural reform. The guidance on debt to equity swap was formally introduced, to adapt to the new economic situation and market environment. In the direction of market-orientation and legal system, and in order to steadily reduce debt risks of enterprises, and to enhance the resilience of medium- and long-term development of the economy, the new round of debt to equity swap put into full play the decisive role of financial market in mitigating excess capacity, corporate mergers and acquisitions, reducing cost of enterprises, as well as deepening enterprise reform. Classified regulation was conducted on a trial basis for corporate bond issuance examination in real estate companies and industries with excess capacity. Meanwhile, regulatory requirements were enhanced on the use of corporate bond fund raised by relevant industries. The introduction of Special Purpose Vehicle (SPV) in the trading structure of Asset-Backed Notes (ABN), realized true sale and bankruptcy isolation, and promoted the launch of innovative trust ABN products. The successful issuance of the first Social Impact Bond (SIB) initiated a new model in solving social problems with bond market capitals, and further made up the weakness of financing in the real economy.

In 2016, importance was attached to the effectiveness of financial markets in serving the real economy, and the efficiency of resource allocation kept improving, which strongly supported the transition and development of the real economy. Innovative startups bonds, renewable corporate bonds and small public offering bonds were issued successfully, which optimized the capital formation mechanism of Small- and Medium-sized Enterprises, and supported the startup and innovation of all kinds of science and technology enterprises, as well as micro- and small- enterprises. Issuance of asset securitization products was increasingly normalized, underlying assets became more diversified, and the scope of market participants was further expanded, which continued to play a role in invigorating stock assets, optimizing resource allocation and serving the real economy. The pilot of "insurance + futures" was further broadened in the futures exchange, insurance companies, futures business institutions and agriculture-related enterprises, and efforts to serve agriculture, rural areas, and farmers were further deepened. Special purpose financial bonds for poverty alleviation by relocation put into play the role of bond market in support of targeted poverty alleviation. A string of policies for green bond development had been launched, and a guiding principle comprehensively covering green finance—*Guidance on Constructing a Green Financial System* was promulgated, a relatively integrated system of green finance policy had been established in China. At the same time, the development of green bond market, carbon financial derivatives and other diversified green financial products gained speed, the type of issuers was enriched, the product category was increased, and the listed market continued to expand, presenting strong potential of growth.

3. Prospects for China's Financial Market Development in 2017

In 2017, the CPC will hold its 19th National Congress, the implementation of the "13th Five-Year" plan will enter an important stage, and the structural reforms on the supply side will be further deepened. Efforts will be made to promote balanced economic, political, cultural, social, and ecological progress and implement the Four-Pronged Comprehensive Strategy, to remain committed to the underlying principle of making progress while keeping performance stable, to gain a strong understanding of and put into practice the new development philosophy, to adapt to, approach in the right way, and steer the new normal in economic development, to give central importance to improving the quality and returns of development, to focus on supply-side structural reform, to further promote innovation, opening-up and regulation, and to maintain sound and stable development of the financial market.

3.1 Financial market reform, opening-up and institution building will continue to deepen

The Central Economic Work Conference set the target of macroeconomic policy in 2017 as to "maintain stable growth, promote reform, make structural adjustments, improve living standards, and guard against risks". For China's financial market, development is still the top priority. But to achieve the development of higher quality and higher level, we should not only expand the size, but also enhance the quality of the financial market. In 2017, China's financial market will focus on further promoting market-oriented reforms of system and mechanism, especially the financial reform in key areas. First, market-based interest rate reform will be further promoted. Market-based interest rate formation, regulation and transmission mechanism will be improved, to enhance central bank's regulatory capacity on interest rate. Efficiency of the central bank operations, including Standing Lending Facility (SLF), Medium-term Lending Facility (MLF), and reverse repurchase, will be improved, to effectively put into play their role as the ceiling of interest rate corridor. Second, market-based RMB exchange rate formation mechanism will be further improved, to enhance the role of market in deciding the exchange rate, and to increase the flexibility of the RMB exchange rate against the US dollar. Efforts will be made to actively guide and stabilize market expectations, to balance cross-border capital flows, and to keep the RMB exchange rate basically stable at a reasonable and balanced level. Third, standardized regulation and steady operation of the financial market will be pushed forward. The establishment of the bond standards committee will be promoted, to unify the information disclosure and access standards of debenture bonds. Regulatory and healthy development of the asset securitization market will be advanced, to steadily expand the pilot program of non-performing assets securitization. Institution reform of the stock market will be carried out, to further develop and improve the multi-layered equity market. Futures and derivatives market will be steadily developed. Institution building of gold market will be strengthened. Construction and standardized management of the bill market will be pushed forward. And opening-up of the financial market will be further advanced. Fourth, pilot program of financial opening-up and innovation in the free trade zone will be moved forward, to promote the construction of green financial system, and steadily push forward debt to equity swap on the market and legal basis.

3.2 Greater importance will be placed on preventing and controlling financial risks

The Central Economic Work Conference has pointed out that, in 2017, greater importance will be attached to curbing financial risk, decisions will be made to resolve a batch of risks, efforts will be taken to prevent asset bubbles, and to improve regulation capacity, so as to forestall systemic financial risks. Therefore, in 2017, efforts will be made in the following aspects. First, to strengthen macro-prudential management, effectively prevent all kinds of asset bubbles. To strengthen financial risks assessment and early warning, focusing on risks in industries with excess capacity, asset quality in banking sector, capital market, local trading sites, cross-market financial businesses, illegal fundraising and etc. To respect for the law of the market, timely defuse potential risks, and achieve sound and steady development of the market under the complex and changing environment. Second, to roll out the coordination mechanism of financial regulation, study and push forward reform of the financial regulatory system. To accelerate the construction of a regulatory system adapting to the development of modern financial market and businesses. To enhance financial regulation coordination with inter-departmental collaboration. To strengthen functional regulation and penetration of regulation on financial business. To establish a sound regulatory system adapting to the characteristics of internet finance. Third, to enhance the soundness of financial institutions and properly handle a number of high-risk financial institutions. To research and formulate regulatory standards and policies on risk assessment and handling of systemically important financial institutions. To explore the market-based mechanism on handling risks of financial institutions. To carry forward the special rectification of risks in internet finance and construction of long-term mechanism for internet finance regulation. Fourth, to practice strict regulation in accordance with the law, crack down on all violations of laws and regulations. To implement the "law-based, strict, and comprehensive" regulatory requirements to maintain the stability of capital market.

3.3 The goal and function for the financial market to serve the real economy will be further highlighted

The Central Economic Work Conference has planed that, in 2017, the economic work will remain committed to the underlying principle of making progress while keeping performance stable, and focus on supply-side structural reform. The fundamental means of supply-side structural reform is to deepen the reform, and improve the mechanism that market plays a decisive role in resources allocation. In order to improve the quality and efficiency of the supply system, and enhance the momentum of sustained economic growth, it is necessary to allocate and utilize financial resources more effectively, so as to improve the efficiency of financial supply. This requires a comprehensive deepening of the financial system reform, increase of financial supply, and improvement of financial efficiency, to let the market play a decisive role in the allocation of resources. In 2017, China's financial market development will adhere to the fundamental purpose of providing service to the real economy. Financial market will play a bigger role in optimizing the allocation of resources, promoting the transformation and upgrading of economic structures, and supporting the supply-side structural reform. First, the financial market will adapt to and steer the new normal in economic development, establish and implement new concept of development, steer toward higher-quality, more efficient, fair, and sustainable economic growth. Second, the financial market will continue to deepen the reform of mechanisms, strengthen market infrastructure, reinforce the incentive and restraint mechanism, improve the operation and service efficiency, so as to put into full play its role of optimizing the allocation of resources, guiding a rational flow of factors of production, managing risks and wealth, and to provide sustainable support for revitalizing the real economy. Third, the financial market will cooperate with the supply-side structural reform, to play a greater role in further promoting the strategic tasks of cutting overcapacity, reducing excess inventory, deleveraging, lowering costs and strengthening areas of weakness. As for the capital market, efforts will be given to further deepen the reform of multi-layered market system, constantly optimize the financing structure, intensify equity financing, and thus provide a variety of financial service to the real economy and reduce the leverage ratio and financing costs of enterprises. Mergers and acquisitions mechanism and market-oriented reforms will be further promoted to better support the economic restructuring and industrial upgrading. Fourth, the financial market, especially the capital market, must maintain a steady growth, during the course of providing support to the real economy. The smooth operation of the financial market is the prerequisite and decisive factor in supporting the real economy, and also the foundation of reforms and development in future.

第二章　货币市场

2016年，货币市场运行平稳，同业拆借市场、债券回购市场、同业存单市场成交量均保持增长。银行间同业拆借市场准入的行政许可取消，提升了市场效率和金融机构的参与热情。票据承兑、贴现、转贴现业务量大幅下降，票据融资规模小幅增长。市场利率水平总体保持平稳，波幅减小。票据市场制度建设稳步推进，《票据交易管理办法》发布，上海票据交易所成立，票据市场功能有望进一步丰富和增强。

一、同业拆借市场

2016年，全国银行间同业拆借市场整体运行平稳，交易量保持稳健快速增长，利率水平稳中小幅上升。3月，取消了“进入全国银行间同业拆借市场审批”行政许可，提高了市场准入效率。市场参与主体持续增长，截至2016年末，同业拆借市场共有市场成员1 725家。

（一）同业拆借市场的运行情况

2016年，同业拆借市场累计成交95.91万亿元，日均成交量为3 821.24亿元，同比增长48.18%。同业拆借全年加权平均利率为2.18%，同比上升14.13个基点。同业拆借日加权利率最高点为12月30日的2.8836%，比2015年的最高点低168.76个基点。最低点为2月19日的2.0139%，比2015年的最低点高82.67个基点。全年利率极差为86.97个基点，

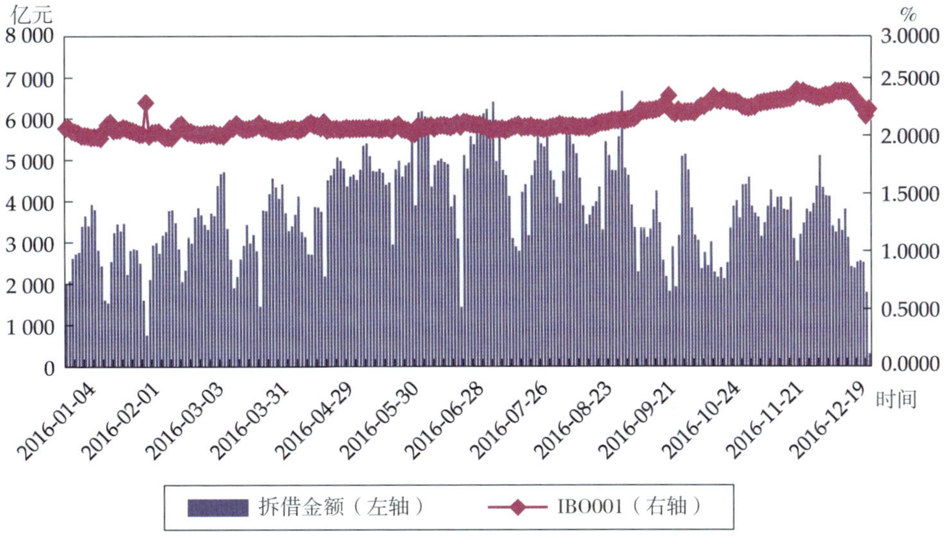

数据来源：全国银行间同业拆借中心。

图2-1　2016年同业拆借交易量和利率走势

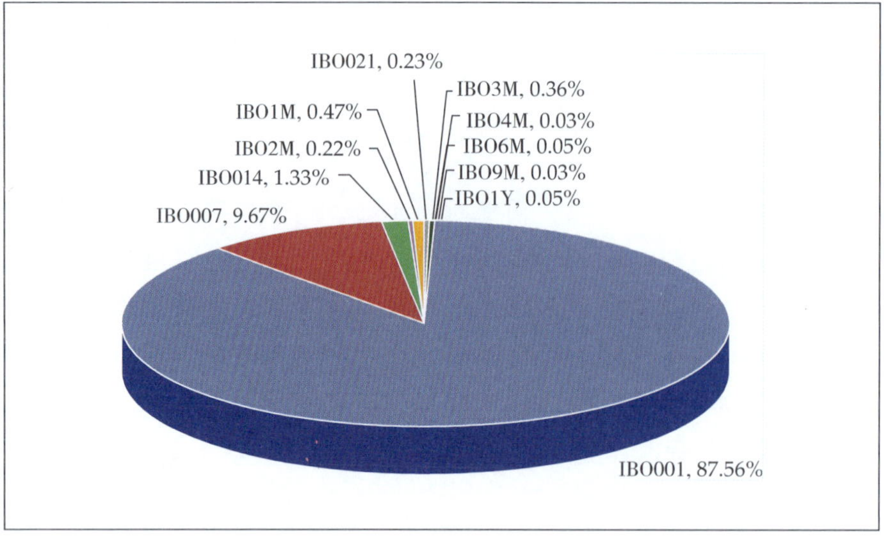

数据来源：全国银行间同业拆借中心。

图2-2 2016年同业拆借交易期限结构

同比缩小251.44个基点，利率曲线趋于平坦化。

同业拆借交易期限结构继续向短期集中，7天期以内交易合计成交93.25万亿元，占总交易量的97.23%，较上年上升1.15个百分点。其中，隔夜交易品种累计成交83.98万亿元，占总交易量的87.56%，较上年上升3.47个百分点；7天期拆借交易占比为9.67%，较上年下降2.32个百分点；14天至3个月期限拆借交易占比为2.61%，较上年下降1.18个百分点；3个月以上期限拆借交易占比为0.16%，较上年上升0.03个百分点。

2016年，同业拆借市场交易主体以银行业金融机构为主，占同业拆借总交易量的86.65%，非银行金融机构交易量占比为13.35%。其中，股份制商业银行的交易量占比最大，为37.91%，较上年上升5.35个百分点；大型商业银行、城市商业银行和政策性银行占比分别为17.17%、14.22%和8.97%；非银行金融机构中，证券公司、财务公司交易较为活跃，交易量占比分别为9.18%和3.30%。

（二）同业拆借市场运行的主要特点

1. 交易规模继续放量

2016年，同业拆借市场交易总量继续放大，月度成交规模由年初的5.72万亿元逐渐上升至年中的10万亿元左右，8月的月度成交规模最高，达到10.73万亿元。9~10月，受季节性因素叠加中秋、国庆双节影响，货币市场资金面收紧，交易规模有所下降，10月成交量为5.52万亿元。随着年末的临近，金融机构流动性管理需求增加，11月和12月成交规模转而上涨。

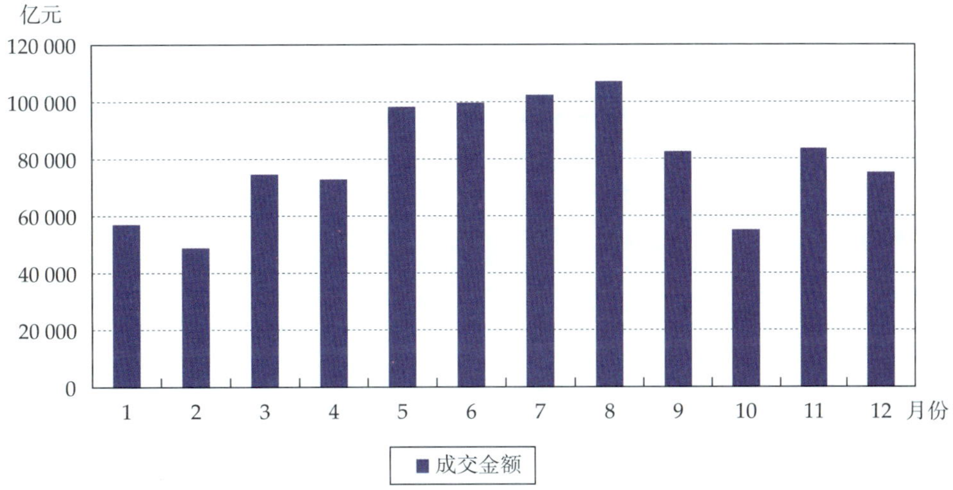

数据来源：全国银行间同业拆借中心。

图2-3　2016年同业拆借市场各月成交规模

数据来源：全国银行间同业拆借中心。

图2-4　2007—2016年同业拆借市场成交情况

2. 利率中枢小幅上移，利率曲线趋于平坦化

2016年，同业拆借市场成交利率整体稳步上行，利率中枢较上年小幅上移。年初，受节日效应影响，利率出现了两次阶段性跳涨，2月同业拆借市场日加权平均利率涨至2.37%，随着季节性因素的消退，利率回落至2.10%左右震荡。从第三季度末起，资金面收紧，各期限利率震荡上行，12月30日达到全年最高点，日加权利率为2.8836%。

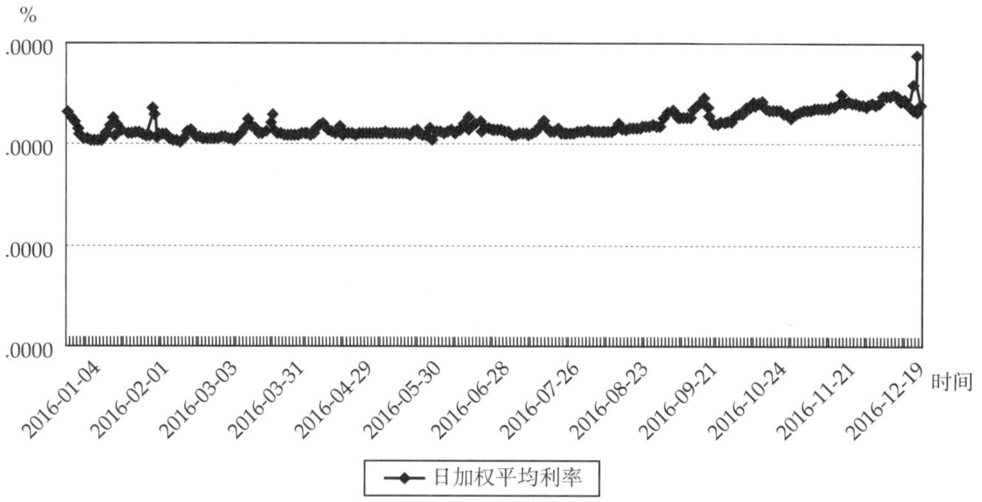

数据来源：全国银行间同业拆借中心。

图2-5 2016年全年日成交量及日加权平均利率走势

3. 融资结构以大型商业银行融出为主

同业拆借市场的融资结构继续保持银行业金融机构融出、非银行金融机构融入的特点。其中，净融出量最大的机构为大型商业银行，全年累计净融出16.28万亿元，占净融出机构融出总量的39.74%。其次是政策性银行和股份制商业银行，净融出量分别为13.68万亿元和9.42万亿元，净融出占比分别为33.39%和23.00%。非银行金融机构中，证券公司和财务公司的净融入量最大，分别为17.58万亿元和5.35万亿元，净融入占比分别为42.91%和13.05%。

（三）同业拆借市场发展展望

随着市场准入行政许可取消，市场参与主体联网入市更加便利，效率得以提高，预计2017年市场成员数量仍将保持比较积极的增长态势，市场成员结构得到进一步优化。同时，取消行政许可不是放松监管，而是监管方式和监管理念向市场化的方向更进一步，同业拆借市场的管理将更加注重事中事后监管，保障市场平稳健康发展。同业拆借市场交易继续保持活跃，在宏观调控及“去杠杆”的政策指导下，预计市场交易量将保持温和增长，交易期限结构更加合理。同业拆借市场将更好地为金融机构管理流动性发挥功能作用，为Shibor基准利率的形成夯实市场交易基础。

二、债券回购市场

2016年，银行间债券回购市场交易规模继续扩大，但增幅放缓，交易期限结构继续呈现短期化特征；回购利率小幅下行，利率波幅明显减小；政策性银行债在回购标的中占比最大；政策性银行、大型商业银行和股份制商业银行表现为资金净融出。

（一）债券回购市场的运行情况

2016年，债券回购市场累计成交817.30万亿元，同比增长41.95%。其中，银行间债券回购市场累计成交601.30万亿元，同比增长31.36%。交易所质押回购市场累计成交216.00万亿元，同比增长85.6%。在银行间债券市场中，质押式回购累计成交568.27万亿元，同比增长31.42%；买断式回购累计成交33.03万亿元，同比增长30.29%。

2016年，银行间债券回购市场回购利率及波动幅度均较上年有所下降。质押式回购加权平均利率为2.19%，较2015年上升了17个基点。最高点为12月30日的3.04%，最低点为2月19日的1.96%，利率极差为108个基点，比2015年下降230个基点。买断式回购日加权平均利率为2.55%，比2015年上升10个基点，利率极差为153个基点，比2015年下降210个基点。2016年，质押式回购利率与买断式回购利率走势保持一致，市场整体利率水平高于2015年。

2016年，交易所质押回购市场利率平均水平较上年上升，波动幅度缩小。1天回购定盘平均利率为2.582%，最高点为13.905%，最低点为0.593%。7天回购定盘平均利率为2.668%，最高点为7.466%，最低点为1.331%。

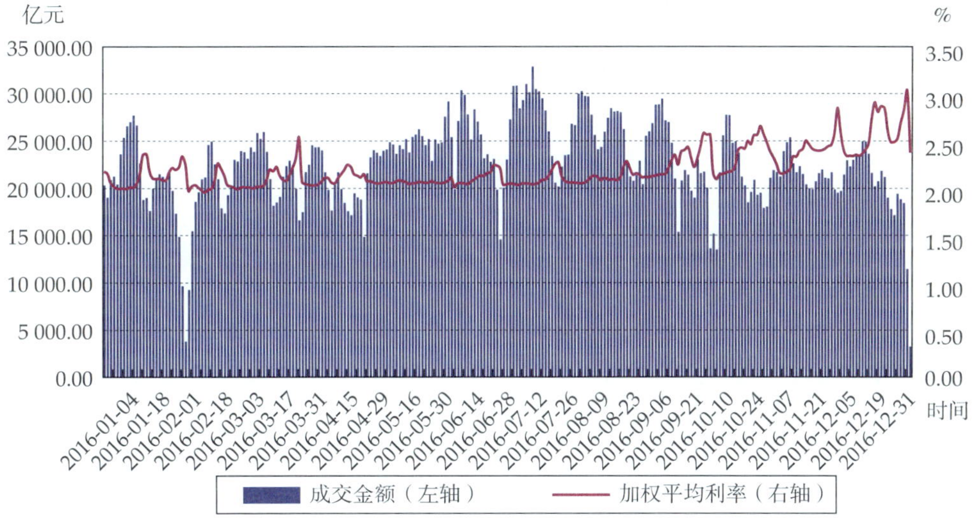

数据来源：中国货币网。

图2-6 2016年银行间质押式回购成交量价

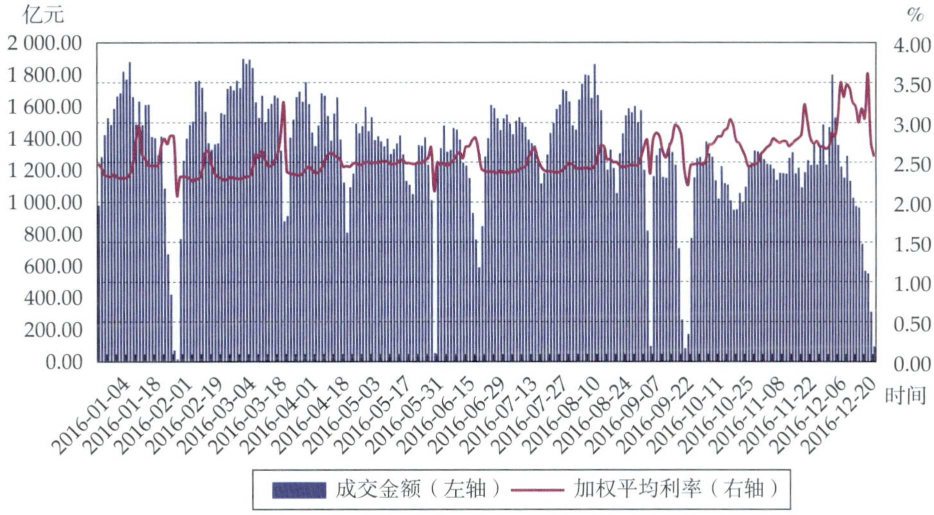

数据来源：中国货币网。

图2-7 2016年银行间买断式回购成交量价

（二）债券回购市场运行的主要特点

1. 回购市场交易规模继续扩大

2016年，银行间债券回购市场成交规模继续扩大，但增幅较上年下降。交易额为601.30万亿元，比上年增加143.54万亿元，增长率较上年下降了72.84个百分点。

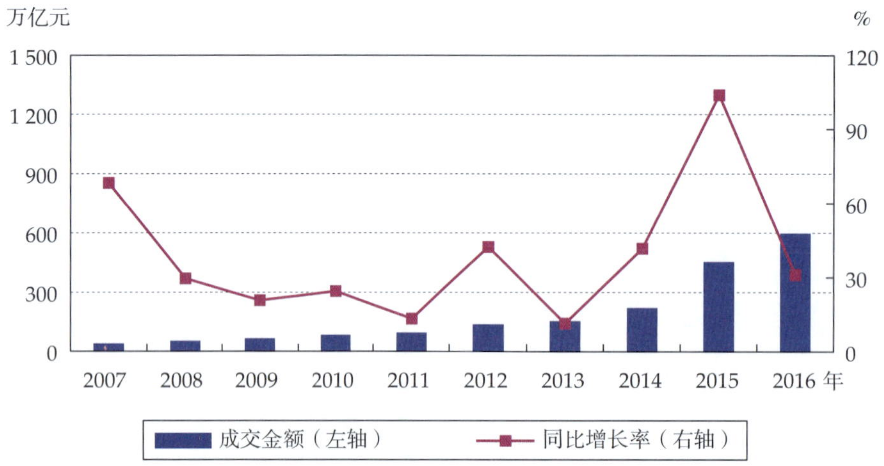

数据来源：中国货币网。

图2-8　2007—2016年银行间债券回购市场交易规模及增长率

2. 交易期限结构继续呈现短期化

在交易期限结构方面，7天以下的质押式回购交易占比达96.43%，较上年小幅增加0.14个百分点。其中，隔夜品种成交继续活跃，共成交486.11万亿元，占质押式回购总成交量的85.54%，与上年的85.59%基本持平；7天品种成交量占比为10.89%，较上年的10.67%小幅增加0.22个百分点。14天以上期限回购交易占比有所下降，其中14天品种成交量占比为2.43%，较上年的2.64%下降0.21个百分点，21天及以上的交易成交占比为1.13%，较上年的1.09%小幅上升0.04个百分点。

买断式回购交易期限结构也在上年的基础上继续呈现短期化，7天以下的交易占总成交量比重达93.41%，较上年的92.49%增加0.92个百分点。

3. 政策性银行债在回购标的中占比最大

2016年，以政府债券、央行票据和政策性银行债为标的的质押式回购占比为75.09%，比上年减少了1.66个百分点。其中，以央行票据作为回购标的的交易占比由上年的0.54%进一步减少至0.47%，延续了自2009年以来的下降趋势；以政策性银行债作为回购标的的交易占比由上年的42.24%小幅下降为42.05%，下降了0.19个百分点；以政府债券作为回购标的的交易占比由上年的35.79%下降到32.57%，下降了3.22个百分点。同时，以短期融资券、超短期融资券、中期票据和企业债券为标的的质押式回购占比为13.71%，比上年下降了1.28个百分点。

2016年，以政府债券、央行票据和政策性银行债为标的的买断式回购占比为47.95%，比上年增加4.38个百分点。其中，

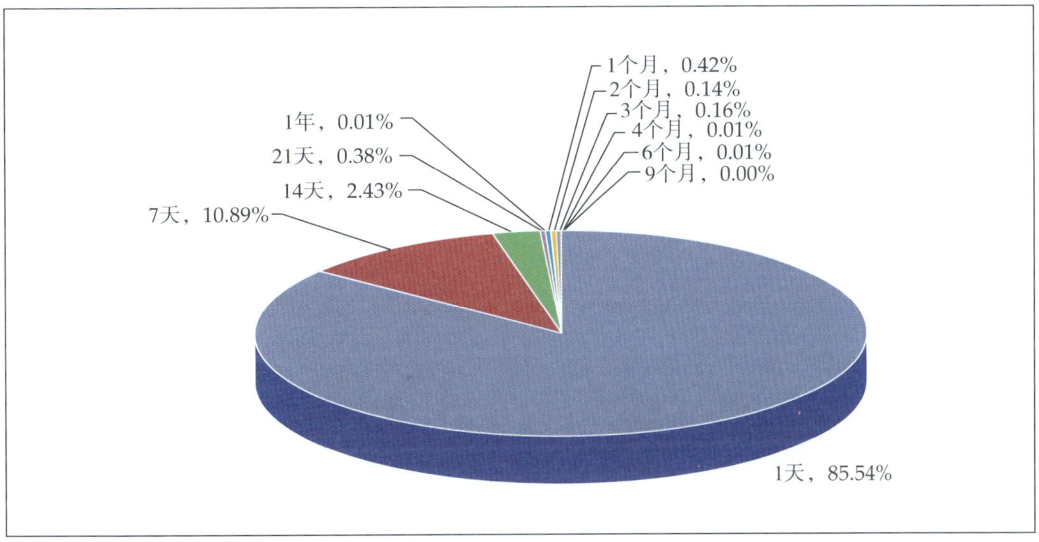

数据来源：中国货币网。

图2-9 2016年债券市场质押式回购交易期限结构

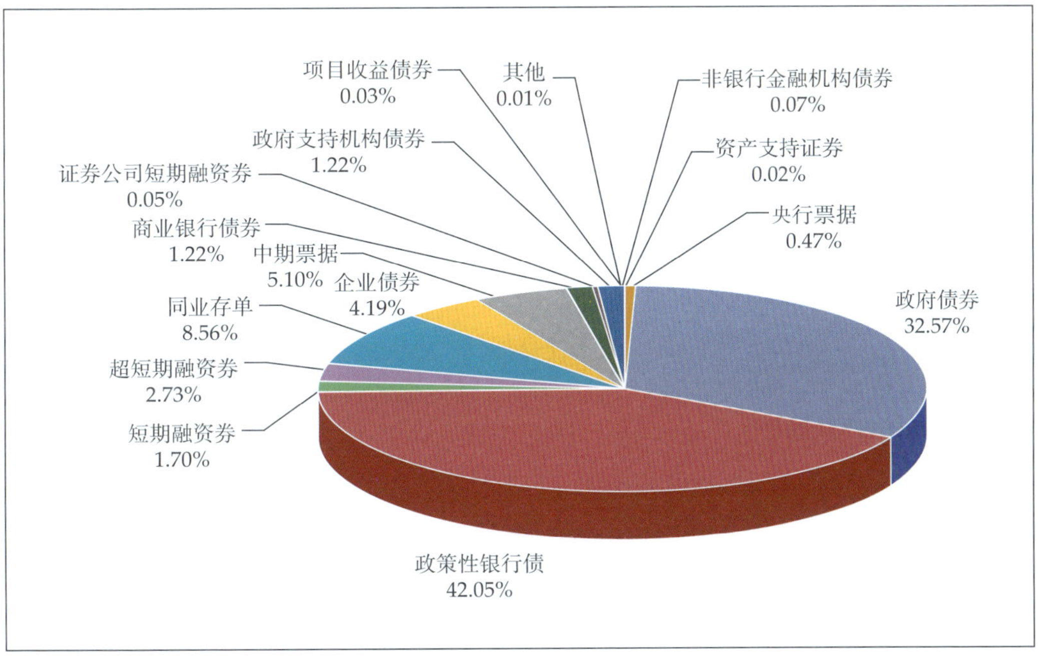

数据来源：中国货币网。

图2-10 2016年债券市场质押式回购交易标的结构

以政府债券作为回购标的的买断式回购占比12.69%，较上年下降了4.29个百分点，以政策性银行债和央行票据作为回购标的的买断式回购占比分别为35.25%和0.01%，分别比上年上升了8.78个百分点和与上年持平。以短期融资券、超短期融资券、中期票据、集合票据和企业债券为标的的买断式回购占比由上年的54.03%下降为44.48%，下降了9.55个百分点。其中，回购标的为企业债券的买断式回购出现较大幅度下降，其成交占比由2015年的23.94%下降为17.93%。

4. 政策性银行、大型商业银行和股份制商业银行资金净融出

从资金净流向来看，融出资金前三位的机构分别是政策性银行、大型商业银行和股份制商业银行，净融出资金分别为137.14万亿元、92.18万亿元和31.22万亿元；净融入资金前三位的机构分别是农村金融机构、非法人金融产品类投资和非银行金融机构，净融入资金分别为81.49万亿元、81.22万亿元和48.03万亿元。

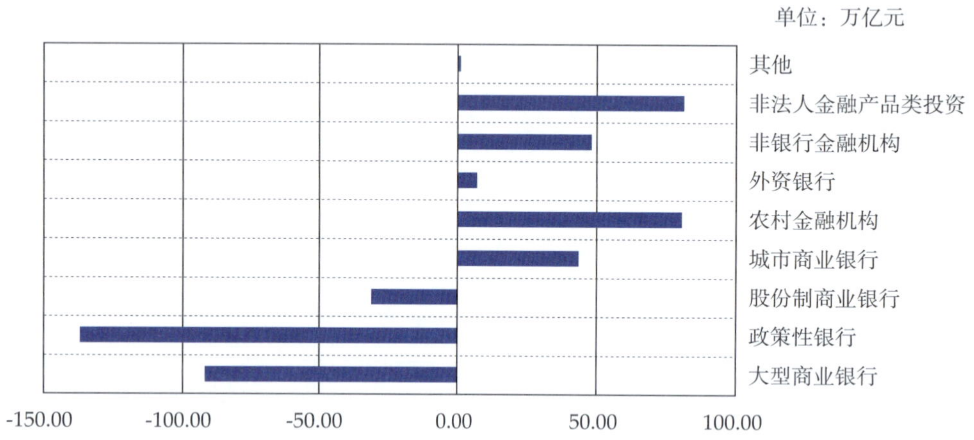

注：1.图中数据为正回购减去逆回购的净回购金额。

2.大型商业银行包含中国工商银行、中国农业银行、中国银行、中国建设银行、交通银行、中国邮政储蓄银行等6家。

3.政策性银行仍包含国家开发银行。

4.股份制商业银行不含交通银行。

5.农村金融机构含农村商业银行和合作银行、农村信用联社、村镇银行。

6.非银行金融机构含证券公司、基金公司、财务公司、保险公司、保险公司的资产管理公司、资产管理公司、信托投资公司等。

7.非法人金融产品类投资含基金、基金公司的特定客户资产管理业务、证券公司的证券资产管理业务、保险公司的保险产品、社保基金、企业年金、商业银行资产管理、信托公司的金融产品、其他投资产品等。

数据来源：中国货币网。

图2-11 2016年债券回购市场机构交易情况

5. 回购利率的平稳性增强

2016年，质押式回购日加权平均利率之间的标准差为0.20，较上年的0.82下降了75.61%；买断式回购日加权平均利率之间的标准差为0.24，较上年的0.83下降了71.08%。以交易占绝对比重的质押式回购日加权利率为例，从日加权平均利率与全年加权平均利率间的绝对差值来看，2016年回购利率的平稳性也显著增强。

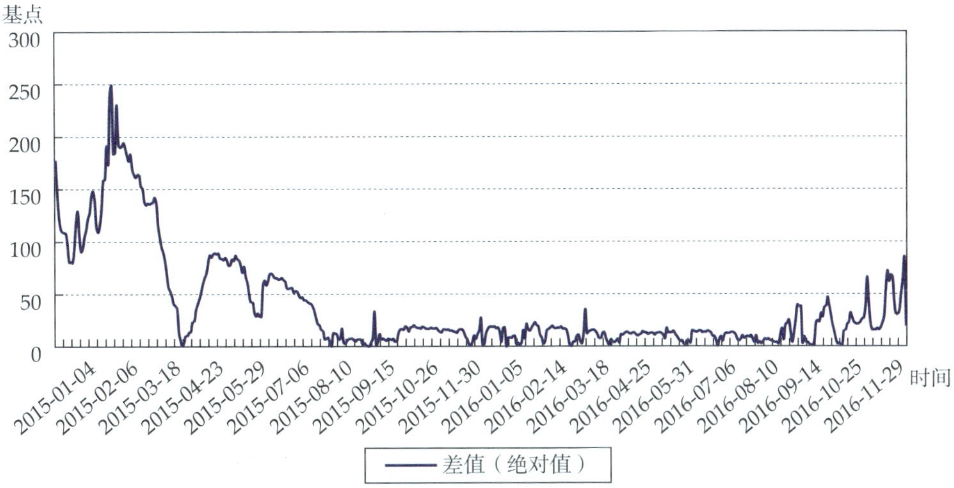

数据来源：中国货币网。

图2-12 2015—2016年债券回购利率与同业拆借利差情况

（三）债券回购市场发展展望

2017年是实施“十三五”规划的重要一年，也是供给侧结构性改革的深化之年，我国经济将进入新的发展阶段，货币政策将保持稳健中性，加强预期引导，全面做好稳增长、促改革、调结构、惠民生、防风险各项工作，促进经济金融平稳健康发展。2017年我国银行间债券回购市场将会保持稳步健康发展。一是在流动性基本稳定的环境下，银行间债券回购市场的交易将保持平稳较快发展，市场规模有望稳步提升。二是随着金融加大服务供给侧结构性改革力度，“双创”、科技、战略性新兴产业等重点领域的企业所发行的债券将可能有所增加，回购标的券种也将会相应增加。三是债券回购市场投资者类型将会进一步丰富。随着我国金融市场的进一步发展以及金融业双向开放的进一步扩大，将会有更多类型的境内外投资者参与到债券回购市场中，非银行金融机构等在债券回购市场的活跃度也将有所提升，债券回购市场投资者类型将进一步多样化。

三、同业存单市场

2016年，同业存单市场整体平稳运行，发行量和托管余额大幅增加，发行利率总体稳定。发行主体有序扩容，认购主体类型更趋丰富。二级市场交投保持活跃，参与主体不断扩大。

（一）同业存单市场的运行情况

2016年，共493家机构发行同业存单16 471只，发行金额达13.04万亿元，同比增长144.34%，共2 124家机构/非法人参与认购。年末托管余额6.28万亿元，较上年末增加3.25万亿元。2016年发行规模中的93.58%由AA级及以上机构发行，其中64.72%由AAA级机构发行。

2016年同业存单发行期限主要集中在1年期以内，以3个月、6个月及1年期为主，且三类期限产品整体结构分布较为均衡。3个月、6个月、1年期的同业存单发行规模分别占总发行金额的27.72%、25.17%和22.91%，同比分别下降3.9个百分点、下降0.87个百分点和上升5.25个百分点。1个月期产品发行量占总发行规模的17.22%。

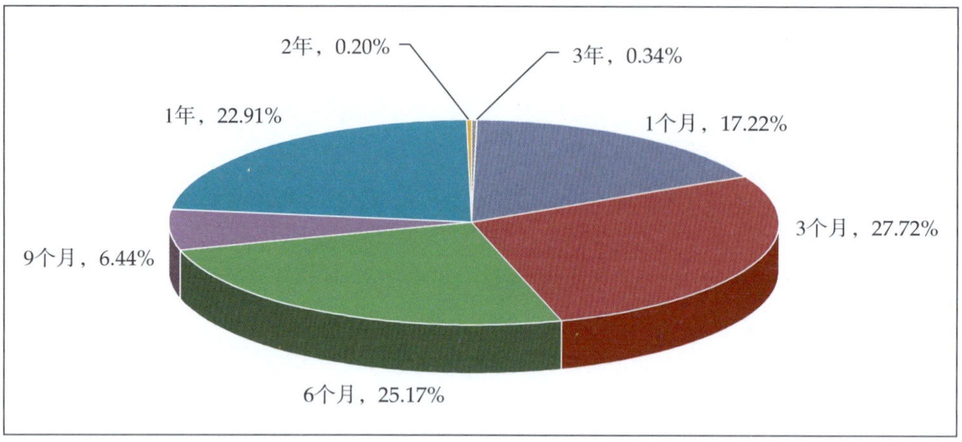

数据来源：中国外汇交易中心。

图2-13　2016年同业存单发行期限分布

2016年，同业存单发行价格整体表现平稳。第四季度受货币市场流动性紧张影响，同业存单发行利率震荡上行，12月达到5%左右。全年发行价格最低值为2.3684%，最高值为5.5850%。年末3个月、6个月和1年期品种发行利率较年初分别上升129个基点、122个基点和88个基点。

2016年，共4 877家机构/非法人参与同业存单二级市场交易，累计成交22.2万笔，成交金额70.40万亿元，同比增长262.89%。月度交易量呈现阶梯式上行，月均交易量达5.86万亿元。交易方式以质押式回购为主，共达成交易48.67万亿元，占总交易额的69.14%；以现券买卖方式达成交易20.03万亿元，占总交

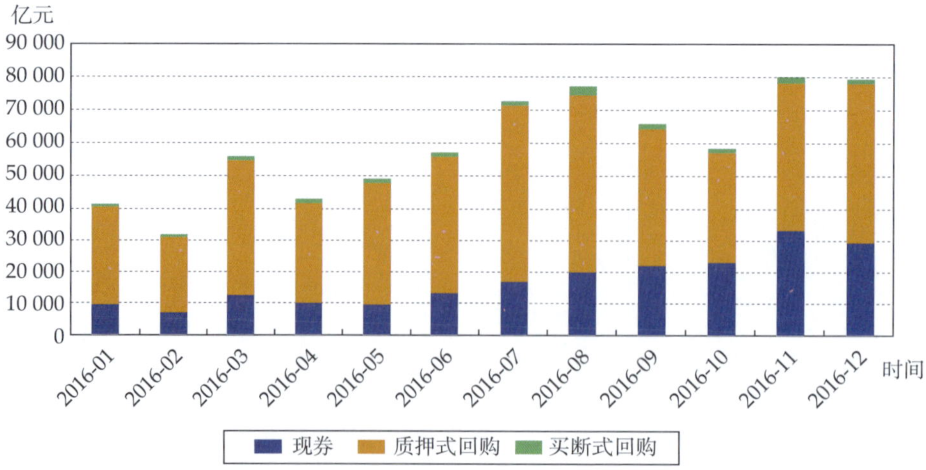

数据来源：中国外汇交易中心。

图2-14　2016年同业存单二级市场月度交易量

易额的28.46%；以买断式回购方式达成交易1.69万亿元。

2016年，同业存单二级市场流动性进一步增强。全年现券换手率达382.72%，较上年增加239.64个百分点，高于记账式国债、中期票据、企业债券等，仅次于短期融资券、超短期融资券等短期品种。回购换手率（月平均）达87.43%，较上年增加46.15个百分点，仅次于记账式国债、政策性银行债、短期融资券等利率债或短期品种。

（二）同业存单市场运行的主要特点

1. 发行主体有序扩容，发行规模大幅增加

同业存单因其高效、灵活、透明度高等特点，受到市场成员的广泛认可，发展速度不断加快。2016年6月，全国银行间同业拆借中心将同业存单发行人范围扩大至2016年合格审慎评估遴选的自律机制核心成员、基础

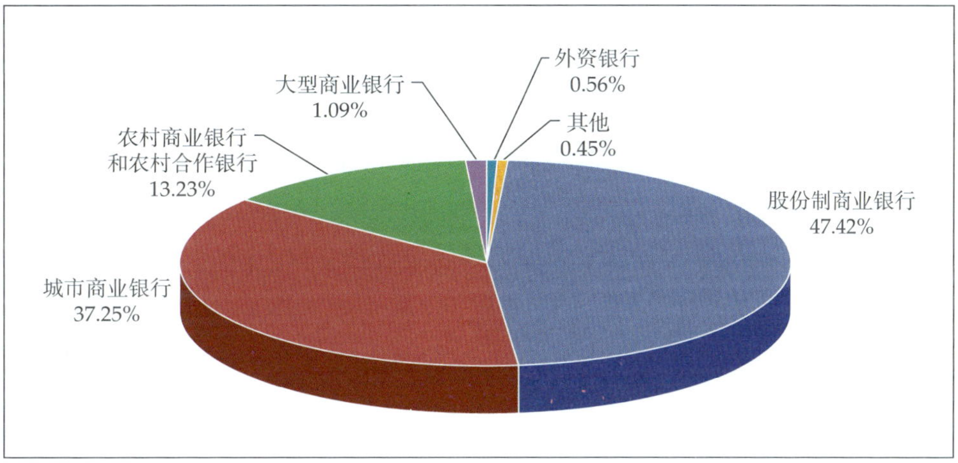

数据来源：中国外汇交易中心。

图2-15 2016年同业存单发行主体结构

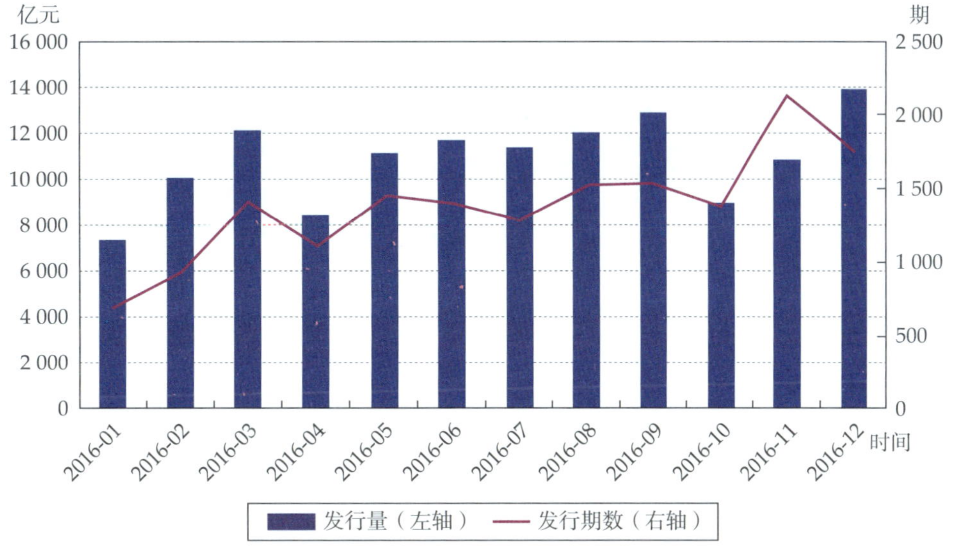

数据来源：中国外汇交易中心。

图2-16 2016年同业存单月度发行情况

成员与观察成员，具备同业存单发行资格的机构个数扩大至1 556家。2016年共有510家机构披露了年度发行计划，占总数的1/3左右。全年实际发行机构较上年增加202家。股份制商业银行和城市商业银行为同业存单发行人主力，发行金额分别占全部发行量的47.42%和37.25%，比上年分别下降7.99个和上升3.66个百分点；农村商业银行和农村合作银行合计发行量占13.23%，比上年上升4.94个百分点。

2016年同业存单发行规模是上年的2.5倍，发行期数同比增加176.06%。受季末、资金面等因素影响，同业存单市场逢季末发行量较大，全年月发行量呈小幅震荡增长态势，月均发行量为1.08万亿元，其中12月发行量达到全年最高，为1.39万亿元。

2. 认购主体类型更趋丰富，非法人机构持有量占比增加

2016年同业存单市场认购主体数量较上年增加了1.7倍，投资者类型也趋于多样化。存款类金融机构认购额占总金额的六成，其中农村信用联社占12.69%，城市商业银行占11.39%，股份制商业银行、国有商业银行、农村商业银行和农村合作银行分别占8.08%、9.79%和9.47%。非法人类产品认购额占比超三成，其中证券投资基金认购金额2.9万亿元，基金管理及其子公司认购金额0.7万亿元。

2016年末商业银行持有同业存单余额3万亿元，占总余额的47.76%。其中股份制商业银行持有0.88万亿元，城市商业银行持有0.75万亿元，国有商业银行持有0.7万亿元，农村商业银行和农村合作银行持有0.54万亿元。2016年1~10月非法人机构的同业存单持有量持续增长，7月末持有余额超过2万亿元，并超越商业银行成为同业存单第一大持有机构。11月、12月非法人机构持续减持同业存单，年末持有余额2.2万亿元，占总余额的35.08%。

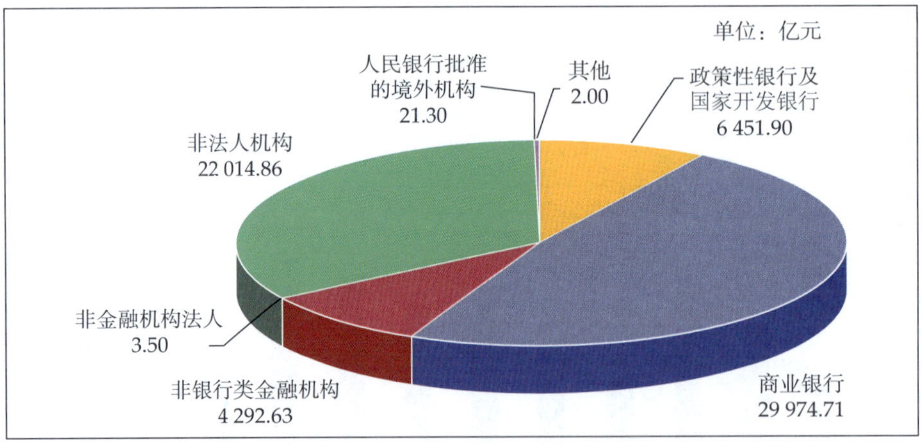

数据来源：上海清算所。

图2–17　2016年末同业存单投资者持有余额

3. 发行价格整体平稳，短期品种波动加剧

2016年1~10月，同业存单发行价格走势平稳，发行利率基本保持在2.60%到3.20%。年末同业资金成本不断攀升，短期品种受影响更大，12月，1个月、3个月、6个月和1年期限品种的平均发行利率环比分别上升150个、92个、88个和64个基点。

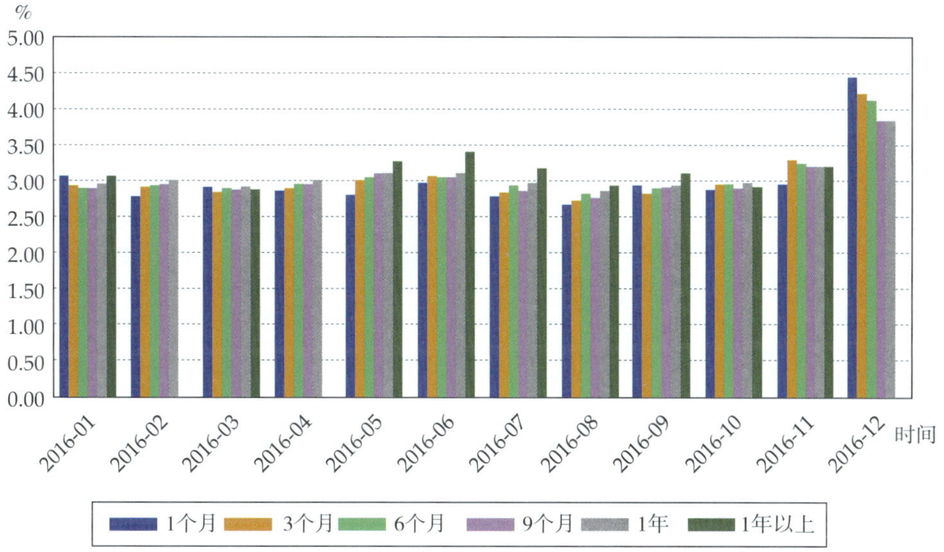

数据来源：上海清算所。

图2-18 2016年各期限同业存单月度平均发行价格

2016年同业存单发行价格基本围绕SHIBOR基准利率波动，年末偏离幅度变大。以股份制商业银行3个月同业存单的发行利率为例，1~10月同业存单发行利率与SHIBOR的利差基本保持在20个基点以内，11月利差逐步攀升，12月利差基本维持在100个基点以上，最高达134个基点。

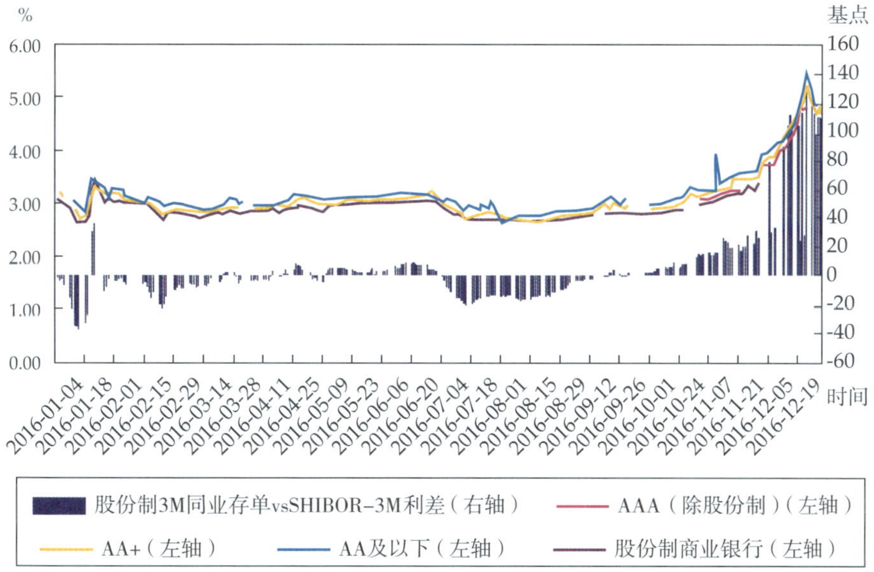

数据来源：中国外汇交易中心。

图2-19 2016年3个月期同业存单发行价格及利差走势

（三）同业存单市场发展展望

从一级市场来看，预计2017年扩大发行主体范围的工作将继续有序进行，参与同业存单实际发行的发行人数量将会继续增加，同业存单市场将保持平稳有序运行。但在稳健中性的货币政策下，叠加此前提出并正在推进的抑制资产泡沫、去杠杆等举措，资金面存在一定的不确定性，预计2017年同业存单的发行规模增速将放缓，发行期限将倾向于短期和长期两端，发行价格波动性将增大。

从二级市场来看，随着同业存单存量的积累和发行规模继续增长，银行间市场准入的不断放开以及同业存单交易机制的不断优化，同业存单各品种交易活跃度将继续保持，参与同业存单二级市场交易的主体范围也将进一步扩大。

四、票据市场

2016年是票据市场发展具有里程碑意义的一年。受宏观经济基本面以及传统票据业务风险隐患加快暴露等因素影响，金融机构票据承兑、贴现、转贴现业务量大幅下降。票据市场利率小幅波动、稳中有降。市场交易结构发生深刻变化，票据回购交易大幅萎缩，电子票据业务占比显著提升。同时，票据业务监管力度持续增强，市场基础设施以及制度建设取得突破性进展，《票据交易管理办法》正式发布以及上海票据交易所设立，标志着全国统一的票据市场逐步形成，票据市场在金融市场体系中的地位以及对实体经济发展的支持作用将进一步增强。

（一）票据市场的运行情况

1. 签发承兑业务

2016年以来，受经济增速下行压力加大、经济结构调整加快的影响，企业的融资需求较为低迷，商业汇票签发量明显下降。同时，由于票据风险案件集中爆发、监管力度持续加大，融资性票据业务受到较大影响，进一步加剧了票据承兑业务的萎缩。2016年，企业累计签发商业汇票18.1万亿元，同比下降19.3%；期末商业汇票未到期金额9.0万亿元，同比下降13.3%。年末承兑余额较年初下降1.4万亿元。从行业结构看，企业签发的银行承兑汇票余额集中在制造业、批发和零售业。从企业结构看，由中小型企业签发的银行承兑汇票约占2/3。与此相反，尽管票据承兑总量呈现收缩迹象，但电子商业汇票（以下简称电票）承兑业务仍保持较快增长。全年电票系统累计签发230.47万笔，出票金额8.34万亿元，同比分别增长71.9%和49.0%，市场占比进一步提升。

2. 贴现交易业务

2016年，面对接连发生的票据业务风险事件和外部监管检查的压力，商业银行在加大票据业务风险管控的同时，适时调整票据交易结构，减少了票据回购交易，加大票据贴现与买断力度以补充信贷规模的不足，促使表外票据逐步回归表内，实现了票据融资规模的较快增长。2016年金融机构累计贴现（含转贴现）84.5万亿元，同比下降17.2%；年末贴现余额为5.5万亿元，仍保持19.6%的正向增长。票据融资增长放缓，年末比年初增加8 946亿元，同比少增7 684亿元。期末票据融资余额占各项贷款的比重为5.1%，同比上升了0.2个百分点。同时，纸票业务风险高发在一定程度上促进了电票业务的快速发展。2016金融机构电票贴现累计83.77万笔、金额5.77万亿元，同比分别增长69.1%和54.5%；累计转贴现325.08万笔、金额49.2万亿元，同比分别增长108.8%和122.3%。

3. 市场利率走势

2016年，在稳健货币政策的大基调下，人民银行通过公开市场操作调节流动性，维持相对中性的货币条件，银行体系流动性总体上合理充裕。票据利率在信贷需求不足导致的价格上限和资金成本产生的价格下限双重制约下，呈低位平缓下行走势，仅在年初年尾两头翘升。2016年初，票据风险事件的发生与监管政策出台，加之节前资金需求旺盛导致流动性紧张，推动利率持续上行。随着节后流动性的缓和与案件因素的淡化，票据价格快速回落。3月到11月票据利率总体呈平缓下行、窄幅波动态势。12月，在去杠杆进程加速推进、外汇占款持续下降等背景下，市场流动性频繁出现紧张态势，带动资金成本中枢上移，票据市场价格一路走高。全年买断式转贴现和回购式转贴现平均报价分别为3.10%和3.96%，较上年下降93个和85个基点。

数据来源：Wind资讯。

图2-20　2016年票据直贴利率走势

数据来源：中国票据网。

图2-21　2016年票据转贴现利率走势

（二）票据市场运行的主要特点

1. 票据承兑量连续增长多年后首现下降

在保持连续多年的正向增长之后，2016年票据承兑量较往年有明显的缩减。2011—2015年，企业累计签发商业汇票分别为15.1万亿元、17.9万亿元、20.3万亿元、22.1万亿元和22.4万亿元，同比分别增长23.8%、18.5%、13.4%、8.9%和1.4%。2016年商业汇票累计签发量跌至18.1万亿元，同比下降19.3%。

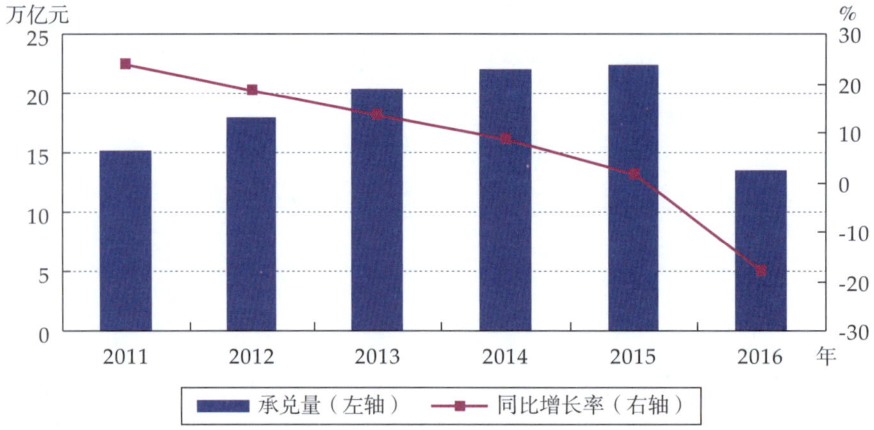

数据来源：中国人民银行。

图2-22 2011—2016年年度票据承兑量

从存量来看，年末承兑余额同比增速也在持续多年的正增长后首度转负。2011—2015年，商业汇票未到期余额分别为6.7万亿元、8.3万亿元、9.0万亿元、9.9万亿元和10.4万亿元，同比分别增长19.6%、23.9%、8.4%、10.0%和5.1%。2016年末，商业汇票未到期余额为9.0万亿元，同比下降13.3%，较年初减少1.4万亿元。

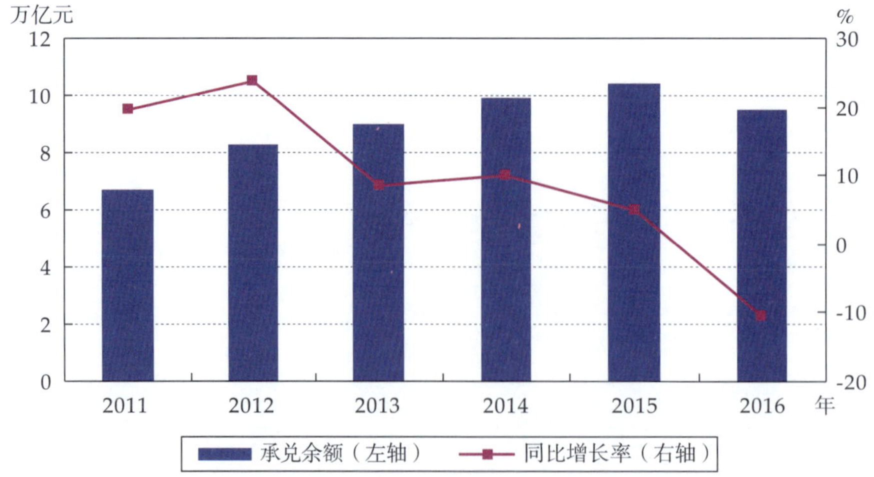

数据来源：中国人民银行。

图2-23 2011—2016年年度票据承兑余额

2016年票据承兑业务下降主要受以下因素的影响。第一，经济增速走低，有效需求不足，企业疲于拓展业务。2016年国内经济维持6.7%的增速，比上年下降0.2个百分点。受此影响，企业扩大生产的意愿不强，开票需求也相应下降。第二，信用环境恶化，逾期垫款增加，银行主动控制风险。为有效控制风险、缓解资金压力，银行对企业授信更趋审慎，有意识地控制了承兑规模的扩张。第三，票据案件爆发，风险集中暴露，监管机构增强整顿力度。自2016年初票据市场相继曝出风险案件，人民银行和银监会多次下发监管文件，票据业务集中进入风险出清和业务整顿的阶段，银行加强对贸易背景真实性等内容的合规性审查，挤压了融资性票据的生存空间，导致承兑业务萎缩。

2. 票据市场对实体经济的支持力度明显增强

2016年，在流动性宽裕的市场条件下，金融机构继续加大票据资产的配置和优质票源的争夺，以票据资产来填补贷款需求不足的影响，通过票据贴现业务来服务实体经济。截至2016年12月末，票据融资余额为5.47万亿元，比年初增加9 000亿元，同比增长19.6%。票据融资余额占人民币贷款余额的比重为5.20%，比上年同期高0.27个百分点。由于中小型企业签发的银行承兑汇票约占总数的三分之二，因此票据市场的发展大大缓解了中小企业“融资难”的问题，且贴现利率持续下行，一般低于同期限贷款利率，一定程度上缓解了企业面临的“融资贵”问题。

票据融资余额占比上升的原因主要有三个方面：一是电票占比的提升拉长融资周期，导致票据融资增量趋减的情况下存量仍保持较高水平。二是在房地产调控、经济下行等背景下总体信贷投放不足，银行主动通过低风险资本占用且流动较强的票据资产进行规模调节，引发票据融资余额在人民币贷款余额中的比重增加。三是监管环境趋严驱使部分表外票据资产重回表内贴现科目，对票据融资的表内余额有一定的扩容作用。

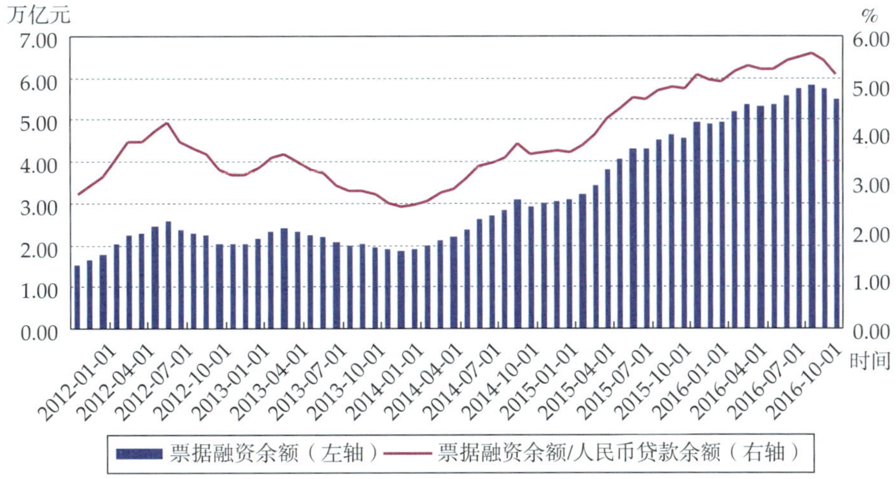

数据来源：中国人民银行。

图2-24 2012—2016年月度票据融资情况

3. 票据交易结构发生显著变化

（1）电子票据业务加速发展。

2016年，电票在签发、直贴和转贴现环节都得到了快速发展，各项业务市场占比大幅提升。一方面，随着纸质票据风险的集中暴露，电子票据以其相对安全透明、便捷高效的优势获得了企业与银行的广泛青睐，催生电子票据的使用意愿。另一方面，人民银行的政策支持以及票据交易所的建立，促进电子票据的业务扩张。2016年9月人民银行发文进一步促进电票业务的发展，12月票据交易所成立，从制度层面和基础设施层面推进了电票的快速发展。2016年，电票系统累计出票金额8.34万亿元，同比增长49.0%；承兑金额8.58万亿元，同比增长48.3%；贴现金额5.77万亿元，同比增长54.5%；转贴现金额49.20万亿元，同比增长122.3%。电票累计出票量和累计贴现量在全部票据累计签发量和累计贴现量中的占比分别达到46.1%和65.1%，同比分别提高了21.0个和39.7个百分点。

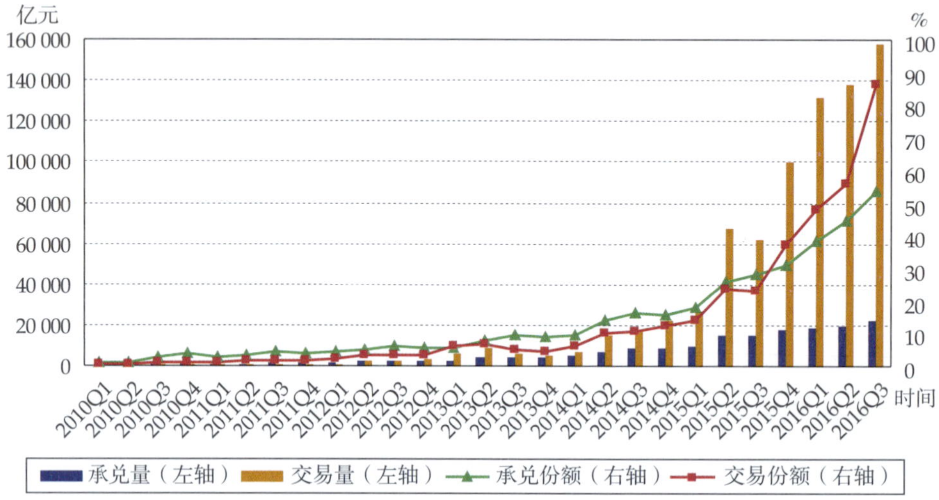

数据来源：中国人民银行。

图2-25 2010—2016年季度电票承兑和交易量及其占比

（2）回购式转贴现业务明显萎缩。

截至2016年上半年，12家主要商业银行①买入返售余额合计为5 234亿元，比年初减少13 617亿元，只占上年同期的18.8%。五大国有银行中，除中国工商银行以外，各行2016年半年度买入返售余额较年初的降幅均在75%以上。2016年“中国票据网”合计报价金额10.8万亿元，同比减少6.2万亿元，降幅为36.5%。其中，买断和卖断报价金额分别为5.66万亿元和3.20万亿元，买断卖断报价金额

① 12家主要商业银行具体为中国工商银行、中国农业银行、中国银行、中国建设银行、交通银行、上海浦东发展银行、招商银行、中国民生银行、兴业银行、中国光大银行、平安银行、华夏银行。

比为1.77，金融机构显现出较强的买票交易意愿。同期，正回购和逆回购合计报价金额1.95万亿元，同比减少3.05万亿元，降幅为61%，反映出在票据业务合规监管趋强的背景下，金融机构主动调整票据回购交易业务发展。

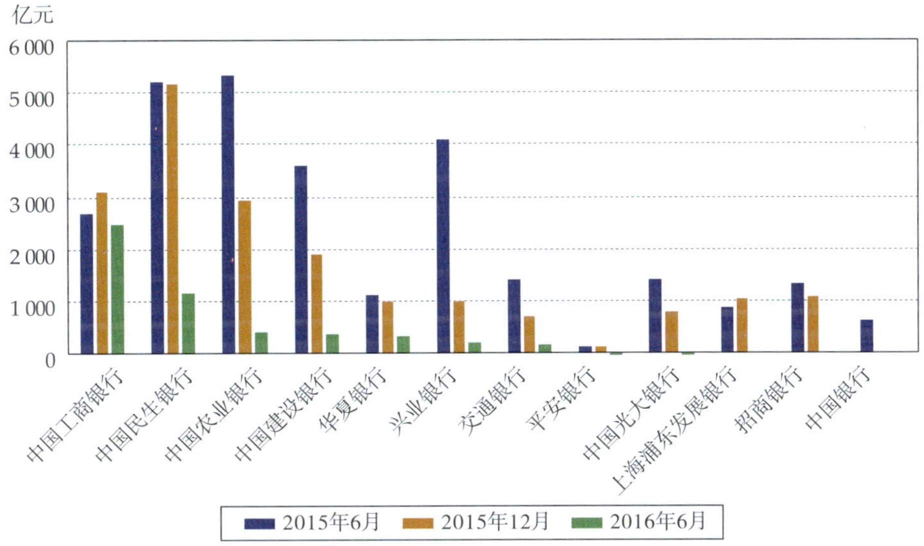

数据来源：各商业银行年报、半年报。

图2-26 2015年以来主要商业银行票据买入返售余额

2016年，票据回购业务大幅收缩除了受监管趋严的影响外，主要受宏观审慎评估体系（MPA）推行的影响。人民银行从2016年起推行的MPA使得票据回购的业务属性回归到同业间真实性的融资需求上。而回购式转贴现的价格受银行内部资金价格的限制，相较于众多非银行机构参与的债券回购市场等，融资价格优势不够突出。因此，回购式转贴现市场急速萎缩。与此同时，商业银行票据资管业务持续发展，个别股份制商业银行资管业务规模达到了数千亿元，资管业务逐步取代回购业务，成为商业银行重要的利润增长点。

4. 票据市场创新方兴未艾

近几年来，在新一轮金融市场深化发展的过程中，金融机构更加注重提升票据业务创新对综合经营效益的贡献。在利率市场化和金融脱媒进程不断加快的背景下，商业银行将跨市场业务创新作为重点，积极加强与信托、证券、基金等金融机构的合作，向市场推出了包括票据资产证券化产品、票据理财、票据资管等多项新型的票据金融产品，有效拓宽了票据业务范围，增强了票据市场深化发展的能力。

（1）票据资产证券化（ABS）初步尝试。

2016年3月29日，全国首单基于票据收益权发行的资产证券化产品——华泰资管—江苏银行“融元1号专项资产支持计划”成功发行，标志着中国票据业务证券化之门正式开启。11月底，招商银行发行规模为200亿元的首单银票ABS——华泰资管—招商银行聚元系列资产支持专项计划。票据资产证券化对商业银行具有非常重要的意义：一方面可以盘活大量优质的存量票据资产，腾出更多的信贷空间更好地支持实体经济融资和产业结构调整；另一方面商业银行通过出售票据资产，既可以转移信用风险，降低风险隐患，又可以释放流动性，加速资金流转，吸纳充裕的社会资金真正进入实体经济，增强银行支持新兴产业的能力。

（2）票据资管、票据理财等票据创新产品成为资金跨市场流动的重要渠道。

近两年来，随着票据收益率大幅下降、同业业务监管力度不断增强，银行传统票据业务经营压力加大，难以再借助规模资金总量扩张、期限错配以及渠道型交易推动业务发展，开始加快多元化票据业务创新，中信银行、平安银行、民生银行、江苏银行等多家银行推出各具特点的票据资管计划或票据收益权转让等产品，获得市场高度关注。票据资管业务作为票据市场银行与非银行金融机构跨市场合作的重要载体，近年来取得了快速的发展。票据资管业务通过对票据资产进行整合托管和运作，在个人投资、企业融资和金融机构票据服务之间建立融资通道，从而提高社会资源的整体配置效能，有效提升了票据业务整体的金融服务功能，有利于银行向集约化的票据经营转型。

（三）票据市场制度和基础设施

长期以来，我国票据市场的制度建设与基础设施建设远远滞后于市场发展的要求，市场透明度低、风险隐患大，特别是一些不法中介的存在严重扰乱了市场秩序，导致近年来票据案件频发。在此背景下，人民银行和银监会多次发文加强对票据市场的监管，但由于缺乏有效手段，监管措施难以落实到位，票据市场主体不断变换花样绕过监管政策，各种违法违规交易屡禁不止。因此，监管部门也意识到只有进一步加强票据市场制度建设和完善市场基础设施，才能从根本上消除票据市场的各种风险隐患。

1. 票据市场制度建设取得突破

2016年4月27日，中国人民银行和银监会共同发布了《关于加强票据业务监管 促进票据市场健康发展的通知》（银发〔2016〕126号，以下简称126号文），要求严格进行贸易背景真实性审查，严格规范同业账户管理，有效防范和控制票据业务风险，促进票据市场健康有序发展。8月27日，中国人民银行下发《关于规范和促进电子商业汇票业务发展的通知》（银发〔2016〕224号，以下简称224号文），明确从2017年1月1日起，单张出票金额在300万元以上的商业汇票必须全部通过电票办理；自2018年1月1日起，原则上单张出票金额在100万元以上的商业汇票必须全部通过电票办理，并对电票贴现、转贴现的交易流程进行简化。12月6日，中国人民银行〔2016〕第29号公告《票据交易管理办法》（以下简称《办法》）正式发布，为上海票据交易所的运行提供制度基础，明确了上海票据交易所在人民银行监督管理下发挥票据交易、登记托管、清算结算和信息服务四大功能，对票据交易规则、票据市场参与者、基础设施、信息电子化、票据登记与托管、交易结算与到期处理等一系列事项进行明确和规范。

一系列政策法规的出台极大地推进了票据市场的制度建设。一是放宽贴现环节贸易的背景审查。224号文和《办法》分别放松了对电票和纸票的贸易背景审查，规定了在贴现环节不再需要企业提供贸易合同和发票。这一规定是票据市场制度的重要突破，极大地简化了企业的贴现流程，提升了企业贴现的积极性，实现票据市场供给端的开源扩容。二是市场参与主体更加多元化。传统的票据市场交易主体较为单一，仅为银行、信托公司、财务公司等金融机构，当市场流动性宽松或趋紧的时候，各参与方的业务需求方向一致，票据交易的同质性、同向性问题严重，容易导致单边市场强势、价格波动剧烈等情况。新规明确向其他金融机构开放电票转贴现市场，其他作为银行间市场交易主体的非银行金融机构可以通过银行业金融机构代理加入电票系统；《办法》明确了在票据交易所模式下，非银行金融机构以及非法人产品可以作为参与主体加入票据交易。多元化的参与主体拆除了票据市场与其他金融市场之间的藩篱，彻底打通了票据资产和其他资产的流通渠道，有利于建立多层次的市场结构，提升市场活跃度，缓和由于市场同质性引起的票据价格剧烈波动。三是转贴现交易更趋便利。此前无论是纸质票据还是电子票据，都要采用线下签订合同的交易模式，而224号文明确了电票转贴现交易无须线下签订合同；《办法》规定票据交易将采取线上签订主协议的方式，这将极大地简化交易流程，提高二级市场交易的活跃度。

2. 票据市场基础设施建设快速推进

近年来我国票据市场发展迅速，票据交易规模已突破百万亿元，成为国内仅次于债券回购的第二大货币子市场。更重要的是，票据作为中小企业极为倚重的融资工具，长期以来由于制度建设与基础设施建设没有及时跟上，交易仍沿用传统的场外一对一询价方式，交易成本高、操作风险大、业务透明度低、风险隐患多。2016年，在票据风险事件不断爆发的背景下，人民银行加快推进全国统一票据市场建设，5月开始票据交易所的筹建工作，11月初人民银行办公厅向各地分支机构、商业银行等机构下发《关于做好票据交易平台接入准备工作的通知》（银办发〔2016〕224号），推进纸票电子化，明确票据交易所系统的试点工作、上线时间等。12月8日票据交易所正式运行，标志着我国统一票据市场建设取得突破性进展。

票据交易所的建立是票据市场乃至整个金融市场一个重大创新，它将形成多方共赢的局面。从监管者角度看，票据交易所的建立有利于提高票据市场的透明度和规范性，便于建立完整、高效的票据市场监管框架，进一步丰富货币政策操作工具，提高货币政策传导的有效性；从市场参与者角度看，票据交易所的建立有利于提高票据市场的交易效率、减少交易成本、降低业务风险，同时通过完善票据市场基础设施、扩充票据市场参与主体，有利于激发票据业务的创新活力，提升票据市场的广度和深度；从企业角度看，票据交易所的建立不仅能够扩大企业承兑和贴现对手的选择面、降低融资难度和融资成本，而且能够通过票据二级市场交易效率的提升推动票据承兑、贴现等一级市场业务的活跃，使得票据更好地为实体经济特别是中小企业融资服务，引导资金“脱虚向实”。

（四）票据市场发展展望

1. 票据市场运行模式将发生根本改变

一方面，随着票据市场制度的完善和票据交易所的建立，票据交易场内化、电子化、信息化、便利化程度将大大提升，票据市场将发展成为以票据交易所为中心，与同业拆借市场、回购市场、短期债券市场等并行独立又相互关联的货币子市场，金融机构的票据业务将成为与金融市场业务、资产管理业务、托管业务相互连接联动的大市场业务，彻底改善以往场外交易模式下票据实物在不同地区传递导致的业务办理时间长、成本高、风险大的局面。另一方面，随着票据市场制度体系和基础设施的逐步完善以及市场主体多元化、票据业务电子化，票据市场运行模式将发生深刻变化，一级市场将实现票据标准化、产品多元化、业务便利化等，票据市场对中小企业的融资功能进一步增强；二级市场将实现对手多元化、流程电子化、业务资金化等，票据市场交易效率将大幅提升，必将促进市场广度和深度的快速扩张。

2. 票据业务综合化经营是大势所趋

随着经济转型升级和票据市场的深化发展，票据融资和服务需求将更加多元化，传统的承兑、贴现、转贴现已难以满足客户需求和市场竞争需要，从而迫使商业银行加大客户挖掘、市场研究和业务创新力度，开展企业综合票据融资服务、跨市场票据资产管理等业务，票据一二级市场集约化、综合化经营的要求越来越高。票据交易所的成立为商业银行票据业务的综合化经营管理创造了条件。商业银行将承兑、贴现、转贴现、再贴现等环节集中到一个票据专营部门进行管理，统筹考虑承兑手续费、保证金、贴现利率和交易价差，有利于提升票据业务的综合回报水平、有效降低融资成本、提升市场竞争力。同时，票据电子化、信息化发展打破了原来的时间和地域限制，交易效率的大幅提升减少了对业务人员的需求，分支机构参与票据二级市场交易的必要性下降，集中决策、专业经营的优势更加突出。因此，大中型商业银行将逐步形成分行贴现、总行专营机构在票据交易所转贴现交易的模式，小银行将更侧重于形成垂直化、扁平化的票据经营体系。与此同时，随着票据交易规范化、合约标准化以及市场透明度的提高，通过票据交易实现监管套利的难度剧增，票据市场对货币政策、市场利率的变动更加敏感，对业务综合回报率要求更高，从而推动票据市场跨市场业务、衍生产品、信用增级、代理经纪、投资咨询等产品和服务的创新发展，业务的复杂性和专业性要求进一步增加，推动票据市场综合化经营的发展。

3. 票据市场风险将得到有效遏制

根据224号文，自2017年起金额在300万元以上的票据均应全部通过电票办理，自2018年起金额在100万元以上的票据均应全部通过电票办理，这将有力地促进电票加快发展，电票市场占有率将迅速上升。低于规定金额的纸质票据，须根据要求在上海票据交易所对票据信息进行电子化登记，且各项业务流程均有严格的信息登记规范操作要求，电子票据发展已经成为必然趋势。与纸质票据相比，电子票据交易信息以电子数据方式存储具有安全性高的优良品质，从而将显著减少票据伪造、变造风险；同时，电子票据交易信息透明度高，将改变部分金融机构依赖票据中介撮合交易的业务模式，有利于金融机构票据业务合规稳健经营，大大降低票据市场的假票风险、操作风险、合规风险等。

专题一 全国银行间同业拆借市场准入管理改革

2016年2月23日，国务院印发《关于取消13项国务院部门行政许可事项的决定》，取消金融机构进入全国银行间同业拆借市场审批。为贯彻落实简政放权、推进行政审批制度改革，3月10日，中国人民银行印发《关于贯彻落实〈国务院关于取消13项国务院部门行政许可事项的决定〉的通知》，停止“金融机构进入全国银行间同业拆借市场审批”。同业拆借行政许可的取消，便利了金融机构，提升了入市热情，同业拆借市场效率进一步提高。

一、改革背景

我国同业拆借业务起步于1984年，1997年形成全国统一的同业拆借市场，并建立起严格准入的管理体系。中国人民银行根据《中华人民共和国中国人民银行法》，履行监督管理银行间同业拆借市场职责，并依据《中华人民共和国行政许可法》实施“进入银行间同业拆借市场审批”行政许可项目。在此基础上，中国人民银行于2007年颁布《同业拆借管理办法》，以审慎监管为原则，以准入管理、期限管理、限额管理、透明度管理为基础，形成了安全与效率相统一的同业拆借市场管理框架。

经过多年发展，同业拆借市场建立起了较健全的法规体系，基础设施完善，市场分层合理，运行有效。随着市场的发展和市场主体的成熟，逐步减少事前的行政手段管理，将市场能够决定的交给市场，维护并优化市场环境，将更有利于市场的升级发展。因此，为贯彻落实党的十八届三中全会提出的“全面深化改革，加快转变政府职能”的统一部署，国务院决定取消“金融机构进入全国银行间同业拆借市场审批”行政许可项目。

二、改革内容

行政许可取消后，金融机构进入全国银行间同业拆借市场不再需要经过行政审批。中国人民银行根据《中华人民共和国中国人民银行法》，监督管理银行间同业拆借市场；全国银行间同业拆借中心提供同业拆借交易联网、交易登记、信息披露管理平台建设等服务；金融机构按照《同业拆借管理办法》规定，合规开展同业拆借业务。

（一）提高入市效率

经中国人民银行同意，全国银行间同业拆借中心发布《全国银行间同业拆借市场业务操作细则》。符合《同业拆借管理办法》规定条件的金融机构可直接至全国银行间同业拆借中心办理联网，办理时限缩短至5个工作日，金融机构联网后即可开展同业拆借交易。

（二）便利额度调整

同业拆借交易期限、限额管理方式从原先由中国人民银行核定改为由全国银行间同业拆借中心按照《同业拆借管理办法》规定，依据金融机构财务信息计算设置。金融机构可结合自身需求，向全国银行间同业拆借中心出具财务信息变更依据予以调整。

（三）加强信息披露

为加强市场透明度建设，《全国银行

间同业拆借市场业务操作细则》明确了各类金融机构在全国银行间同业拆借市场中的信息披露要求。全国银行间同业拆借中心提供平台和监测服务，中国人民银行对金融机构信息披露情况进行监督管理。

（四）强化履约管理

金融机构应当确保交易信息真实、有效，交易达成后应当按约定履行交易。若出现未按约定履行交易的情形，交易双方应当在结算日次一工作日向全国银行间同业拆借中心提交书面报备，以便于监管机构及时防范和化解市场风险。

三、行政审批取消后的市场运行情况

同业拆借行政审批制度改革实施以来，金融机构入市热情明显提高，市场活跃度稳步提升，成交规模大幅增长，同业拆借交易在货币市场交易中的占比进一步增加。

（一）市场成员快速增长

2016年末，全国银行间同业拆借市场成员机构共计1 725家，较上年末增长25%；当年新入市机构343家，是上年的1.9倍。

（二）交易规模大幅提升

全年，同业拆借业务成交规模达95.91万亿元，同比增长48.18%，是近五年同业拆借交易年均增长规模的2.7倍，在货币市场各子市场中增幅最大。

（三）市场占比稳步提高

2016年，同业拆借交易在货币市场交易中占比为13.76%，较上年提高1.27个百分点。

四、展望

同业拆借行政许可的取消，提高了同业拆借市场准入效率，便利了金融机构，提升了其参与市场热情，是货币市场改革开放的重要举措，也是行政体制改革的一项成功尝试。下一步，中国人民银行将继续推进简政放权、放管结合、优化服务，推动市场自律机制和透明度建设，完善定价形成机制，激发同业拆借市场活力，建立并完善事中事后监督管理机制，推动市场平稳发展，切实防范市场风险。

第三章　债券市场

2016年，我国债券市场继续保持良好的发展态势。债券市场增量和存量规模持续增长，地方政府债券发行规模增长较快，公司信用类债券发行量增速放缓；债券价格有所波动，收益率较年初有所上升；创新产品不断涌现，投资者结构更趋多元，非法人投资者及境外投资者对债券市场的参与度更加深入；发行和交易制度建设进一步完善，市场规范力度加大，开放程度进一步提高。

一、债券市场的运行情况

（一）债券发行规模继续增大

1. 债券发行量整体快速增长

2016年，债券市场各类债券累计发行36.14万亿元，同比增长54.20%。其中，全国银行间债券市场发行量为32.20万亿元，同比增长53.8%，占债券市场发行总量的比重为89.1%；交易所发行量为3.94万亿元，占债券市场发行总量的比重为10.9%。

分券种看，发行量最大的三个券种依次是同业存单、地方政府债券和非金融企业债务融资工具，发行量分别为12.99万亿元、6.04万亿元和5.03万亿元。其中，同业存单和地方政府债券同比分别增长145.3%和57.6%，非金融企业债务融资工具发行量下降6.3%。

表3-1　2016年债券市场主要券种发行量

券种	发行量（亿元）	同比增长率（%）	券种	发行量（亿元）	同比增长率（%）
国债	29 457.7	48.2	非金融企业债务融资工具	50 297.9	-6.3
地方政府债券	60 428.4	57.6	企业债券	5 917.7	72.5
政府支持机构债券	2 250.0	-6.3	公司债券	25 770.0	93.9
政策性银行债	33 529.7	30.0	资产支持证券	8 647.0	40.4
金融债券	13 896.5	-24.1	国际机构债券	1 266.4	1 001.2
同业存单	129 931.0	145.3	合计	361 392.1	54.2

数据来源：中国证监会、中央国债登记结算有限责任公司、上海清算所。

2. 债券托管量平稳增长

截至2016年末，债券市场托管余额为63.66万亿元，较上年增加15.76万亿元，同比增幅为32.91%。其中，银行间债券市场托管余额为56.33万亿元，同比增长27.84%，占全国债券市场托管量的88.5%；交易所市场的各类债券托管余额为7.33万亿元，同比增长91.24%，占全国债券市场托管量的11.5%。

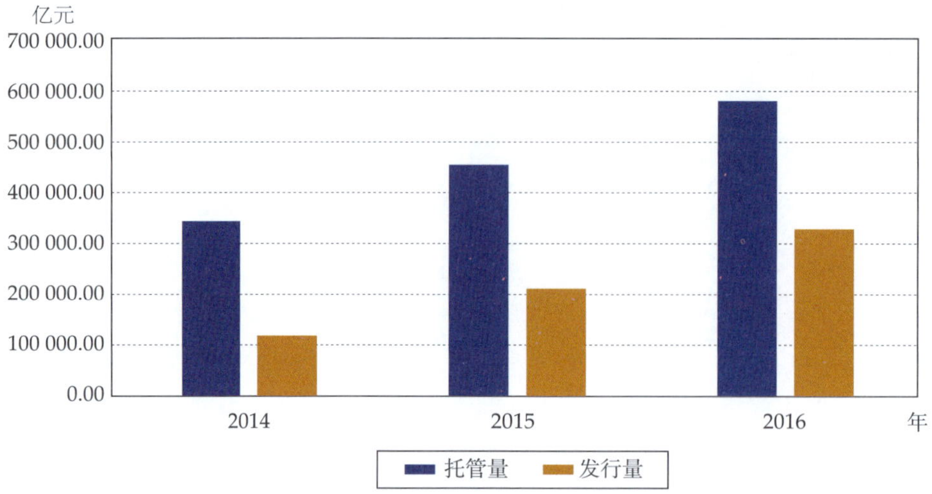

数据来源：中央国债登记结算有限责任公司、上海清算所。

图3-1 银行间债券市场发行量与托管量历史趋势

（二）债券交易规模稳步增长

1. 现券交易规模继续上升

2016年，债券市场现券累计成交132.23万亿元，同比增长46.6%。其中，银行间债券市场现券累计成交127.10万亿元，同比增长46.5%，占全国债券市场现券成交量的96.1%；交易所现券累计成交5.13万亿元，同比增长50.8%，占全国债券市场现券成交量的3.9%。

从银行间债券市场现券交易的券种结构来看，政策性银行债、同业存单和国债是成交占比前三位的券种，成交金额分别为56.1万亿元、19.8万亿元和12.6万亿元，市场占比分别为43.84%、16.07%和9.94%；中期票据、超短期融资券、企业债券、短期融资券等四类主要的公司信用类债券成交金额为32.2万亿元，市场占比为25.65%。

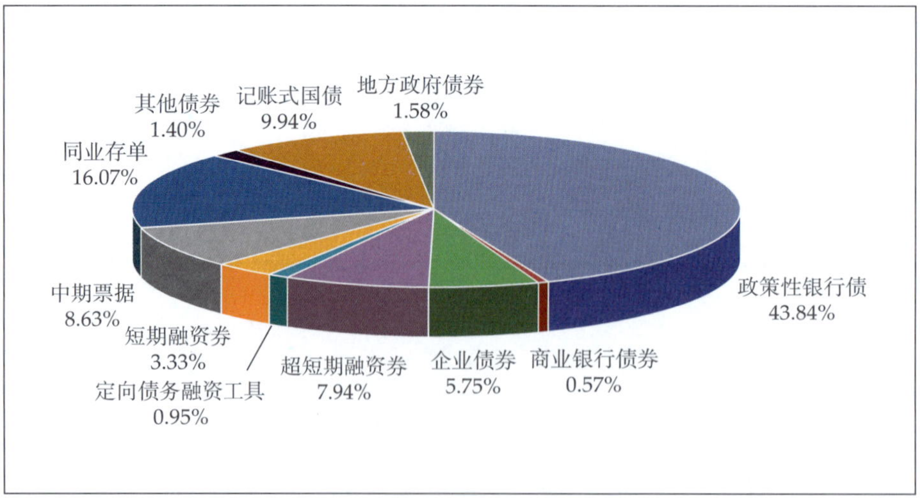

数据来源：中央国债登记结算有限责任公司、上海清算所。

图3-2 2016年银行间债券市场现券交易券种结构

从银行间债券市场现券交易的期限结构来看，待偿期为1年期以下、1~5年期、5~7年期、7~10年期和10年期以上成交金额分别为51万亿元、41.5万亿元、9.3万亿元、21万亿元和4.3万亿元，市场占比分别为40.1%、32.7%、7.3%、16.5%和3.4%。

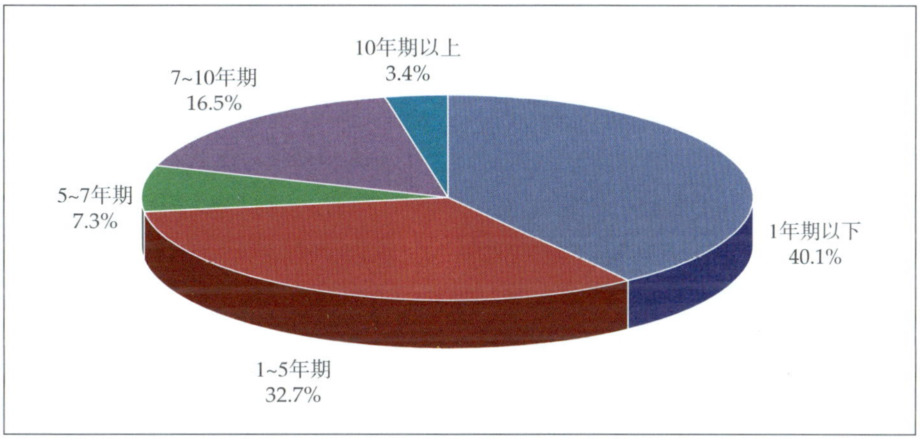

数据来源：中央国债登记结算有限责任公司、上海清算所。

图3-3　2016年银行间债券市场现券交易期限结构

2. 债券价格指数于年末大幅调整

中债总财富指数（总值）年初167.74，在10月达到最高点174.47，在12月回落至最低点167.12，接近年初水平，随后略有上升。上海清算所银行间信用债综合指数（总收益）年初107.09，上行趋势过后，于12月回落至109.12。全年债券价格指数于10月出现拐点，于12月初加速下滑至全年底部，于月末稍有回升，总体而言，12月债券市场发生了较大幅度的调整。

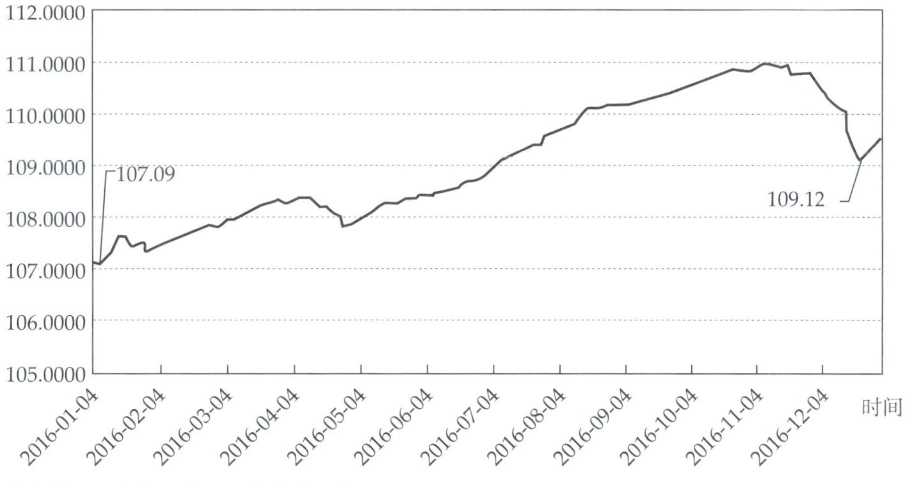

数据来源：上海清算所、中央国债登记结算有限责任公司。

图3-4　银行间信用债综合指数月度变化趋势

3. 银行间债市投资者结构保持相对稳定

2016年，银行间债券市场投资者结构基本稳定。截至年末，存款类金融机构持债规模为34.05万亿元，占市场托管总量的比重为60.4%，比上年下降1.8个百分点。在存款类金融机构中，国有控股商业银行持有14.91万亿元，占比为43.8%，比上年下降了4.6个百分点；股份制商业银行持有9.40万亿元，占比为27.6%，比上年上升了2.9个百分点；城市商业银行、农村商业银行和农村合作银行持有7.83万亿元，占比为23.0%，比上年上升了2.7个百分点。非法人机构投资者持债总规模为14.47万亿元，占市场托管总量的比重为25.7%，比上年上升了5.5个百分点。其中，证券投资基金持有3.05万亿元，占比为21.1%，比上年下降了2.6个百分点；证券公司资产管理计划持债占比上升了2个百分点，达到21.1%；基金管理公司特定客户资产管理组合持债占比上升了3.7个百分点，达到15.6%。

二、 债券市场运行的主要特点

（一）地方政府债务置换有序展开，发行规模稳步扩大

根据财政部在2016年1月发布的地方政府债券发行工作安排，地方政府债务置换在限额管理下有序展开，全年地方政府债券发行规模共计6.04万亿元，同比增长57.6%。其中，置换债4.87万亿元，置换规模同比增长约52%。地方政府债券发行量大幅增长是带动市场发行总量增长的重要因素。

截至2016年末，地方政府债余额达到10.63万亿元，从投资者来看，地方政府债最主要的投资主体依次是国有控股商业银行、股份制商业银行，以及城市商业银行、农村商业银行和农村合作银行，持有量分别为5.64万亿元、2.65万亿元和1.07万亿元，占地方政府债券余额的比重分别为53.1%、24.9%和10.1%。

（二）公司信用类债券增速放缓，发行期限更趋短期化

2016年，公司信用类债券共计发行8.19万亿元，同比增长16.48%，增速较上年下降19.8个百分点。其中，公司债券、企业债券发行量增幅较大，公司债券发行2.57万亿元，同比增长93.9%；企业债券发行5 917.7亿元，同比增长72.5%。非金融企业债务融资工具发行5.03万亿元，同比有所下降。

短期化趋势在2016年更加明显。1年期及以下债券发行量占比从2015年的48.0%上升至55.1%；1~3年期和3~5年期债券发行量占比分别从2015年的13.7%和14.3%下降至10.4%和12.5%；5~10年期债券发行量从2015年的21.2%下降至19.1%，10年期以上品种占比基本不变。

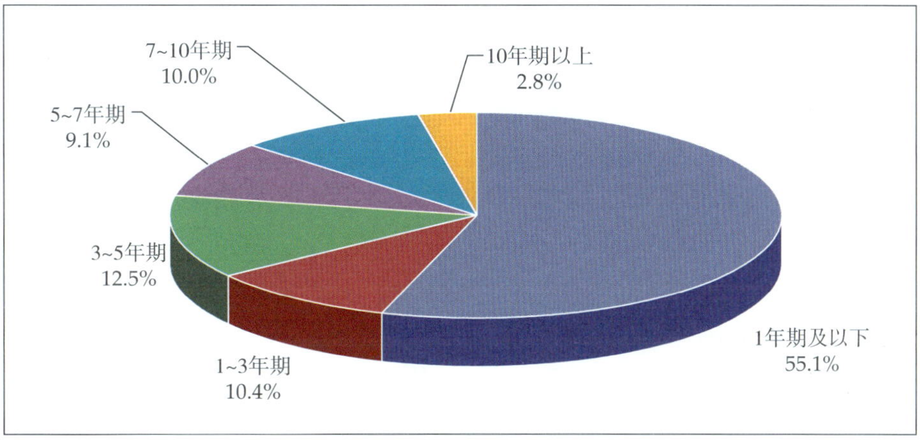

数据来源：中央国债登记结算有限责任公司、上海清算所。

图3-5 2016年银行间债券市场发行期限结构

（三）债券市场走势先强后弱，收益率整体大幅上行

2016年，债券市场波动加大，国债收益率曲线整体大幅上移。2016年初到3月中上旬，银行间债券市场总体运行较为平稳。截至3月20日，1年期和3年期国债到期收益率均较年初下降20个基点左右，7年期和10年期国债到期收益率均与年初基本持平。3月下旬至4月下旬，国开债和AAA级中期票据到期收益率曲线均整体上升40个基点左右，此后，收益率维持震荡。6月中旬后，市场交投活跃，收益率持续下行，期限利差、信用利差不断压缩，10月21日前后，3年期国债、10年期国债和30年期国债到期收益率均下跌至年内最低水平。进入11月，债券市场收益率快速大幅上行，12月20日，3年期国债、10年期国债和30年期国债到期收益率最高分别升至

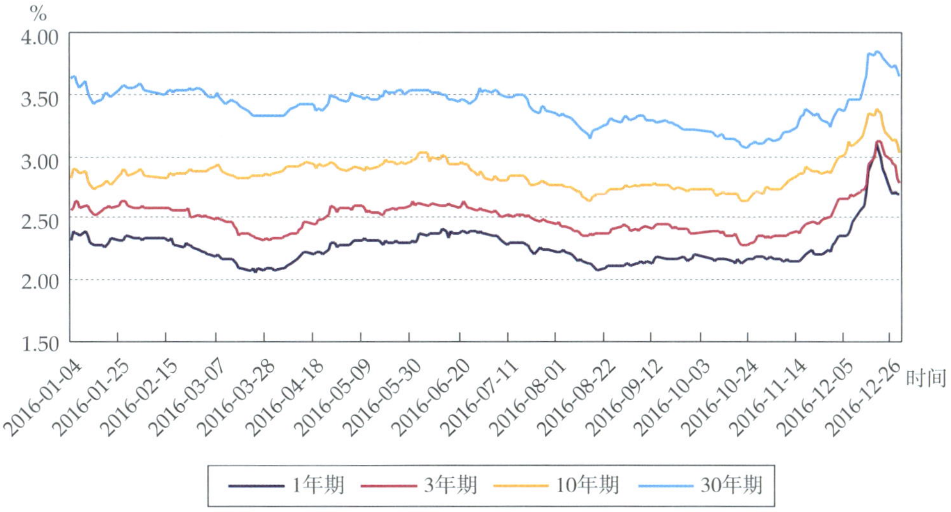

数据来源：中国外汇交易中心。

图3-6 2016年银行间债券市场国债收益率走势图

3.13%、3.38%和3.86%，分别较10月的年内低点上升85个、74个和78个基点。年末，债券市场收益率有所回落，3年期国债、10年期国债和30年期国债到期收益率分别为2.78%、3.02%和3.64%，分别较年初上升23个、19个和2个基点。

（四）投资者类型更加丰富，非法人机构持有比例继续提高

2016年，人民银行发布相关公告，进一步明确境内外机构投资者参与银行间债券市场的相关规定，简化了合格机构投资者进入银行间债券市场的流程，市场成员规模不断增长，非法人合格机构投资者和境外合格机构投资者的占比上升，投资者类型更加丰富。截至2016年末，银行间债券市场各类参与主体合计14 127家，较上年末增加4 491家。其中，境内非法人类机构11 391家，增加4 151家，增幅为57.33%；境内法人类机构2 329家，增加235家，增幅为11.22%；境外机构407家，增幅为34.77%。

非法人机构持有比例继续升高。银行间债券市场信用债券主要持有人中，非法人机构持有量占比从2015年的53.2%上升至63.5%；商业银行持有量占比从2015年的33.3%下降至26.2%。利率债券主要持有人中，非法人机构持有量占比从2015年的9.0%上升至15.3%，上升幅度明显。

（五）交易活跃度有所上升，短期债券保持较高换手率

2016年，银行间债券市场的现券累计换手率达到220.07%，较上年提高24.56个百分点，债券市场流动性稳步提高。主要债券品种政策性银行债和企业债券保持着较好的流动性，年度换手率分别为439.42%和201.81%，分别较上年提高83.97个百分点和基本持平。短期融资券与超短期融资券作为企业短期融资的工具，也具有较高流动性，其换手率分别为688.09%和653.06%。其余依次为中期票据、外国债券、记账式国债、非银行金融机构债券、商业银行债券、政府支持机构债券、资本工具、资产支持证券和地方政府债券。

表3–2　银行间债券市场2016年与2015年主要券种换手率之比较

券种	2016年（%）	2015年（%）	与上年相比换手率增加（个百分点）
记账式国债	114.46	99.72	14.74
地方政府债券	18.45	5.59	12.85
央行票据	3 398.98	145.09	3 253.89
政策性银行债	439.42	355.45	83.97
政府支持机构债券	34.42	70.21	-35.80
商业银行债券	43.33	30.60	12.73
资本工具	25.93	21.70	4.23
非银行金融机构债券	86.89	86.07	0.82

（续）

券种	2016年（%）	2015年（%）	与上年相比换手率增加（个百分点）
企业债券	201.81	202.01	-0.21
短期融资券	688.09	480.86	207.23
超短期融资券	653.06	480.65	172.41
资产支持证券	24.93	7.44	17.49
中期票据	160.41	197.67	-37.26
集合票据	—	1 124.55	—
外国债券	146.25	0.00	146.25
同业存单	312.94	140.94	172.00

数据来源：中央国债登记结算有限责任公司、上海清算所。

（六）债券市场信用风险整体可控，信用风险管理工具进一步丰富

2016年，受宏观经济增速下行和产业转型升级影响，债券市场信用风险事件有所增加，全年发生债务违约的发行人共34家，涉及债券79只，涉及规模398.94亿元。随着2016年债券市场信用风险的释放，市场各方对于违约事件的认识加深，重视程度不断提高，应对措施和经验有所增强。2016年底的中央经济工作会议明确了“稳中求进”的工作原则，强调“要把防控金融风险放到更加重要的位置”。在此背景下，债市风险依然可控，发生系统性风险的可能性低。以债务融资工具市场为例，2016年债务融资工具累计违约金额占全部存量规模的比重约为0.35%，远低于2016年末商业银行1.76%的不良贷款率，信用风险整体可控。

为进一步完善信用风险市场化分担机制，2016年，中国银行间市场交易商协会（以下简称交易商协会）组织市场成员结合国内银行间市场特点推出信用违约互换（CDS）、信用联结票据（CLN）两项新产品，推动信用风险缓释工具创新，进一步完善信用风险市场化分担机制。

三、债券市场创新

（一）产品创新持续活跃

1. 资产证券化继续延伸发展

一是开展不良资产证券化试点，有助于进一步拓宽商业银行不良资产处置渠道，提高不良资产价格发现能力和透明度。截至2016年末，首批试点银行均已完成首单项目发行，累计发行14单产品，发行规模156亿元，处置不良资产461亿元。

二是首单信托型ABN注册发行。交易商协会组织修订了《非金融企业资产支持票据指引》及配套表格体系，对ABN基础资产、交易结构、参与主体等方面进行重点规范。2016年6月21日，首单信托型ABN——远东国际租赁有限公司2016年度第一期信托资产支

持票据成功发行，金额为20.68亿元。

2. 绿色债券产品创新不断

自2015年底中国人民银行发布第39号公告提出在银行间债券市场推出绿色金融债券以来，绿色债券受到市场的高度关注。2016年，绿色债券的规模持续扩大，种类日益丰富，对我国经济绿色化程度的提高有重要作用。

在金融债券方面，1月，浦发银行成功簿记发行了200亿元国内首单绿色金融债券，实现了绿色金融债券从制度框架到产品发行的落地。其后，青岛银行、中国进出口银行也先后发行了绿色金融债券。在非金融企业债务融资工具方面，5月，新疆金风科技股份有限公司10亿元国内首单绿色永续中期票据在银行间债券市场成功发行。10月，武汉地铁集团有限公司又发行了国内首单采取“债贷基”模式的银行间债券市场绿色债务融资工具，进一步丰富了绿色债券创新品种。在企业债券方面，4月，北京汽车股份有限公司成功发行25亿元国内首单绿色企业债券。在公司债券方面，6月，浙江嘉化能源化工股份有限公司发行的3亿元公司债券成为首单在上海证券交易所上市的绿色公司债券。随后，博天环境集团、格林美股份有限公司、北京清新环境技术股份有限公司也先后成功发行绿色公司债券。绿色债券市场整体呈现良好的发展态势。

3. 银行间债券市场发行首只SDR计价债券

2016年8月，世界银行通过簿记建档方式在全国银行间债券市场发行了第一期SDR计价债券。本期发行的SDR计价债券金额为5亿特别提款权（SDR），是世界银行获准在中国大陆发行的共计20亿元SDR债券中的第一期。本期债券的期限为三年，固定利率，每年付息一次，发行利率为0.49%，发行方式为簿记建档。本期债券属于国际开发债券，风险资产权重为0。本期债券仅计价采用SDR，投资者购买及世界银行还本付息时均使用人民币。两者之间的换算是依据发行及还本付息前一天的外汇中间价，再根据当时SDR篮子中各种货币所占的比重，将投资者应向世界银行支付的投资款及世界银行应向投资者支付的利息及本金由SDR换算为人民币进行结算。

此次世界银行发行SDR计价债券是1981年以来全球范围内首只SDR计价债券，也是在我国发行的首只SDR计价债券，其发行具有重要的里程碑意义。一是有利于境内外投资者开展多样性的资产配置，规避单一货币的利率汇率风险。二是有利于推动SDR金融工具市场化。三是有利于丰富中国债券市场交易品种，促进中国债券市场的开放与发展。四是有利于扩大SDR使用，增强国际货币体系的稳定性和韧性。

4. 推出信用违约互换等信用风险管理工具

2016年9月23日，交易商协会发布新修订的《银行间市场信用风险缓释工具试点业务规则》以及相关产品指引，在保留原有的信用风险缓释合约（CRMA）和信用风险缓释凭证（CRMW）两项产品的同时，推出信用违约互换（CDS）与信用联结票据（CLN）两项信用风险缓释工具（CRM）创新产品。

2016年10月31日，银行间债券市场达成首批CDS交易，名义本金总计3.0亿元，交易参考实体涉及石油、天然气、电力、水务、煤炭、电信、食品、航空等行业，交易期限一年至两年不等。随着我国银行间债券市场信用事件逐渐增加，CDS等创新产品的推出，满足了债券市场投资者主动管理信用风险的需求，为市场参与者提供了信用风险保护和对冲工具，逐步建立银行间债券市场信用风险分散分担机制。同时，CRM产品对于提高商业银行资本管理能力具有重要意义，并有助于完善信用风险的价格形成机制，提高债券市场信用定价水平，实现信用风险的合理配置，维护宏观经济金融稳定。

5. 首次引入社会效应债券

2016年12月21日，交易商协会按照相关自律管理规则接受国内首单社会效应债券的注册申请，注册金额5亿元。2016年12月23日，首单社会效应债券成功发行，募集资金专项用于山东省沂南县125个重点贫困村的精准扶贫项目，票面利率为固定利率+浮动利率，固定利率根据簿记建档结果确定为3.75%，浮动利率根据扶贫实施效果按年核定，以体现投资的社会效应，扶贫效果由第三方专业机构定期进行评估。通过试点发行社会效应债券开展精准扶贫工作，能够帮助村民脱贫增收，加大金融精准扶贫力度，加快脱贫攻坚步伐。

（二）发行与交易机制创新不断推出

1. 银行间债券市场推出现券匿名点击成交业务

为进一步满足市场需求，推动银行间债券市场合理分层、提升交易效率、优化价格发现功能，2016年9月，全国银行间同业拆借中心在X-Swap和X-Repo的基础上，结合现券市场特点，推出了银行间债券市场现券匿名点击成交业务X-Bond。

X-Bond定位于做市机构、活跃机构等交易商之间；参与机构匿名报价、报价基于双边授信自动匹配成交，未匹配报价可供其他参与机构点击成交；展示逐笔成交信息，优先展示活跃债券报价成交行情，提高了现券价格透明度和基准性。随着X-Bond的推出，基于双边授信的匿名点击交易平台X系列，基本实现对银行间货币市场、债券市场和衍生品市场的覆盖，现货市场和衍生品市场之间的联动性进一步提高。截至2016年末，X-Bond参与机构139家；X-Bond报价8 288笔，成交755笔，成交券面总额845亿元；报价成交机构多为现券市场活跃机构；报价成交券种以国开债、国债等品种为主。

2. 银行间债券市场开办预发行业务

2016年12月15日至19日，国家开发银行对其拟于20日发行的两期债券成功开展了预发行。根据中国人民银行2014年12月发布的业务管理办法，参与银行间债券市场现券买卖的投资者均可参与预发行交易，且券种覆盖了在银行间债券市场发行的全部债券品种。预发行的价格发现功能有助于为即将发行的债券价格提供合理预期，也可为正式发行时的投标者提供更为有效的定价依据，能进一步促进市场形成合理的债券发行价格预期，对于进一步完善我国债券发行市场具有重要意义。

四、债券市场制度建设

（一）规范与完善债券市场发行管理

1. 国务院统一公司信用类债券发行标准和审核规则

2016年8月，国务院印发《降低实体经济企业成本工作方案》，指出改革完善公司信用类债券发行管理制度，合理扩大债券发行规模，提高直接融资比例，在投资者分类趋同的原则下，分别统一公司信用类债券市场发行准入标准和审核规则。统一公司信用类债券市场发行准入标准和审核规则有利于增强市场透明度，降低监管套利可能性，促进市场健康有序发展。

2. 完善开发性银行和政策性银行金融债券发行

为鼓励开发性银行、政策性银行通过发行金融债券的方式筹集中长期稳定资金，支持国家重点领域项目建设、服务国家战略，中国人民银行于2016年9月发布了《关于完善开发性银行和政策性银行金融债券发行有关事宜的通知》，简化政策性金融债券发行程序，赋予债券发行人更多自主空间。

3. 进一步完善地方债相关管理办法

2016年，财政部发布一系列涉及地方政府债务管理方面的政策措施。1月，财政部发布《关于对地方政府债务实行限额管理的实施意见》以及《关于做好2016年地方政府债券发行工作的通知》，明确对地方债务余额和年债务置换量实行限额管理，提出建立健全地方政府债务风险防控机制和妥善处理存量债务。7月，财政部和中国人民银行联合发布《关于中央和地方国库现金管理商业银行定期存款质押品管理有关事宜的通知》，将地方政府债券纳入中央国库现金管理和地方国库现金管理质押品范围，地方政府债券不受发行主体限制，可以跨地域质押。12月，财政部公布了《地方政府一般债务预算管理办法》和《地方政府专项债务预算管理办法》，从债务限额确定、预算编制和批复、预算执行和决算、非债券形式债务纳入预算、监督管理等方面，提出了规范地方政府债务预算管理的工作要求。

4. 进一步规范非金融企业债务融资工具发行机制

为更好地贯彻落实党中央、国务院关于“稳增长、调结构、促改革、惠民生、防风险”系列政策要求，积极发挥债务融资工具市场对实体经济发展的支持作用，交易商协会组织市场成员修订了《非金融企业债务融资工具注册发行规则》、《非金融企业债务融资工具公开发行注册工作规程》和《非金融企业债务融资工具公开发行注册文件表格体系》，并于2016年2月19日正式发布实施。上述制度修订坚持“以信息披露为核心”的注册制基本原则，从机制流程、信息披露、管理方式三方面优化，构建“分层分类”注册发行管理体系，注册发行工作的效率和质量均得到有效提升。

5. 交易所市场加强公司债券监管

一是证监会批复公司债券簿记建档指引。2016年9月，中国证监会批复了上海证券交易所和深圳证券交易所发布实施《上海证券交易所公司债券簿记建档发行业务指引》、《深圳证券交易所公司债券簿记建档发行业务指引》，具体规范了簿记建档内控制度、簿记建档现场管理、簿记建档流程和自律管理要求。

二是交易所加强对公司债券发行的监管。2016年10月，上海证券交易所对房地产、产能过剩行业公司债券发行审核试行分类监管，主要涉及房地产公司、煤炭和钢铁等过剩行业发行的公司债券。此次监管标准采取“基础范围（行业政策）和综合指标评价”两项，并依据综合指标评价触发频次将企业分为正常类、关注类、风险类。

6. 进一步促进债券市场柜台业务发展

2016年2月14日，中国人民银行发布《全国银行间债券市场柜台业务管理办法》（以下简称《办法》）。《办法》规定，除符合条件的金融机构和企业外，年收入不低于50

万元，名下金融资产不少于300万元，具有两年以上证券投资经验的个人投资者，也可投资银行间债券市场柜台业务的全部债券品种和交易品种。而对于不满足上述条件的个人投资者，可以买卖发行人主体评级或债项评级较低者不低于AAA的债券，以及参与债券回购交易。个人投资者的引入，有利于丰富债券投资人的种类，弥补银行间债券市场投资人类型相对单一的缺陷，可增强银行间债券市场的活跃度和债券投资需求，促进直接融资比重的提高。根据《办法》要求，9月，中国（上海）自由贸易试验区债券市场柜台业务推出，为区内、境外投资人提供了新的资产配置渠道。中国银行作为首家接入的承办银行，在中国人民银行批准额度内将其在银行间市场持有的存量债券划转至上海自贸区内，通过其区内柜台、网站报价销售，首笔交易标的为超短期融资券。

（二）规范与完善债券市场交易管理

1. 进一步规范合格机构投资者进入银行间债券市场

（1）规范境内机构投资者投资银行间债券市场。

2016年4月27日，中国人民银行发布2016年第8号公告，明确境内合格机构投资者的标准，大幅拓宽银行间债券市场投资者范围，进一步优化备案、开户、联网流程，强调业务检查要求和自律管理要求，提高市场准入管理效率，促进市场规范健康发展。公告显著促进了非法人机构投资者入市投资。此前，银行理财产品中只有16家上市银行发行的可以入市。根据公告规定，非法人类合格机构投资者指金融机构等作为资产管理人，在依法合规的前提下，接受客户的委托或授权，按照与客户约定的投资计划和方式开展资产管理或投资业务所设立的各类投资产品。

（2）促进和规范境外机构投资者投资银行间债券市场。

2016年2月17日，中国人民银行发布2016年第3号公告，在银行间债券市场引入更多符合条件的境外机构投资者，取消投资额度限制，简化管理流程。根据公告规定，在中华人民共和国境外依法注册成立的各类金融机构及其依法合规面向客户发行的投资产品，以及养老基金、慈善基金、捐赠基金等中国人民银行认可的其他中长期机构投资者，均可投资银行间债券市场，没有额度限制。

（3）规范非金融机构投资银行间债券市场。

2016年，经中国人民银行同意，交易商协会对非金融机构投资人入市门槛进行调整，将净资产要求不低于3 000万元调整为1 000万元，在推动银行间债券市场投资人有序扩容的同时，也更好地满足了市场投融资需求，有利于促进债务融资工具市场全面发展。

2. 优化做市业务制度与评价指标体系

（1）财政部、中国人民银行发布《国债做市支持操作规则》。

2016年9月，财政部会同中国人民银行发布了《关于印发〈国债做市支持操作规则〉的通知》，对建立国债做市支持机制作出规定。国债做市支持机制是指财政部在银行间债券市场运用随买、随卖等工具，支持银行间债券市场做市商对新近发行的关键期限国债做市的市场行为。建立国债做市支持机制可以进一步提高国债的流动性，保障国债二级市场连续不断运行。

（2）《银行间债券市场做市业务指引》

及《银行间债券市场做市业务评价指标体系》发布。

根据中国人民银行发布的《全国银行间债券市场做市商管理规定》，交易商协会组织市场成员修订并发布《银行间债券市场做市业务指引》及《银行间债券市场做市业务评价指标体系》两份自律文本，启动了新规则下的做市业务评价工作。新发布的做市业务自律文本对原有评价规则做出以下完善：一是为中国人民银行对做市商资质实施动态管理提供决策参考，将银行间市场全部做市商及尝试做市机构纳入被评价范围，对开展做市业务的做市机构进行统一评价；二是为体现不同做市机构做市业务特点及做市券种偏好，搭建“综合+专项”的评价体系，评价并公布做市机构分别在利率债、信用债的做市情况，为市场参与者更高效地寻找交易对手方提供有益参考。

3. 进一步完善债券市场投资人保护制度

2016年9月，交易商协会完成《投资人保护条款范例》（以下简称《范例》）的制定。《范例》要点主要包括以下几个方面：一是设置“交叉保护条款”、“事先约束条款”和“控制权变更条款”三类投资人保护条款，并分别设置对应的投资人保护安排。二是事先在募集说明书中约定发生触发情形后的处理程序以及发行人、投资人和主承销商的各方权责，增强持有人会议可执行力。三是分类细化具体触发情形和违反约定责任，市场各方可根据发行人具体情况确定相应阈值，并针对不同类型条款设置差异化的违反约定责任类型。四是首次引入“违反约定救济工具箱”和“资产池承诺”条款，更好地保护投资人合法权益。《范例》将推动解决争议法治化、提升持有人会议效力，有利于进一步完善债券市场投资人保护制度，对促进债务融资工具市场持续规范健康发展具有积极意义。

4. 进一步完善债券价格指数和债券收益率曲线

（1）加快推动完善国债收益率曲线。

2016年6月，中债国债及其他债券收益率曲线在中国人民银行中英文网站发布；10月，财政部和中国人民银行官方网站首次发布30年期国债收益率，国际货币基金组织（IMF）正式采用三个月期限中债国债收益率作为代表性利率纳入特别提款权（SDR）利率计算。

（2）进一步完善收益率曲线和指数的编制应用。

2016年，中国发布了首批绿色系列债券指数，其中包括2只绿色债券指数和1只气候相关债券指数；发布了外币计价指数，同时跟踪境内人民币债券的收益和外汇的收益。银行间债券市场还正式推出非公开定向债务融资工具（PPN）综合指数。这些指数的应用也进一步扩展：中国银行伦敦分行在境外发行了绿色资产担保债券，是境内绿色债券指数在国际市场中的首个应用；平安资产管理有限公司使用平安—中债可投资级信用债指数和中债—银行间国债指数发行了两只私募型资管产品；易方达基金和广发基金使用中债—7~10年国家开发银行债券指数发行了基金产品，合计规模约50亿元。

5. 完善信贷资产支持证券信息披露制度

2016年，交易商协会发布《不良贷款资产支持证券信息披露指引（试行）》及《微小企业贷款资产支持证券信息披露指引（试行）》，进一步丰富了基础资产种类，明确了信息披露标准。

11月，交易商协会发布《信贷资产支持证券信息披露工作评价规程（试行）》（以下简称《规程》），明确主要对采用注册制发行的资产证券化产品注册、发行及存续期信息披露工作进行评价，评价结果将作为判断该机构是否能够以注册方式发行信贷资产支持证券的重要参考。《规程》的出台推动建立了市场化的信息披露工作后续跟踪评价机制，进一步完善了信贷资产支持证券信息披露事中事后监管机制，有利于推动资产证券化市场的规范化、常态化发展。

（三）推动中国（上海）自贸区债券业务创新发展

为贯彻落实党中央、国务院关于进一步深化上海自贸区改革开放的相关政策精神，2016年，中国人民银行批复了交易商协会、中国外汇交易中心、上海清算所、中央国债登记结算有限责任公司等自律组织和中介机构创新发展上海自贸区债券业务。业务的发展以全国银行间债券市场的制度框架为基础，符合银行间债券市场合格投资者要求的区内及境外投资者通过自由贸易账户（以下简称FT账户）或非居民账户（以下简称NRA账户），以中国外汇交易中心的国际金融资产交易平台为依托，参与上海自贸区债券的发行和交易业务，托管清算机构通过FT账户或NRA账户为投资者提供相关的服务。12月，经财政部批准，上海市财政局在财政部下达的上海市地方债年度限额内，通过公开招标方式，面向上海自贸区内已开立FT账户的区内及境外机构投资者发行了30亿元地方政府债券。上海自贸区相关债券业务的创新发展也提高了区内注册企业参与债券市场的积极性，2016年，在上海自贸区注册的各类企业共发行了9 650.42亿元公司信用类债券，较2015年增加了60.48%，高于债券市场公司信用类债券整体16.48%的增幅。

上海自贸区债券业务的创新发展，有利于贯彻落实党中央、国务院关于进一步深化上海自贸区改革开放的相关政策精神及中国人民银行关于推进上海自贸区金融改革试点的系列要求，支持实体经济发展；有利于推动债券市场创新和制度完善，促进银行间债券市场成熟发展；有利于扩大银行间债券市场对外开放，提升国际化水平。

（四）发布促进绿色债券市场发展的相关制度

为贯彻落实国务院《生态文明体制改革总体方案》和党的十八届五中全会精神，2015年12月15日，中国人民银行发布第39号公告，在银行间债券市场推出绿色金融债券。2016年，中国人民银行、国家发展改革委、财政部、证监会等多个部委联合或单独发布了支持和促进绿色债券发展的相关文件，明确节能减排技术改造项目、绿色城镇化项目等12大项为未来绿色债券的支持重点，并要求统一绿色债券标准，提出推动证券市场支持绿色投资和丰富融资工具等方面的行动要求。在系列制度的推动下，2016年，我国绿色债券市场发展迅速，全年累计发行了53只绿色债券，金额总计为2 052.31亿元，占同期全球发行总规模的36%，只用了一年时间就成为全球最大的绿色债券市场。目前我国绿色债券品种覆盖金融债券、企业债券、公司债券、债务融资工具和信贷资产支持证券等，其中绿色金融债券发行量占比最高，发行量为1 550亿元，占75.52%。绿色债券的发行有利于构建绿色金融体系，增加绿色金融供给，贯彻落实“五大发展理念”和发挥金融服务供给侧结构性改革的作用。

五、债券市场发展展望

（一）整体发行规模将继续增长

2017年，在财政政策要更加积极有效的背景下，中央与地方政府的各项公共支出将可能会进一步扩大。同时，为降低企业经营成本，2017年将会在减税和降费方面加大工作力度。此外，根据国务院相关规定，目前还有6.27万亿元地方政府存量债务需要进行置换。在这一系列政策的共同作用下，中央与地方政府可能会适度加大举债力度。在公司信用类债券方面，随着债券市场信用风险处置机制的不断健全，各市场主体对信用风险的甄别和处置能力将不断提高，也将为公司信用类债券市场的规范健康发展提供有效的保障，促进公司信用类债券发行规模的平稳增长。

（二）产品和机制将围绕实体经济需求持续推进

2017年，债券市场将继续做好为供给侧结构性改革提供金融服务的工作，加大对“双创”、科技、战略性新兴产业等重点领域以及保障性安居工作、脱贫攻坚、“三农”、健康养老、小微企业、就业、少数民族等薄弱环节的金融支持力度。绿色债券市场将进一步发展，支持扶贫行业、创新行业、“一带一路”、京津冀协同发展、资产证券化等领域的产品创新将进一步丰富。此外，随着我国自贸区建设的进一步深化以及人民币国际化的稳步推进，人民币合格境外机构投资者试点范围将进一步拓展，我国债券市场中的发行人及投资者类型也将进一步多元化，这也要求我国债券市场不断通过机制等创新来适应这一发展变化。

（三）债券市场信用风险处置机制将不断完善

2017年，我国债券市场信用风险处置机制将得到进一步完善，交易监测和风险预警能力不断加强，信息披露和信用评级等市场化的约束机制不断健全；市场化信用风险分散机制将更加高效，担保体系作用发挥更好，信用衍生品市场发展合理有序；信用增进市场将稳步发展，市场风险承受度不断提升；全环链信用风险预警处置机制将不断更新，从而保障我国债券市场的安全运行和整体稳定，牢牢守住不发生系统性风险的底线。

（四）债券市场改革开放将深入推进

2017年，我国债券市场将继续落实和完善开放政策，稳步推进开放进程。境外投资者在银行间债券市场准入备案、开户联网、交易投资、清算结算，以及资金汇出入、税收缴纳等各环节的配套政策将更加完善，操作运行将更加便利。具体包括：研究拓宽跨境合作和直接投资的可行方式，为境外机构提供更多的选择；适时丰富和优化交易工具，满足境外投资者合理交易需求；推动建立备案、开户、联网等一站式服务，进一步提升入市便利度；明晰境外投资者相关的税收规定和外汇管理政策等。未来一年，银行间债券市场政策制度和基础设施将不断优化，境外投资者实际需求将得以满足，境外投资者在数量、活跃度和市场占比方面有望继续提高，市场国际化程度将持续提升。

专题二 债券市场对外开放

伴随人民币国际化和资本项目开放进程，我国债券市场对外开放稳步推进。自2010年以来，中国人民银行先后允许符合条件的境外央行或货币当局、主权财富基金、国际金融组织、人民币境外清算行和参加行、境外保险机构、RQFII和QFII投资银行间债券市场。境外发行主体也从国际开发机构逐步扩大到金融机构和企业，市场开放步伐不断加快。2016年，债券市场对外开放政策进一步放开，大幅拓宽了境外投资者主体范围，取消了投资额度限制，境外投融资主体参与度显著提升，标志着我国债券市场对外开放进入一个新的阶段。

一、制度创新驱动开放进程加快

（一）引入更多类型的境外机构投资者

2016年2月，为进一步推动银行间债券市场对外开放，便利境外机构投资者投资银行间债券市场，中国人民银行发布了2016年第3号公告。主要内容包括：一是拓宽投资者范围。公告明确，在中华人民共和国境外依法注册成立的各类金融机构及其依法合规面向客户发行的投资产品，以及养老基金、慈善基金、捐赠基金等中国人民银行认可的其他中长期机构投资者，均可投资银行间债券市场。二是取消投资额度限制、丰富交易工具。明确各类境外机构投资者投资银行间债券市场均没有额度限制，现阶段均可在银行间债券市场开展现券交易，并可基于套期保值需求开展债券借贷、债券远期、远期利率协议及利率互换等交易。境外人民币业务清算行和参加行还可在银行间债券市场开展债券回购交易。三是简化管理流程。符合条件的境外机构通过银行间市场结算代理人完成备案、开户等手续后，即可成为银行间债券市场参与者。

公告出台后，为配合做好境外机构投资者入市相关工作，国家外汇管理局印发了《关于境外机构投资者投资银行间债券市场有关外汇管理问题的通知》（汇发〔2016〕12号），中国人民银行上海总部出台了《境外机构投资者投资银行间债券市场备案管理实施细则》（中国人民银行上海总部公告〔2016〕第2号），中央国债登记结算有限责任公司、全国银行间同业拆借中心和银行间市场清算所股份有限公司三家中介机构联合发布了《境外机构投资者进入银行间市场联网和开户操作指引》（中债字〔2016〕52号），在各环节上明确操作要求。

公告和一系列配套措施的发布，大大便利了境外机构投资者特别是中长期投资者投资银行间债券市场，提升了我国债券市场在国际上的知名度和认可度，为境外投资主体的进一步丰富和市场国际化水平的提高提供了良好的制度环境和保障。

（二）创新推出SDR计价债券

2016年8月，世界银行通过簿记建档方式在全国银行间债券市场发行了第一期SDR计价债券，规模为5亿SDR，品种为固定利率，这是1981年以来国际金融市场首只SDR计价债券，也是在我国发行的首只

SDR计价债券。此后，渣打银行也面向银行间债券市场发行了1亿SDR计价债券。SDR计价债券由上海清算所负责托管和清算，投资者购买和发行人还本付息均由SDR换算为人民币进行结算。

SDR计价债券的发行，有助于为国内投资者提供更多的投资选择，也为需要对冲SDR负债的国际投资者提供了更好的投资渠道；有利于丰富中国债券市场交易品种，促进中国债券市场的开放与发展；也有利于扩大SDR的使用，增强国际货币体系的稳定性。

二、对外开放成效显著

（一）熊猫债显著增加，境外人民币债券稳步推进

2016年，我国银行间债券市场熊猫债发行规模增长，发行主体范围拓展。全年共16家境外机构发行21期熊猫债，规模合计452亿元。其中，1月，加拿大不列颠哥伦比亚省发行人民币债券，该债券成为首只在银行间市场发行的境外地方政府人民币债券。7月，新开发银行发行30亿元绿色金融债券，是多边开发机构首次在中国发行绿色金融债券。8月，波兰共和国作为欧洲首个主权国家在银行间市场发行30亿元人民币主权债券。9月，法国威立雅环境集团在银行间市场发行10亿元人民币债券，是法国企业在境内银行间债券市场发行的第一只人民币债券。加拿大国民银行在银行间市场发行35亿元人民币债券。

2016年，境外市场人民币债券发行稳步推进，全年发行366只，总规模1 002.1亿元，较2015年下降33.9%，但人民币债券品种和发行地区进一步扩大。4月，匈牙利政府成功发行10亿元人民币债券，期限3年，这是中东欧地区发行的首只主权离岸人民币债券。5月，财政部宣布在伦敦发行30亿元人民币国债，票面利率3.28%，期限3年，是财政部首次在中国香港以外的境外市场发行人民币国债。中国农业银行纽约分行成功发行在美中资金融机构首笔人民币债券，发行规模1.17亿元人民币，期限1年，票面利率3.35%。7月，中国银行成功完成境外30亿等值美元绿色债券发行定价，由中国银行卢森堡分行、纽约分行同步发行，覆盖美元、欧元、人民币三个币种及2年、3年、5年三个期限，发行金额分别为22.5亿美元、5亿欧元、15亿元人民币，将分别在卢森堡债券交易所、香港联交所挂牌上市。

（二）境外机构投资者数量增多，类型丰富

截至2016年末，银行间债券市场境外机构共计407家[①]，占市场投资者总量的2.97%，同比增加39.38%。

其中，央行类机构58家，境外商业银行112家（境外人民币清算行12家、其他境外商业银行100家），非银行类金融机构28家（保险公司21家、证券公司4家、其他资产管理机构3家），中长期机构投资者5家

① 境外机构家数统计为实际已进入银行间债券市场的数目，且统计口径为在交易中心开户的账户数。其中新加坡政府投资有限公司、国际货币基金组织（IMF）分别开立2个账户。

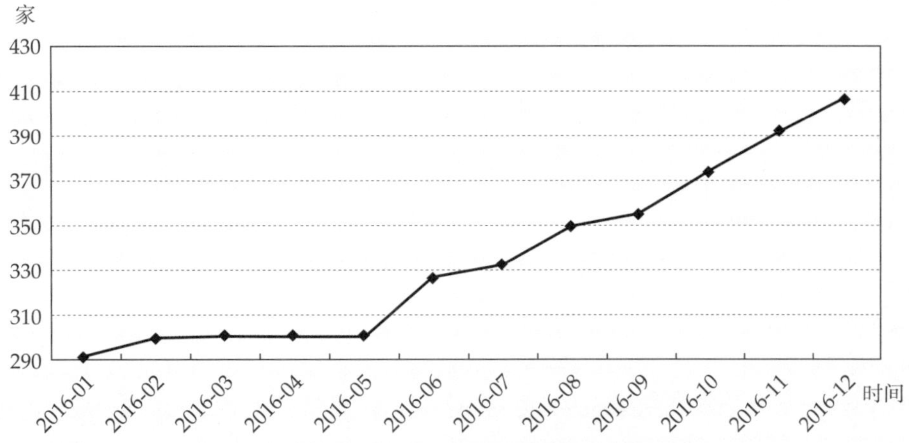

图3-7 2016年1~12月入市机构数变化情况

（养老基金1家、其他中长期机构投资者4家），金融机构产品类投资者204家（保险公司产品2家、证券公司产品30家、基金管理公司产品49家、其他资产管理机构产品123家）。

境外投资者地区分布更加广泛。以非央行类境外机构为例，截至2016年末，境外投资者地域分布扩大到31个国家和地区，遍布亚洲、欧洲、美洲、澳洲等。

（三）境外机构交易量增长，活跃度提升

2016年，境外机构在银行间债券市场累计交易量为1.25万亿元[①]，占市场现券交易总量的比重约为1%。尤其是在6月后，随着相关政策及实施细则的落地，市场预期明确，交易意愿上升，交易量明显增长，9月达到1 666亿元。

境外机构在银行间债券市场以买入为主。全年买入债券5 911笔，券面总额8 745.33亿元，卖出债券4 213笔，券面总额3 774.98亿元，买入债券的交易量约为卖出债券交易量的2.32倍，表明了境外机构增持债券的意愿。

从机构类型上看，以境外商业银行、央行类机构以及金融机构产品类投资者为主。境外商业银行现券交易量为6 932.7亿元，占比54%；境外央行类机构现券交易量为4 229亿元，占境外机构交易量的比重为33%；境外金融机构产品类投资者现券交易量为1 440亿元，占比11%。

境外机构交易工具有所丰富。2016年9月，境外机构首次在银行间债券市场开展债券回购交易。全年共发生回购24笔，交易金额为251亿元。

（四）境外机构债券托管量增加，持债结构稳定

境外机构在银行间债券市场的债券托管总量逐月递增。截至2016年末，境外机

① 以双边计算。

构债券托管量为8 000.31亿元，同比增加23.38%。境外机构托管量占市场托管总量的比重也不断提高。1月末，境外机构托管量占比为1.30%，至12月末，境外机构托管量占比上升到1.42%。

境外机构投资品种以国债、国开行金融债券以及政策性银行债为主。截至2016年末，境外机构持有国债4 236.51亿元，占全部券种的52.95%；持有国开行金融债券1 624.59亿元，占比为20.31%；持有政策性银行债1 421.43亿元，占比为17.77%；持有公司信用类债券495.76亿元，仅占6.20%。

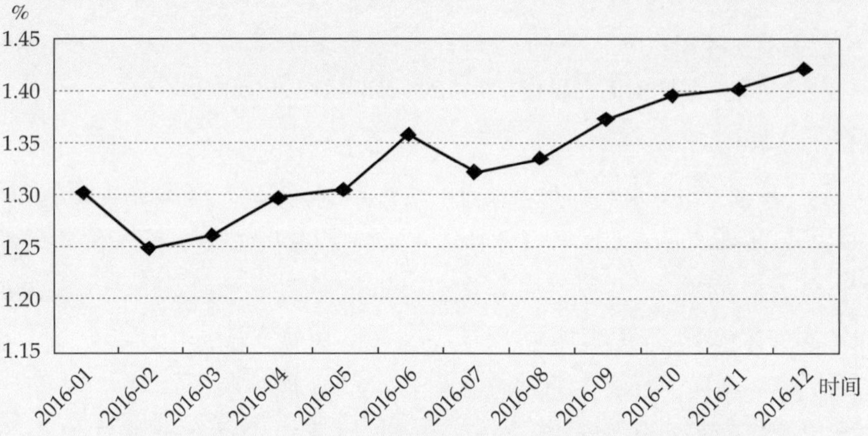

图3-8 2016年1~12月境外机构托管量占比变化情况

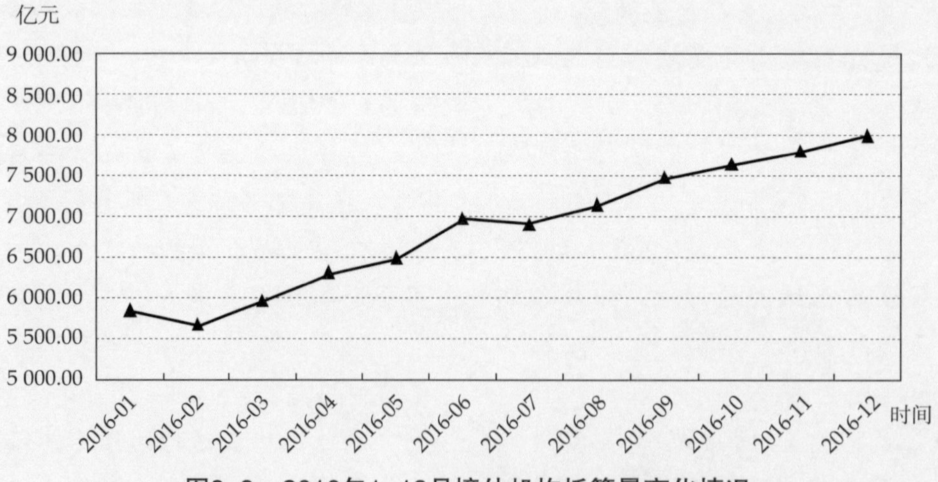

图3-9 2016年1~12月境外机构托管量变化情况

专题三 完善注册发行制度 推进分层分类管理体系

自2008年中国人民银行授权交易商协会对债务融资工具注册发行实施自律管理以来，交易商协会坚持市场化、注册制理念，秉持“自律、创新、服务”的宗旨，持续推进制度创新，逐步建立了较为完善的自律管理制度体系，推动债务融资工具市场持续快速健康发展。随着市场广度和深度的不断拓展、发行主体数量的不断增加、产品类型的日益丰富，部分注册工作流程和要求已不能充分适应市场和业务发展的新要求。很多市场认可度高、多次发行的企业反复报送内容基本一致的文件，浪费人力、物力资源，影响市场运行效率；单一化、平面化的信息披露要求不利于充分展示不同类型主体和产品的个性特点，造成冗余信息增多，既影响工作效率，也不便于投资人高效提取有效信息；前期部分行之有效的优化措施尚没有制度化、体系化，影响了实际执行效果。

为更好地贯彻落实国家关于“稳增长、调结构、促改革、惠民生、防风险”系列政策精神，交易商协会自2014年下半年以来多次组织市场成员召开座谈会，先后赴江苏、山东、四川、安徽、福建等地进行调研，研究进一步发挥债务融资工具市场对实体经济发展的支持作用。在历时一年的工作过程中对既有制度体系进行了系统梳理总结，提炼固化前期行之有效的实践做法，同时吸收借鉴发达市场管理经验，对机制优化设计方案进行反复研究论证，在此基础上完成了相关制度修订。

一、分层分类管理体系的基本原则

本次制度完善坚持“以信息披露为核心”的注册制基本原则，构建分层分类注册发行管理体系。遵循“简化、优化、强化、细化”的原则，对制度流程与信息披露要求既做减法，又做加法：一是简化、优化注册发行流程，但不降低注册发行自律管理的基本要求；二是简化、优化信息披露表格体系，但不降低风险揭示的标准；三是强化、细化风险行业、企业、事项的信息披露要求，加强对投资人合法权益的保护；四是强化对主承销商等中介机构的日常评议管理，细化对注册发行相关人员的工作要求。

二、分层分类管理体系的主要机制设计

本次制度完善从“机制流程优化、信息披露优化、管理方式优化”三个方面来构建注册发行分层分类管理体系，在做好风险揭示及投资人保护的前提下，进一步完善了现行储架发行制度，提升了企业储架发行便利，通过制度设计提升了注册发行工作效率和质量。

（一）实行“主体分层、产品分类”注册发行管理

按照市场化、规范化、透明化的原则，从主体资质、信息披露成熟程度、合规性等角度遴选分层指标，将发行人分为第一类企业、第二类企业进行管理。在整体注册发行机制流程和信息披露优化基础上，第一类企业将比第二类企业享受更多

的注册发行便利。

第一类企业应符合以下要求：(1) 市场认可度高，行业地位显著，经营财务状况稳健，最近两个会计年度未发生连续亏损；(2) 最近36个月内累计公开发行不少于三期，发行规模不少于100亿元；(3) 最近24个月内无债务融资工具或者其他债务违约或者延迟支付本息的事实，控股股东、控股子公司无债务融资工具违约或者延迟支付本息的事实；(4) 最近12个月内未被相关主管部门采取限制直接债务融资业务等行政处罚，未受到交易商协会警告及以上自律处分；(5) 交易商协会根据投资者保护的需要规定的其他条件等。不符合第一类要求的为第二类企业。

针对第一类企业应满足“市场认可度高，行业地位显著，经营财务状况稳健”的要求，交易商协会组织市场成员研究搭建了一套简洁清晰、操作性强、主要基于经营财务指标测算的分层标准体系，并在《非金融企业债务融资工具公开发行注册工作规程》中以附件形式明确发布相关指标，实际操作中由企业和相关中介机构结合经营财务情况以及发行次数和规模等其他指标自行判断是否符合第一类企业要求。

债务融资工具产品丰富多样，既包括超短期融资券、短期融资券、中期票据等常规产品，也包括永续票据、资产支持票据、项目收益票据、可转换票据等特殊结构化品种，还包括并购票据、房地产企业中期票据等特殊用途品种。鉴于结构化品种以及特殊用途品种在注册发行流程、信息披露方面有专项要求，与常规品种有一定差异，应对产品进行分类管理。其中，与短期融资券、中期票据相比，超短期融资券定位为补充企业短期营运资金，注册发行便利程度更高；资产支持票据、项目收益票据、并购票据等产品含特殊结构设计或特殊用途，在常规产品基础上适当增加针对性的信息披露要求，设计差异化的储架发行要求。

（二）提高储架发行便利程度

实施分层分类注册发行管理体系后，所有企业的储架发行便利程度有所提高。第一类企业可就公开发行常规品种债务融资工具（超短期融资券、短期融资券、中期票据及永续票据）进行统一注册，并在注册有效期内自主择机发行。注册时可不确定注册额度，但发行时应明确发行品种、发行期限、发行规模等要素，发行规模应符合法律法规和交易商协会相关规则指引要求；可在注册时设立主承销商团，每期发行指定一家牵头主承销商，并可设一家联席主承销商。第二类企业可按品种分别注册，常规品种注册完成后12个月（含）内可自主择机发行，12个月后发行应先向交易商协会备案。分层分类管理在为企业提供更多注册发行便利的同时，也有利于将评议工作重心转向首次注册、风险突出的行业企业项目以及各类结构化品种项目，强化针对性信息披露评议，做好风险揭示与防范工作。

（三）优化注册评议机制流程

一是注册预评流程在继续实行双人负责制的基础上，由先初评后复核流程改为双人同步评议。同时评议时效也作出相应调整，第一类企业首次反馈须在5日内出具意见，第二类企业10日内首次反馈。针对企业补充文件的后续反馈须在5日内出具意见，预评工作效率得到有效提高。二是进一步完善了注册会议评议机制，优化了注册会议决策程序，完善了注册会议会后事项处理机制。

（四）规范发行自律管理

在发行管理方面，引入了“自主发行期”设置，以便利企业把握发行时间窗口。具体要求为：企业首次在银行间市场公开发行债务融资工具，应至少于发行日前3个工作日公布发行文件；企业非首次在银行间市场公开发行债务融资工具，应至少于发行日前2个工作日公布发行文件；企业公开发行超短期融资券，应至少于发行日前1个工作日公布发行文件。另外，对非金融企业债务融资工具使用集中簿记建档系统规范开展相关工作进行了明确。

（五）完善信息披露要求

新版表格体系引入了补充募集说明书，对既有表格进行分类、归纳、汇总，搭建了立体式、差异化的信息披露架构，实现了从发行方式、发行主体、工作流程、发行频率、注册品种等五个维度满足不同类别、不同环节、不同产品、不同情形的信息披露要求，在减少重复冗余信息披露的同时，强化了重要事项等风险揭示披露要求，有助于发行人、投资人等市场参与各方简洁、快速、高效地使用信息。为进一步强化投资人保护机制安排，明确企业应按照投资者保护条款信息披露子表格披露交叉违约条款、事先约束条款、财务指标承诺条款等。

（六）加强事中事后管理

本次修订在提升企业注册发行便利的同时，对事中事后相关管理要求进行了强化。一是进一步明确了对企业、中介机构等市场参与各方的自律规范要求；二是完善了注册有效期内企业发生重大事项以及其他重要事项的处理机制，明确要求主承销商应持续跟踪企业经营财务情况，督促企业做好补充信息披露工作；三是交易商协会将对企业发行文件信息披露质量进行抽查评议；四是交易商协会将开展对主承销商注册承销业务、后续管理业务的评议管理等工作，强化中介机构尽职履责义务，推动其充分发挥项目筛选和信用风险防范方面的专业能力。注册发行制度完善及分层分类管理体系构建，坚持了“以信息披露为核心”的注册制基本原则，进一步丰富了注册制在我国债务融资工具市场发展中的内涵和外延，推动了自律管理方式由“事前管理为主”向“事前、事中、事后管理相结合”的转变，在强化风险防范和投资人保护的前提下，更充分地发挥了市场在资源配置中的决定性作用，有利于提升注册发行工作效率和质量，切实发挥债务融资工具服务市场、服务实体经济发展的作用。

第四章 股票市场

2016年，中国股票市场融资规模继续增长，IPO家数和融资额创近五年来新高，增发仍是股票市场融资的主要方式。各股票指数均在年初出现较大下跌，之后一直处于箱体运行，波动性明显下降。新三板分层制度正式推出，沪深港市场互联互通加速。监管部门多措并举推动健全资本市场制度体系，进一步加强对投资者权益的保护，切实防范股票市场风险，规范股票市场运行，确保资本市场稳中求进。

一、股票市场的运行情况

（一）股票发行与融资

2016年，中国股票市场融资规模保持增长。全年共发生股票融资982例，募集资金17 395.23亿元，同比增长12.54%。从融资方式看，全年完成首次公开发行227例，较2015年略有提升，合计IPO募集资金1 496.08亿元，同比减少5.09%；全年完成增发745例，同比下降13.07%，合计增发募集资金15 723.22亿元，同比增长14.57%；全年完成配股10例，较2015年增加5例，合计配股募集资金175.94亿元，同比增加11.62%。总体来看，增发依旧是股票市场最主要的融资方式，占全年股票融资总额的90.39%，IPO及配股的占比分别为8.60%和1.01%。

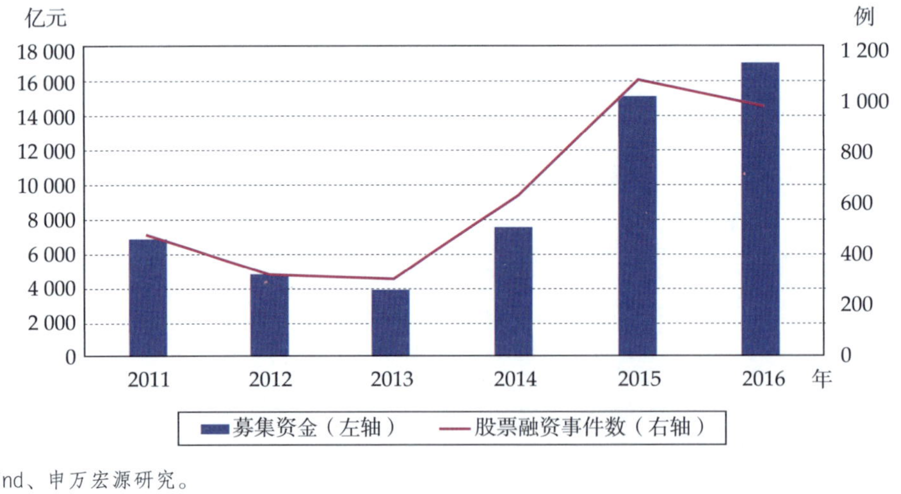

数据来源：Wind、申万宏源研究。

图4-1　2011—2016年股票市场融资情况

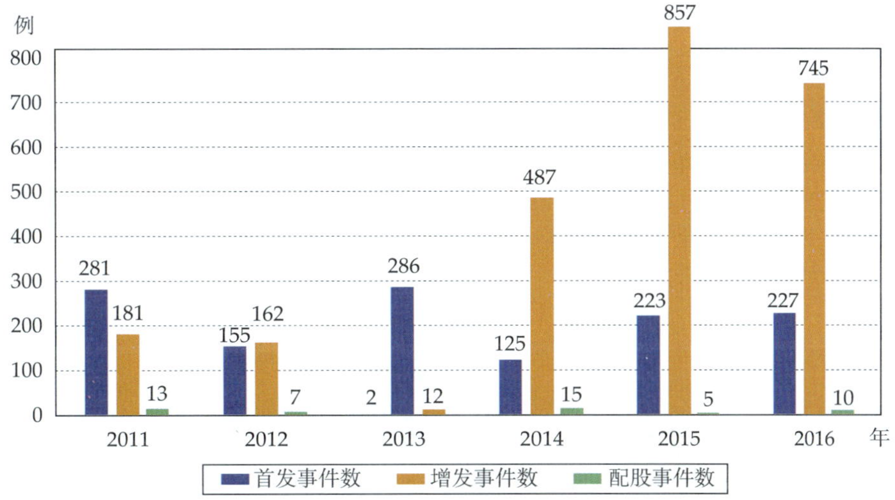

数据来源：Wind、申万宏源研究。

图4-2　2011—2016年股票市场各类融资事件数

（二）股票指数与交易

截至2016年底，沪、深两市共有上市公司3 052家，比上年末增加225家，上市股票3 134只，比上年末增加225只，其中A股3 034只、B股100只。两市股票总市值50.77万亿元，比上年末减少2.36万亿元，减少4.45%；股票流通市值39.34万亿元，比上年末减少2.45万亿元，减少5.87%。市场总股本4.88万亿股，比上年末增长13.34%；流通股本4.11万亿股，比上年末增长11.05%，占全部股本的84.38%，股本流通率较上年末略有下降。

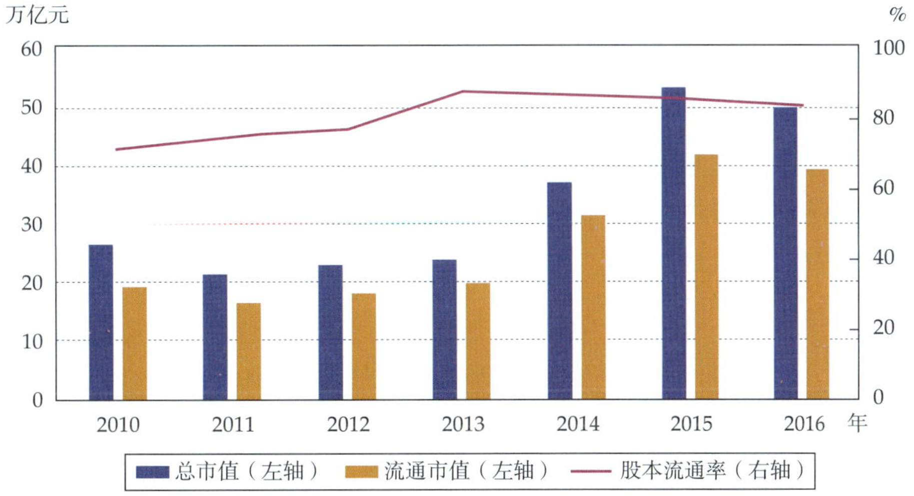

数据来源：Wind、申万宏源研究。

图4-3　2010—2016年股票市值及股本流通率情况

2016年末，上证综合指数、深证成份指数、中小板指数和创业板指数分别收于3 103.64点、10 177.14点、6 472.23点和1 962.06点，同比分别下跌12.31%、19.64%、22.89%和27.71%。股指涨幅在全球主要市场中位于末尾，市值缩水超过2万亿元，其中创业板市值缩水程度最为显著。

数据来源：Wind、申万宏源研究。

图4-4　2016年上证综合指数、深证成份指数走势

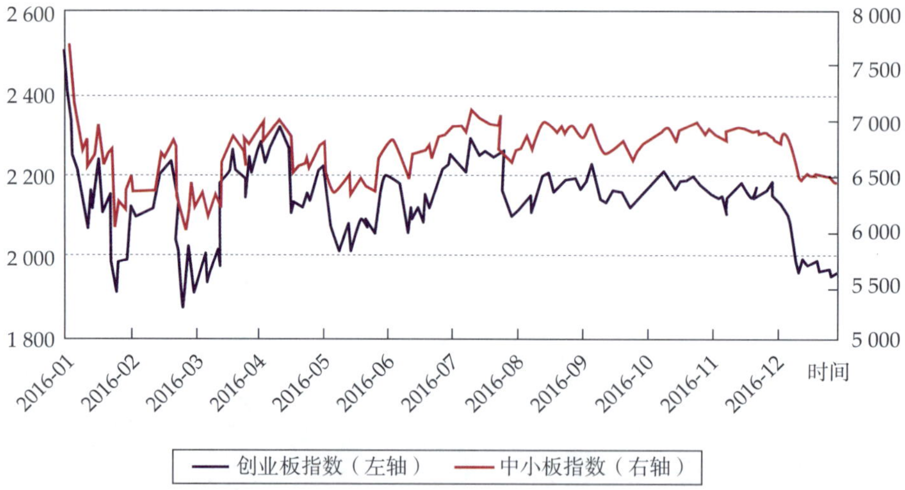

数据来源：Wind、申万宏源研究。

图4-5　2016年创业板指数、中小板指数走势

2016年，全部A股累计成交量9.39万亿股，同比下降44.65%；累计成交金额126.51万亿元，同比下降50.05%。其中，沪、深主板市场股票累计成交数量6.42万亿股，同比下降52.38%，累计成交金额为70.91万亿元，同比下降59.63%；中小板累计成交数量2.03亿

股，同比下降18.90%，累计成交金额34.06万亿元，同比下降30.86%；创业板累计成交数量0.94万亿股，同比下降4.55%，累计成交金额21.54万亿元，同比下降24.13%。

二、股票市场运行的主要特点

（一）股票市场走势稳定，波动性明显下降

在经历2015年市场大幅波动以来，2016年初股票指数熔断机制经历试错，年初再度出现了千股跌停的现象，随着市场情绪逐步回归稳定，整体来看，2016年股票市场波动性明显下降。以上证综指为例，2015年全年，共有81个交易日的涨跌幅超过2%，另有15个交易日的涨跌幅超过5%；而2016年3月以来，涨跌幅超过2%的交易日仅有11个，也未出现单日涨跌幅超过5%的现象，市场波动幅度明显收窄，投资者信心增强，市场运行趋于稳定。

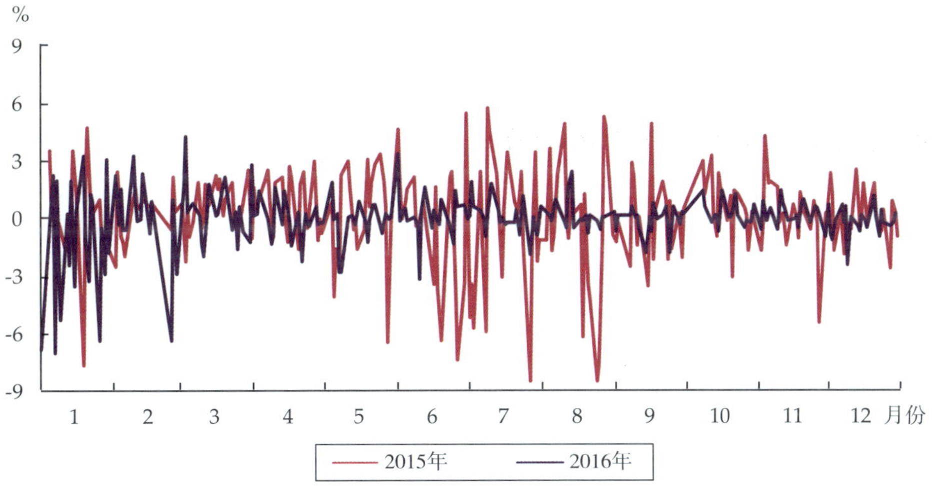

数据来源：Wind、申万宏源研究。

图4-6　2015年、2016年上证综指日涨跌幅

（二）新股网下申购政策调整，融资融券余额相对稳定

2016年，新股网下申购预缴款取消，网下投资者申购账户数由年初的1 000户增长至2016年10月高峰时期的5 000户。2016年融资融券余额相对稳定，全年在8 000亿~10 000亿元的区间波动，截至2016年末融资融券余额约9 392亿元，占A股总市值的比重约为1.9%。股票质押快速增长，2016年共质押股票3 067.64亿股，较2015年大幅增长近50%，股票质押参考市值约41 465.71亿元，较2015年增长2.35%，其中主板参考市值18 278.51亿元，同比增幅相对最大。

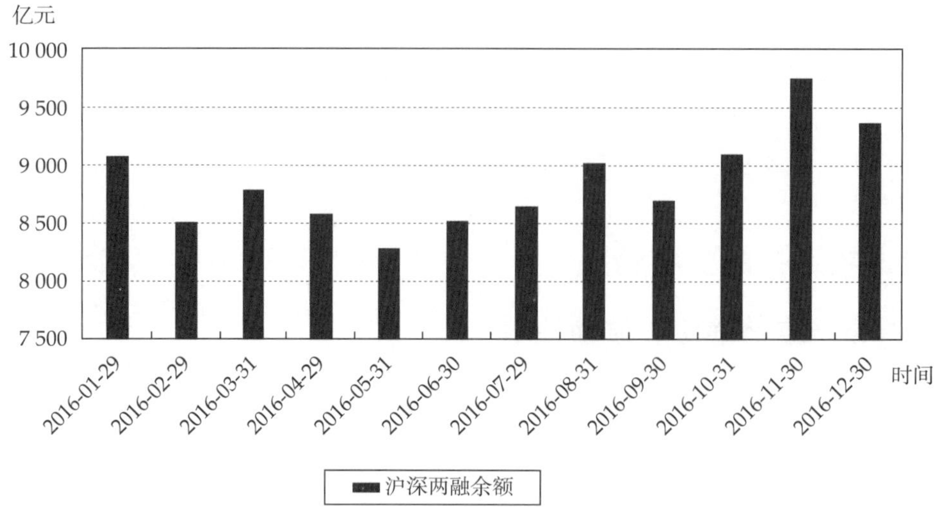

数据来源：Wind、申万宏源研究。

图4-7 2016年沪深两市各月两融余额

（三）沪港通平稳运行，两地市场互补性显现

2016年沪港通累计交易金额14 565.5亿元，其中，沪股通累计成交7 452.7亿元，港股通累计成交7 112.8亿元，交易、登记结算、换汇和公司行为等各项业务处理顺畅，业务和技术系统运行平稳。沪港通的平稳运行不仅带来了资金的相互流通，更带动了两地市场格局的深刻变化。从投资偏好来看，内地投资者的投资理念更趋于成熟理性；从股指差异来看，恒生AH股溢价指数持续走低，表明内地与香港市场的估值差异正在逐步缩小；从市场开放来看，自2016年8月16日起沪港通不再设置总额度限制，有利于进一步促进两地资本市场的互联互通。

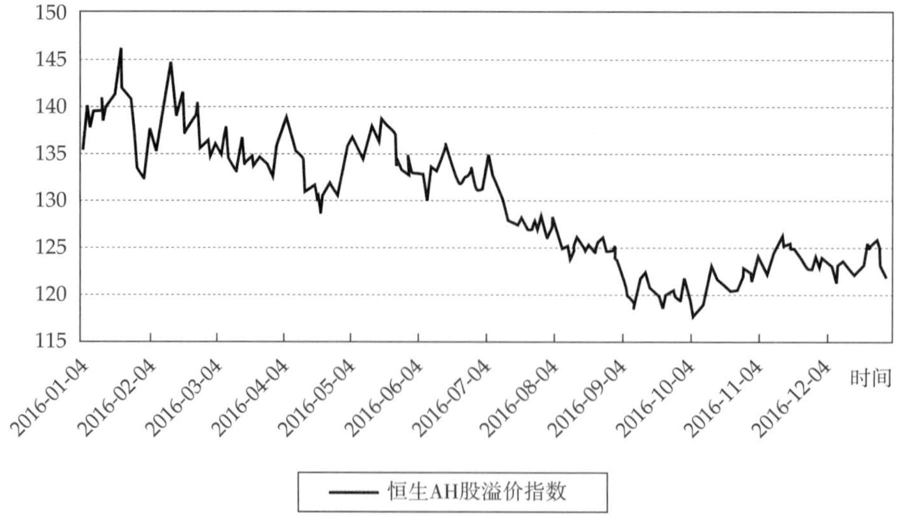

数据来源：Wind、申万宏源研究。

图4-8 2016年恒生AH股溢价指数

（四）债转股助力市场去杠杆，可交换债成为市场亮点

2016年10月10日，国务院发布《关于积极稳妥降低企业杠杆率的意见》（国发〔2016〕54号），并同时发布《关于市场化银行债权转股权的指导意见》，支持银行充分利用现有符合条件的所属机构，或允许申请设立符合规定的新机构开展市场化债转股。此后，农业银行、工商银行、建设银行、中国银行纷纷设立资产管理子公司，专门经营与债转股相关的债权收购、债权转股权以及持有、管理、处置转股企业股权等业务。据不完全统计，2016年10月以来四大国有银行落地的债转股项目达16单，已公布金额的11单规模达1 620亿元，另有5单已签署框架协议。

2016年，可交换债发行出现井喷式增长，全年共发行可交换债91只，同比增长175.76%；合计发行金额890.56亿元，同比增长207.32%。一方面，可交换债不新增股票，换股的股票为原股东抵押部分，因此债券的风险与发行人的信用关系不大，信用较差、难以发行债券融资的发行人如果拥有上市公司的股权，也可以通过发行可交换债的方式融资。另一方面，可交换债的融资成本显著低于股票质押，并且通常可以募集到股票市值70%~100%的金额。此外，用于可交换债发行的抵押品可以是处于禁售状态的股票，无疑解决了上市公司股东因参与定增而面临较长锁定期的难题。

三、股票市场制度建设

（一）规范上市公司停复牌制度，促进上市公司信息披露质量

2016年5月27日，上交所发布《上市公司筹划重大事项停复牌业务指引》（上证发〔2016〕19号），从扩大停牌规范范围、严格控制停牌时间和细化停牌期间的信息披露和延期复牌程序要求等三方面完善上市公司停复牌业务；同日，深交所发布《上市公司停复牌业务备忘录》，从明确相关重大事项的最长停牌时间、加大投资者对长期停牌行为的监督、细化停复牌事项的信息披露要求、强化停牌约束和加强中介机构作用等五个方面对上市公司停复牌业务予以规范，加强停复牌制度监管。停复牌制度是我国资本市场健康发展的一项重要基础制度，规范停复牌制度对于切实维护市场交易效率，保护投资者知情权和交易权，促进上市公司提高信息披露质量等方面都具有积极意义。

（二）并购重组明确五大监管方向，引导市场规范发展

2016年9月9日，证监会发布《关于修改〈上市公司重大资产重组管理办法〉的决定》（证监会〔第127号令〕），进一步规范重组上市行为，明确并购重组的五大监管方向。一是强化信息披露，弱化实质审核；二是流程简化、分道审批；三是支持并购重组创新，完善机制安排；四是分类审核，严格借壳上市审查；五是提高并购重组审核透明度。上市公司重大资产重组的再规范，将大幅压缩炒卖“伪壳”、“垃圾壳”的牟利空间，有利于上市公司通过正常的并购重组提高质量、推动行业整合和产业升级。同时，规则提高了“借壳”门槛和“卖壳”成本，有助于强化退市制度刚性，缓解“退市难”的局面，有利于股市上“僵尸企业”的清理，推进上市公司优胜劣汰，提升市场资源配置效率。

（三）加强同业业务去通道，严防系统性金融风险

2016年7月14日，证监会发布《证券期货经营机构私募资产管理业务运作管理暂行规定》（证监会公告〔2016〕13号），针对证券公司、基金管理公司等开展私募资管业务中暴露出的问题进行了明确规范，主要内容包括：扩大适用主体的范围，将私募证券投资基金管理人一并纳入监管体系；明确规定结构化产品负债端的杠杆倍数；限制结构化和非结构化集合资产管理计划的融资杠杆上限；禁止预期收益率宣传，禁止对优先级提供保本保收益安排；禁止嵌套和资金池操作以及加强对第三方投顾的监管。此外，银监会发布了《关于规范金融资产管理公司不良资产收购业务的通知》（银监办发〔2016〕56号），限制金融资产管理公司为银行不良资产处置提供通道。保监会发布了《中国保监会关于清理规范保险资产管理公司通道类业务有关事项的通知》（保监资金〔2016〕98号），要求各保险资管公司清理规范银行存款通道等业务。上述监管规定的出台对于加强同业业务去通道，促进金融机构回归本位，防范系统性金融风险有着积极的意义。

表4-1 2016年沪深交易所停复牌新规梳理

	公告事项	停牌时间	备注
深交所	重大资产重组（首次申请）	1个月	每五个交易日披露一次进展
	重大资产重组（继续停牌）	累计不超过2个月；经董事会批准累计不超过3个月；经股东大会批准累计不超过6个月	
	非公开发行（涉及重大资产购买）	10个交易日	
	非公开发行（不涉及重大资产购买）	1个月	
	筹划购买或出售资产	10个交易日	
	签订重大合同或战略性协议	10个交易日	
上交所	筹划重大资产重组	原则上不超过3个月，最多不超过5个月	每五个交易日披露一次进展
	终止筹划重大资产重组（停牌不足一个月）	披露终止公告当日复牌	
	终止筹划重大资产重组（停牌超过一个月）	披露投资者说明会结果当日复牌	
	要约收购（符合上市条件）	期限届满次日连续停牌直至收购结果披露当日	
	要约收购（不符合上市条件）	收购结果披露至解决方案披露不超过5个交易日	

资料来源：沪深交易所、申万宏源研究。

（四）新三板分层制度正式推出，推进场外市场多层次建设

2016年5月27日，全国股转公司公布《全国中小企业股份转让系统挂牌公司分层管理办法（试行）》（股转系统公告〔2016〕37号）（以下简称《分层管理办法》），并公布自6月27日起对新三板挂牌公司施行分层管理，区分为创新层和基础层，这标志着新三板分层方案正式落定。《分层管理办法》设置了三套并行标准，旨在筛选出市场关注的不同类型公司进入创新层：标准一侧重于挂牌公司的盈利要求；标准二侧重于挂牌公司的成长性要求；标准三侧重于挂牌公司的做市市值要求。三板分层制度的推出为处于不同发展阶段和具有不同市场需求的挂牌公司提供了相适应的资本市场平台，同时对于改善三板市场流动性、合理分配监管资源具有积极意义。截至2016年12月31日，新三板挂牌企业中共有952家创新层企业。分层制度的推出对于进一步完善新三板市场功能、降低投资者信息收集成本、提高风险控制能力、审慎推进市场创新具有积极意义。

表4-2　新三板分层制度主要内容

	主要内容
明确了创新层的准入标准	《分层管理办法》设置了三套并行标准。标准一侧重于挂牌公司的盈利要求，以满足盈利能力较强、相对成熟挂牌公司的分层需求；标准二侧重于挂牌公司的成长性要求，以满足处于初创期、高速成长的中小企业的分层需求；标准三侧重于挂牌公司的做市市值要求，以满足商业模式新颖、创新创业型企业的分层需求。除了上述三套差异化准入标准，进入创新层的挂牌公司还需满足公司治理、合法合规性以及交易或者融资要求。
就申请挂牌公司进入创新层设置了准入标准	申请挂牌公司进入创新层的标准与已挂牌公司进入创新层的三套标准基本一致。但考虑申请挂牌公司尚未经过挂牌后的规范化运作和持续监管，尚未公开交易和分散股权，也没有做市交易市值，因此，《分层管理办法》就申请挂牌公司进入创新层的标准作了适当调整。
就创新层设置了维持标准	为保证市场分层的动态管理，《分层管理办法》就创新层挂牌公司设置了维持标准。层级调整时，创新层挂牌公司如果不能满足三套维持标准之一的，将被调整到基础层。
明确了挂牌公司的层级划分和调整机制	《分层管理办法》规定挂牌公司每年进行一次层级调整，未来可视市场需要逐步提高或降低层级调整的频率。层级调整时，挂牌公司可以就分层结果提出异议或者自愿放弃进入创新层。此外，为防止部分挂牌公司通过虚假信息披露、市场操纵等不合规手段进入创新层，《分层管理办法》还规定了强制调整的情形。

资料来源：全国股转公司、申万宏源研究。

四、股票市场对外开放

（一）深港通正式推出，沪深港一体化加速推进

2016年12月5日，经过两年多筹备的深港通正式启动，标志着中国资本市场在法治化、市场化和国际化方向上又迈出了坚实一步。深港通的开启将在改善境内市场投资者结构、提升流动性、平复A股和H股估值差异、拓展金融产品和交易品种等方面起到促

进作用：其一，带来投资者结构的变化，深港通有利于吸引更多境外长期资金进入A股市场，继而改善A股市场投资者结构；其二，带来流动性的变化，总额度限制的放开将有效提升金融产品的流动性，满足投资者多样化的跨境投资以及风险管理需求；其三，带来价差收窄的变化，由于投资者结构、交易机制等原因，年末A股、H股之间的折价约在124%的水平，未来价差有望进一步收窄；其四，带来金融产品和交易品种的丰富，ETF、债券纳入互联互通有望在2017年取得重要进展。截至2016年12月30日收市，港股通合计买入79.43亿港元，卖出12.21亿港元；深股通合计买入206.79亿元，卖出55.11亿元。

（二）QFII、RQFII额度持续增加，外资投资便利性更趋完善

2016年2月，国家外汇管理局发布《合格境外机构投资者境内证券投资外汇管理规定》（国家外汇管理局公告2016年第1号），进一步放宽合格境外机构投资者（QFII）额度限制，并简化审批流程。9月，中国人民银行、国家外汇管理局发布《关于人民币合格境外机构投资者境内证券投资管理有关问题的通知》（银发〔2016〕227号），进一步提高对RQFII和QFII机构外汇管理的一致性，推动境内金融市场开放。主要内容包括：一是参照QFII管理，将机构资产规模一定比例作为获取额度（基础额度）的依据，额度管理方式统一调整为余额管理；二是简化额度审批管理，对机构基础额度内的额度申请采取备案管理并自动获取；三是便利RQFII资金汇出入，在资金汇入上与QFII管理相同，不对资金汇入设置期限要求，在资金汇出上不设比例与分期汇出的要求，对开放式基金不设锁定期，允许按日汇出，对其他产品或资金，将锁定期由1年缩短为3个月，允许每日汇出；四是取消购汇汇出，要求RQFII以人民币方式汇出入；五是简化数据报送要求，通过资本项目信息系统进行数据采集和监测。相关政策实施以后，市场反映良好，截至2016年末，QFII累计投资投资额度为873.10亿美元，RQFII累计投资额度为5 284.75亿元人民币。

五、股票市场发展展望

（一）IPO发行常态化，定增监管维持趋紧态势

为有效缓解新股“堰塞湖”，强化市场融资功能，提升资本市场对实体经济的服务能力，2017年新股或将保持一定的发行节奏，但为了缓解新股发行对二级市场的冲击，新股发行融资规模可能继续受限。同时，定增监管将持续趋严，抑制高折价、规范并购重组、严控配套募资用途和规模仍将是定增市场的监管重点。

（二）完善场外市场建设，助力中小企业发展

加快完善新三板市场，规范发展区域性股权市场，有序扩大和更加便利中小微企业股权融资，是推进供给侧结构性改革的重要举措，对完善多层次资本市场体系，使金融更好地服务实体经济转型升级，深入实施创新驱动发展战略，促进大众创业、万众创新，具有重要意义。2017年场外市场建设有望进一步提速。一是在新三板选择部分优质企业引入集中竞价交易机制，提升三板市场流动性。二是加快推进新三板向创业板转板试点，逐步建立各层次市场间的有机联系。

三是规范发展区域性股权市场，区域性股权市场有望纳入多层次资本市场体系，实现三板和四板的合作对接与协同发展。

（三）以开放促改革，完善互联互通机制

2017年在沪港通、深港通的基础上，境内外资本市场的互联互通将进一步深化。一方面，境内市场与香港市场的互联互通将覆盖更多资产类别；另一方面，“沪伦通”的可行性研究已取得阶段性成果，有望在2017年得到进一步推进和落实。

（四）去通道去杠杆下，积极推进产品创新

2017年，对于产品创新的监管思路将延续“遏制套利型产品创新，鼓励原创型产品创新”的总基调，在当前“抑制资产泡沫、防范金融风险”的背景下，产品创新将更多地围绕加快中小企业发展、推动供给侧结构性改革、助力经济增长等维度展开。一是将贯彻精准扶贫基本方针，发挥资本市场行业优势，为贫困地区首次公开发行、新三板挂牌、发行债券、并购重组等开辟绿色通道；二是将大力发展资产证券化，推动供给侧结构性改革；三是将继续研究建立以市场需求为导向的产品创新机制，丰富健全多层次产品体系。

专题四 股票市场投资者结构变化研究

一、近年来我国投资者持股结构状况

（一）个人投资者在账户数量上占据绝对优势

在我国股票市场中，个人投资者所持股票交易账户数量占绝对优势。中证登数据显示，2016年末我国股票市场账户总额11 811.04万户，其中个人投资者11 778.42万户，占比为99.72%；非自然人账户数量为30.32万户，占比为0.28%。

表4-3 2016年末投资者市值分布

期末已上市的A股流通市值	自然人		非自然人		合计	
	投资者数（户）	占比（%）	投资者数（户）	占比（%）	投资者数（户）	占比（%）
a.1万元以下	12 017 997	24.37	4 536	6.30	12 022 533	24.35
b.1万~10万元	23 627 616	47.92	8 288	11.51	23 635 904	47.87
c.10万~50万元	10 513 794	21.32	10 978	15.25	10 524 772	21.31
d.50万~100万元	1 791 721	3.63	6 055	8.41	1 797 776	3.64
e.100万~500万元	1 195 312	2.42	13 360	18.56	1 208 672	2.45
f.500万~1 000万元	97 822	0.20	5 257	7.30	103 079	0.21
g.1 000万~1亿元	58 960	0.12	13 499	18.75	72 459	0.15
h.1亿元以上	4 680	0.01	10 009	13.90	14 689	0.03
合计	49 307 902	100.00	71 982	100.00	49 379 884	100.00

资料来源：中证登、申万宏源研究。

从账户市值来看，个人投资者依旧以小散户为主，机构投资者持股规模结构较多元化，各个层次较平均。根据2016年底已上市A股流通市值测算，有超过72%的个人投资者账户市值低于10万元，50万元以上的仅占6.35%。机构投资者所持上市A股流通市值分布较为均匀，无占绝对优势类别。

（二）专业机构投资者持股占比下降

A股投资者分为三类：个人投资者、一般法人和保险、基金、券商、QFII等专业机构投资者。从市值占比数据来看，截至2016年第三季度末，个人投资者持股占比为43.6%，先后经历了2008年以来的快速下降到近几年的稳中有升；一般法人的持股占比为49.8%，股权分置改革带来的大量限售股解禁以及定增带来的增量股份使得一般法人持股占比在2009年之后呈现快速增长；以基金、保险等为代表的专业机构投资者持股占比约为6.6%，近年来呈现稳中有降的趋势。

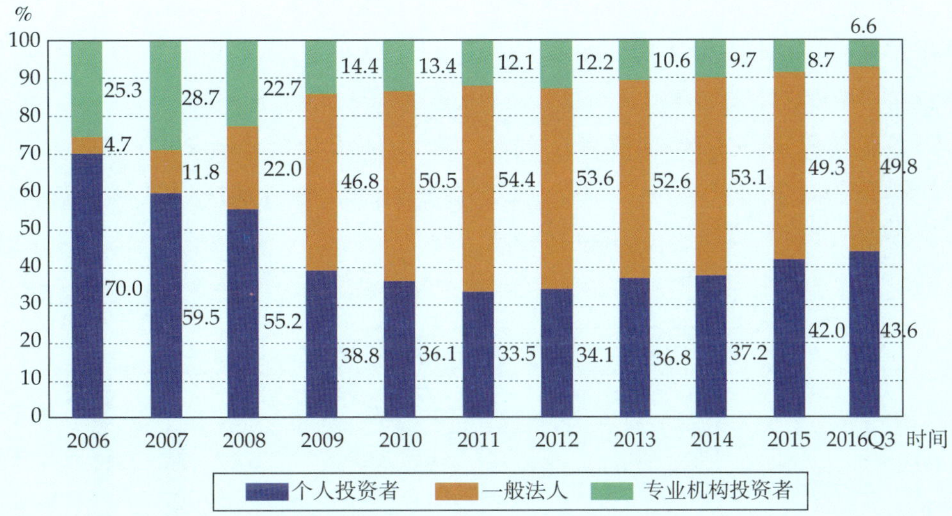

注：持股占比，是指占流通市值比重；专业机构投资者包括基金公司、保险公司、证券公司、社保基金、信托公司、企业年金、QFII等。

数据来源：Wind、申万宏源研究。

图4-9 我国股票市场投资者市值占比

二、股权分置改革带动产业资本占比上升

（一）限售股解禁释放了20多万亿元的流通市值

从存量角度来看，A股解禁限售股规模上升带动了产业资本持股占比的上升。自2006年大小非解禁以来，市场共释放了26.61万亿元的流通市值，尤其是2009—2010年间，解禁市值迭创高峰。与此同时，一般法人的持股市值占流通市值的比

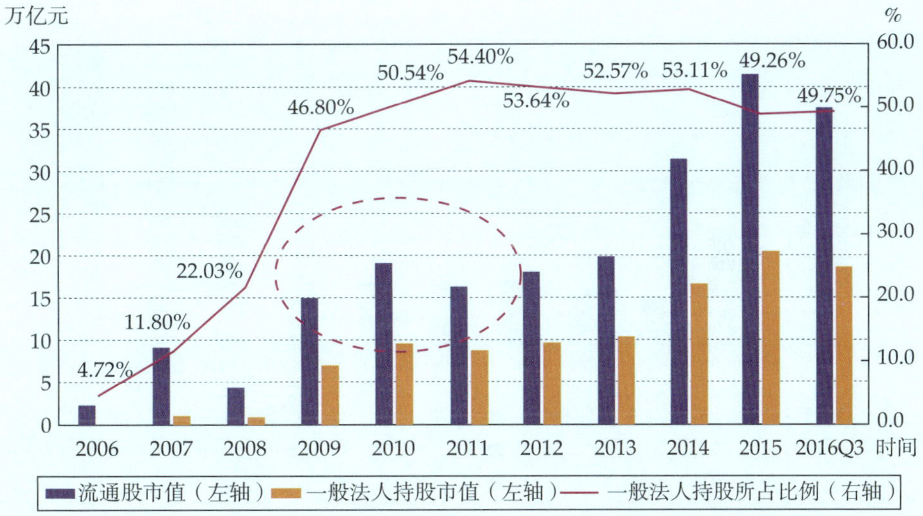

数据来源：Wind、申万宏源研究。

图4-10 2006—2016年一般法人持股情况

例亦从2008年末的22.0%增长至2010年末的50.5%。截至2016年第三季度末，一般法人合计持股18.8万亿元，占整体流通市值的49.75%。

（二）增量方面，不断扩容的定增主要配售对象是一般法人

从增量角度来看，近年来，定向增发规模已远超同期IPO规模，成为市场主要

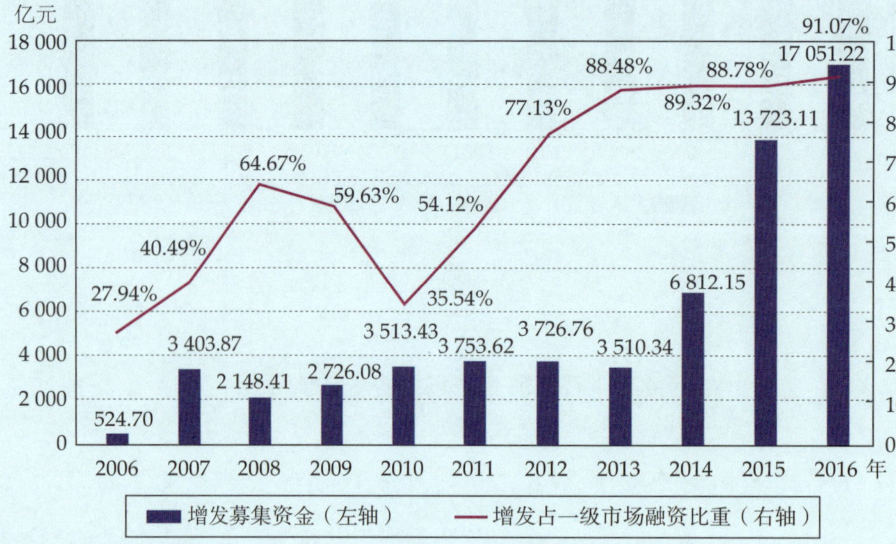

数据来源：Wind、申万宏源研究。

图4-11　增发占一级市场融资比重

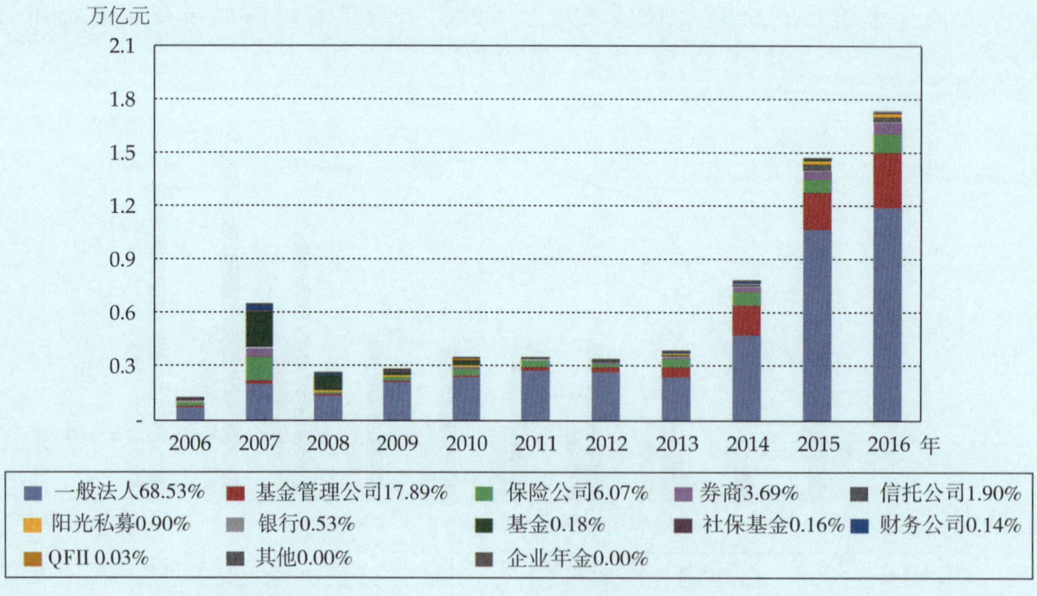

数据来源：Wind、申万宏源研究。

图4-12　企业日益成为增发配售的主要对象

的增量资金来源。Wind数据显示，2011年以来，超过五成的一级市场融资通过增发完成，并且近三年来上市公司增发募资规模呈现快速增长，增发融资占一级市场融资比重的近九成。2016年，共实现定向增发融资17 051.22亿元，占一级市场融资规模的91.07%。从定向增发的配售对象进一步分析，一般法人是定向增发的主要配售对象，因此一般法人的持股市值得以进一步提高。2016年，共实现增发配售1.74万亿元，其中有超过68%的股票向一般法人配售，另有不到1/3的增发股票对基金、保险、券商等金融机构进行配售。

三、我国机构投资者的多元化特征已经显现

（一）保险公司已成为超越公募基金的重要力量

从专业机构投资者的内部持股占比来看，十年前，机构投资者以基金公司独大，公募基金所持股票市值占全体机构投资者的80%以上，而伴随着泛资管时代的到来以及机构投资者队伍的不断壮大，保险、公募基金、社保基金、QFII、证券公司等纷纷加大了入市的步伐，成为资本市场重要的参与主体。截至2016年第三季度，保险公司所持股票市值占全体机构投资者的41.19%，公募和专户基金的占比为37.73%，社保基金、QFII、券商的占比依次为6.80%、4.91%和5.34%。

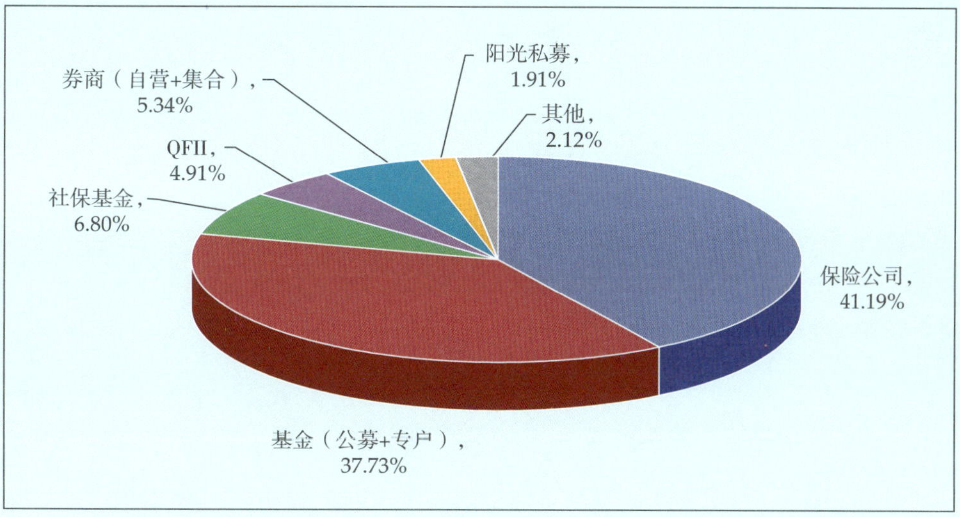

数据来源：Wind、申万宏源研究。

图4-13　专业机构投资者内部持股占比（截至2016年第三季度）

（二）公募基金占比下降

近年来公募基金规模虽出现了持续上升，但公募基金股票持仓比例呈现显著下降，致使公募基金不再成为股票市场唯一有话语权的机构投资者，截至2016年末，公募基金股票市值规模1.66万亿元，股票市

值占基金净值的比重为18.51%。另外，伴随着泛资管时代的到来，保险资金、社保基金、阳光私募、信托公司等正成为资本市场机构投资者中的新兴力量，我国股票市场投资者的多元化特征已经逐步显现。

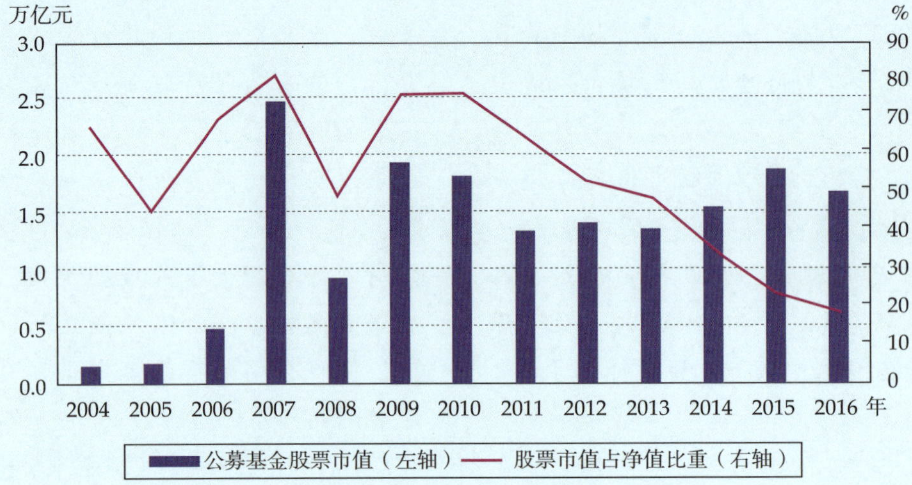

数据来源：Wind、申万宏源研究。

图4-14 2004—2016年公募基金股票持仓情况

第五章　外汇市场

2016年，我国外汇市场总体运行平稳。人民币对一篮子货币小幅贬值，双向浮动特征明显，汇率弹性增强。外汇市场成交活跃，流动性提升，直接交易币种进一步丰富，交易主体及结构进一步扩展和改善。市场运行机制、外汇管理体制等制度建设不断推进，人民币汇率形成机制改革朝着市场化方向不断深化。

一、外汇市场的运行情况

（一）人民币对一篮子货币小幅贬值

2016年，人民币对一篮子货币小幅贬值。12月末，CFETS人民币汇率指数为94.83，较年初贬值5.1%；参考BIS货币篮子和SDR货币篮子的人民币汇率指数分别为96.24和95.50，分别较年初贬值4.6%和2.2%。2016年12月，人民币名义有效汇率指数为118.55，人民币实际有效汇率指数为122.81，与年初相比，分别贬值5.1%和5.4%；2005年人民币汇率形成机制改革以来至2016年12月，人民币名义有效汇率升值34.8%，实际有效汇率升值44.4%。

人民币对主要货币汇率有贬有升。2016年12月末，人民币兑美元汇率中间价为6.9370元，比年初贬值6.3%。2005年人民币汇率形成机制改革以来至2016年末，人民币兑美元汇率中间价累计升值19.3%。12月末，人民币兑欧元、日元、英镑、澳元、加元汇率中间价分别为1欧元兑7.3068元人民币、100日元兑5.9591元人民币、1英镑兑8.5094元人民币、1澳元兑5.0157元人民币、1加元兑5.1406元人民币，分别较年初贬值 3.5%、贬值9.4%、升值12.5 %、贬值5.6%和贬值8.8%；人民币兑马来西亚林吉特、俄罗斯卢布中间价分别为1人民币兑0.64406林吉特、1人民币兑8.6906卢布，分别较年初贬值2.7%和23.0%。

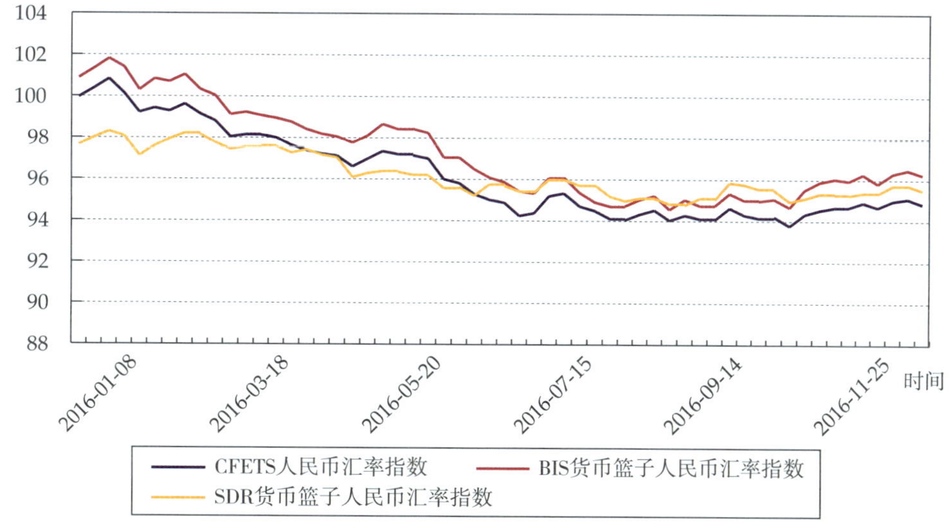

数据来源：中国外汇交易中心。

图5-1　2016年人民币汇率指数波动

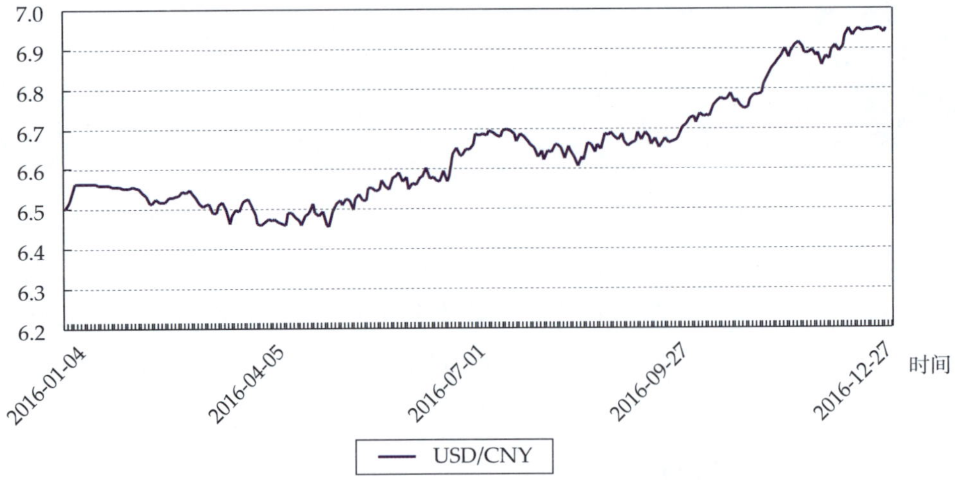

数据来源：中国外汇交易中心。

图5-2　2016年人民币兑美元中间价波动

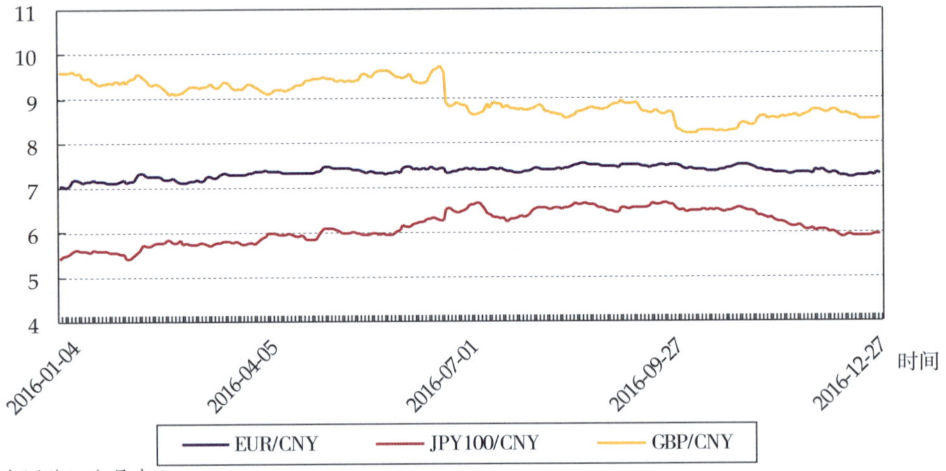

数据来源：中国外汇交易中心。

图5-3　2016年人民币兑主要发达经济体汇率中间价波动

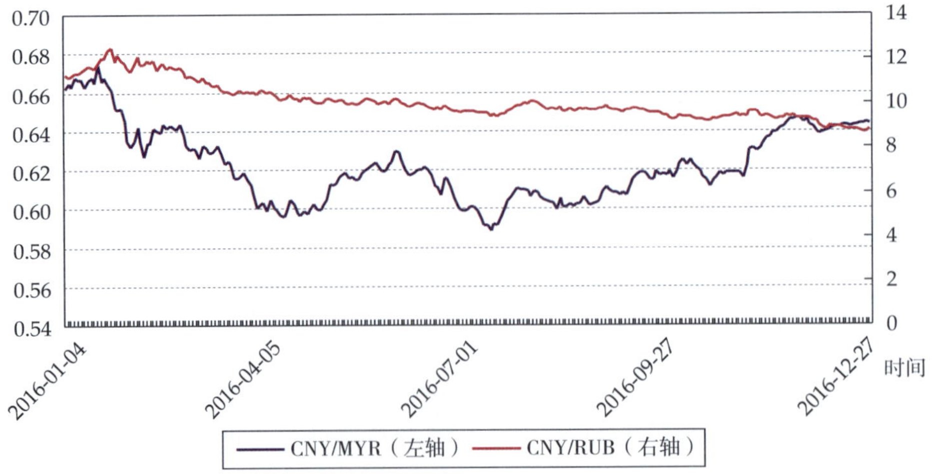

数据来源：中国外汇交易中心。

图5-4　2016年人民币兑新兴市场货币汇率中间价波动

（二）人民币外汇市场交易量增大

1. 人民币外汇即期市场交易情况

2016年，人民币外汇市场共成交约16.85万亿美元，同比增长24.4%。其中，人民币外汇即期市场成交5.93万亿美元，同比增长21.9%。

从成交币种来看，人民币兑美元成交5.73万亿美元，同比增长24.3%；人民币兑欧元成交690.87亿美元，同比增长1.9%；人民币兑日元成交492.92亿美元，同比下降8.1%；人民币兑英镑成交73.54亿美元，同比下降41.0%；人民币兑俄罗斯卢布成交17.61亿美元，同比下降50.1%；人民币兑马来西亚林吉特成交5.12亿美元，同比上升115.3%。

2016年末，人民币外汇市场会员共计597家，较上年末增加79家，增长15.3%。其中，境外央行类机构、境外清算行和境外参加行等境外会员机构达59家。

2. 外币拆借市场成交情况

2016年，银行间外币拆借市场发展迅速，外币拆借会员数量持续增加。全年，外币拆借市场成交共计折合人民币11.05万亿元，较上年增长18倍。其中，银行间外币拆借市场共拆入/拆出16 505.31亿美元、297.27亿港元、24.61亿欧元，美元拆借交易占外币拆借总交易的98%以上。截至年末，外币拆借市场共有会员413家，较上年末增长44.4%。

（三）外币对市场发展平稳

2016年，银行间外币对市场发展平稳。全年外币对市场共成交1 159.45亿美元，同比下降3.5%，其中，欧元/美元和美元/日元仍为交易最活跃的货币对，交易量分别为397.86亿美元和293.31亿美元。分币种来看，2016年美元/日元和美元/瑞士法郎货币对交易量增长较快，较上年分别增长1.1倍和3.4倍，欧元/美元、美元/港元、欧元/日元等货币对交易量则有所下滑，较上年分别下降29.5%、46.7%和58.4%。截至年末，外币对会员达161家，较上年末增加12.6%。

二、外汇市场运行的主要特点

（一）人民币兑美元汇率中间价形成机制运行良好

2016年，人民币汇率在稳定的前提下弹性加大，初步形成了"收盘汇率+一篮子货币汇率变化"的人民币兑美元汇率中间价形成机制，以市场供求为基础、参考一篮子货币进行调节的特征更加清晰。

从收盘汇率看，2016年以来受企业外币负债去杠杆以及海外兼并收购意愿不断升温等因素影响，我国外汇市场整体呈现供小于求的局面，人民币兑美元收盘汇率大多偏向较中间价贬值的方向。从参考一篮子货币汇率变化看，5月之前，在全球经济复苏乏力、国际金融市场波动加大的背景下，市场对美联储加息预期降温，美元指数下跌，相应的人民币兑美元汇率中间价较上日收盘汇率有所升值。5月以后，市场对美联储加息预期再次升温，英国"脱欧"又引发了国际金融市场的不确定性，美元指数由弱转强，人民币兑美元汇率中间价较前日收盘汇率的调升幅度也相应收窄。11月美国总统大选后，美元显著走强，人民币兑美元汇率贬值，但无论是与新兴市场经济体货币还是与发达经济体货币相比，人民币贬值幅度都相对较小，因此11月以来CFETS人民币汇率指数反而小幅走升。总的来看，"收盘汇率+一篮子货币汇率变化”的机制提高了人民币兑美元汇率中间价形成的规则性、透明度和市场化水平，在稳定市场预期方面发挥了积极作用。

随着市场对新机制的理解更为深入，市场预期趋于平稳。国内外汇贷款集中偿还压力明显减弱，境外机构则继续增持境内债券，总体来看，跨境资金流动中的积极变化也在不断显现。

数据来源：中国外汇交易中心。

图5-5 人民币兑美元中间价与前一天收盘价

（二）人民币汇率弹性增强

2016年，人民币兑美元汇率中间价形成机制更加市场化，市场交易价与中间价不断收敛，银行间外汇市场即期交易价相对中间价日间波幅日平均为0.07%，最大为0.58%，波幅均值较2015年下降0.7个百分点。

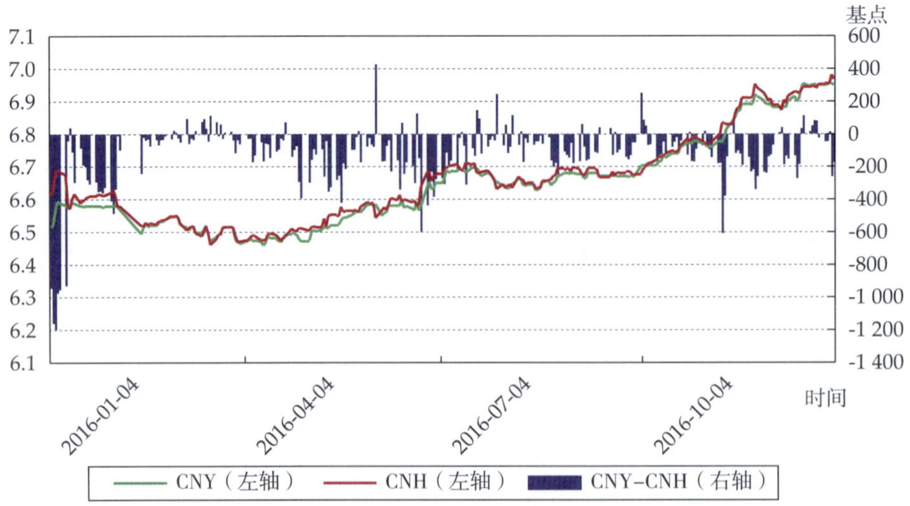

数据来源：中国外汇交易中心。

图5-6 境内外人民币兑美元汇率走势及价差

人民币汇率双向浮动弹性明显增强。2016年12月，1年期期权隐含波动率为5.045%，较年初上升0.355个百分点，较2015年8月汇改前上升2.23个百分点，显示人民币汇率弹性进一步增强。

“8·11汇改”以来，CNH表现出较CNY更大的贬值趋势，市场套利机制反向运作，人民币资金由离岸市场回流在岸市场。与此同时，境外投资者对持有人民币汇率信心减弱，部分人民币存款转回美元、港元资产。两者共同作用，香港人民币存款从高峰时期的10 035亿元跌至6 529亿元。受此影响，境外人民币流动性紧张，离岸人民币拆借利率上升，2016年部分交易日出现较为明显的境内外价差倒挂。

（三）外汇市场直接交易币种更加丰富

2016年，银行间外汇市场持续发展和扩大人民币外汇直接交易，扩大可交易货币供给，促进市场币种结构多元化。2016年6月推出人民币对南非兰特和韩国韩元直接交易，9月推出人民币对阿联酋迪拉姆、沙特里亚尔直接交易，11月发展人民币对加元直接交易，12月推出人民币对墨西哥比索、波兰兹罗提、丹麦克朗、匈牙利福林、土耳其里拉、挪威克朗、瑞典克朗直接交易。银行间外汇市场挂牌交易的货币对总数增至近30对，涵盖国际主要储备货币、新兴市场经济体货币以及“一带一路”沿线货币。大力发展直接交易，在促进中国与相关国家和地区的双多边贸易和投资、便利人民币和相关货币在贸易投资结算中的使用、满足经济主体降低汇兑成本需要的同时，也促进了市场币种结构的优化。

三、外汇市场的制度建设

（一）外汇市场参与主体进一步丰富

2016年，外汇市场进一步加大开放力度。2016年1月，银行间外汇市场向符合条件的人民币购售业务境外参加行开放。9月，银行间外币拆借市场也向境外机构开放。至此，银行间外汇市场的各个子市场、各类产品都已向境外机构开放。现已有59家境外主体成为银行间外汇市场会员，占会员总数的10%，既丰富了银行间外汇市场交易主体类型，也成为增进市场流动性和市场融合的重要力量。其中，境外央行类机构在银行间外汇市场的交易已不受交易额度、交易品种、交易方式、清算方式等限制。与此同时，外汇市场提供直连、代理等多种交易渠道供选择，参与者便利程度显著提高。

2016年9月，华为技术有限公司获国家外汇管理局备案同意进入银行间人民币外汇市场，成为继重庆力帆实业（集团）进出口有限公司后银行间外汇市场中的第二家非金融企业类型即期会员。

在基于实需的背景下，我国银行间外汇市场的会员以商业银行为主，非银行金融机构和非金融企业占比相对较小。这在一定程度上使得国内外汇交易的交易方向趋同，从而降低了外汇衍生品资产配置需求。随着境内银行间外汇市场对内对外开放步伐的加快，市场会员的种类和数量也在增加，目前已有少量券商、基金等非银行金融机构以及非金融企业成为银行间外汇市场会员，此外还有包括境外央行类机构、境外清算行和境外参加行在内的境外主体进入境内银行间外汇市场。外汇市场参与主体的进一步扩大将极大地丰富外汇市场的流动性来源，提高市场效率。

（二）银行间外汇市场交易时间延长

国际外汇市场是一个分散在全球的OTC市场，由于时差的存在，不同国家和地区的外汇市场交易时段首尾相连，形成了全天24小时连续交易的市场。以北京时间的一天为基准，每天4点新西兰的惠灵顿外汇市场开市，经过澳大利亚悉尼、日本东京、德国法兰克福、英国伦敦等几个市场的接力，最终美国纽约市场在北京时间次日的4：00闭市，连接成为24小时的全球外汇市场。

为便利境外机构交易，自2016年1月起，银行间外汇市场外汇交易时间延长至北京时间23：30，覆盖欧洲交易时段。在夜盘交易时段（16：30~23：30），人民币汇率中间价及浮动幅度、做市商报价等市场管理制度仍然适用，交易后处理及市场服务支持时间也相应延长。交易时间延长以来，做市商在夜盘交易时段持续提供买卖双边报价，市场流动性总体平稳，各交易品种在夜盘时段均有成交。

（三）外汇市场交易后业务发展迅速

2016年，银行间外汇市场交易确认的规模稳步增长，市场份额稳步提升。2016年2月，中国外汇交易中心开发的ISO 20022（金融服务：金融业通用报文方案）外汇交易确认和交易获取报文正式注册发布，这是国际标准组织（ISO）首次发布中国金融领域的相关报文，填补了ISO 20022标准在外汇交易后相关业务过程上的空白。2016年5月，外汇交易确认接口服务投入运营。目前，各接口使用机构的确认自动化程度均保持在90%以上，部分机构达到98%以上，实现了交易执行、交易确认和资金支付直通式处理，节省了大量的人力和时间资源，同时也在很大程度上降低了相关业务的操作风险。

该业务标准基于银行间市场业务数据交换协议（IMIX协议）开发，经过多轮ISO 20022专家评审和答辩，成为国际金融领域普遍适用的标准，这是中国银行间市场参与国际标准制定修订工作的一个重大突破，标志着我国银行间外汇市场建立起从交易执行、交易获取、交易确认到资金支付的直通式处理机制，实现了对金融交易生命周期的有效管理，也极大地提高了我国市场在全球治理中的制度性话语权。

（四）外汇市场基础设施不断完善

随着人民币汇率市场化改革、人民币国际化的推进，外汇市场的社会关注度和影响力不断提高，市场环境更加错综复杂。2016年，中国外汇交易中心积极配合监管部门，继续推进银行间外汇市场基础设施建设，包括完善人民币汇率形成机制，强化市场沟通，提高市场透明度；编制和发布人民币汇率指数，引导市场预期，更好地保持人民币对一篮子货币汇率基本稳定；配合人民币加入SDR货币篮子，银行间外汇市场计算和发布多币种、多时点参考汇率，并按照IMF“数据公布特殊标准”（SDDS）发布人民币汇率数据，为包括国际金融组织在内的各国投资者提供定价参考。

2016年6月，全国外汇市场自律机制成立，标志着我国外汇市场从他律为主向他律和自律并重的转变，有利于维护外汇市场正当竞争和健康有序运作。目前，共有14家中外资银行加入自律机制核心成员。随着汇率市场化改革的继续推进，市场将在汇率形成中发挥更加重要的作用，外汇市场自律机制将有助于以更低的社会成本、更有效的管理方式来维护市场秩序，避免监管套利。

（五）人民币纳入SDR货币篮子

2016年10月1日，人民币正式纳入特别提款权（SDR）货币篮子，SDR货币篮子相应扩大至美元、欧元、人民币、日元、英镑五种货币，人民币在SDR货币篮子中的权重为10.92%，美元、欧元、日元和英镑的权重分别为41.73%、30.93%、8.33%和8.09%。人民币纳入SDR货币篮子是中国经济融入全球金融体系的一个重要里程碑，是对中国当局过去多年来在改革其货币和金融体系方面取得成就的认可，中国在这一领域的持续推进和深化将推动建立一个更加充满活力的国际货币和金融体系，这又会支持中国和全球经济的发展和稳定。

总的来看，人民币加入SDR有助于增强SDR的代表性和吸引力，完善现行国际货币体系，对中国和世界是双赢的结果；有助于巩固人民币计价结算货币的地位，促进人民币在金融交易中的使用；有助于更多国家将人民币纳入外汇储备；有助于推动中国按照既定目标，进一步提高人民币资本项目可兑换程度；有助于中国加快推动金融改革和对外开放，加强金融宏观审慎管理制度建设，为促进全球经济增长、维护全球金融稳定、完善全球经济治理作出积极贡献。

四、外汇市场发展展望

（一）人民币汇率形成机制改革进一步推进，外汇市场加快完善

将继续按照主动性、可控性和渐进性原则，进一步完善人民币汇率市场化形成机制，加大市场决定汇率的力度，增强人民币汇率双向浮动弹性，保持人民币在合理、均衡水平上的基本稳定。未来，人民币汇率将继续按照以市场化供求为基础、参考一篮子货币进行调节的机制有序运行，并有条件继续在合理均衡水平上保持基本稳定。同时，我国外汇市场也将加快发展，坚持金融服务实体经济和支持供给侧结构性改革的原则，稳步拓宽人民币流出和回流渠道，推进人民币对其他货币直接交易市场发展，更好地为人民币的跨境使用和降低微观经济主体的汇兑成本提供服务。

（二）外汇市场对外开放加大，市场容量提升

中国境内银行间外汇市场发展至今，广度、深度和流动性等方面均有了显著提升。随着人民币正式加入SDR，境外投资者将有更多增持人民币资产的需求，会有更多境外机构进入银行间市场，外汇市场成员结构将得到进一步丰富，参与主体将进一步增加，市场交易量也将得到进一步提升。

（三）交易系统升级，市场效率提高

2017年中国外汇交易中心将全面升级现有交易系统CFETS FX2009，新的交易系统将具备更加全面的交易属性，无论是在交易分组设置、做市商与会员利益机制权衡还是授信额度管理方面均有大幅改进，将极大地便利交易员的操作，对提高整个市场效率起到积极的推动作用。此外，新平台综合考虑了国际市场现状，对部分功能进行了优化，对性能进行了提升，尽可能引导国内外汇市场的交易习惯向国际市场靠拢，从而为国内外汇市场未来发展和人民币国际化提供相应支持。

专题五 人民币加入SDR

2015年11月30日，国际货币基金组织（IMF）执董会决定将人民币纳入SDR货币篮子，并于2016年10月1日正式生效。人民币成功入篮是中国金融体制改革开放和SDR发展进程中的一个重要里程碑，对中国和世界都具有重要意义和深远影响。这是国际社会对中国综合国力和中国金融体系数十年来改革开放成就的认可，有利于促进中国在更深层次和更广领域参与全球经济、融入国际金融体系，推动人民币稳步走向国际化，也将进一步扩大SDR自身的影响力，完善现行国际货币体系。同时，人民币加入SDR也意味着人民币利率、汇率和资产更容易受到国际因素的影响，中国要承担更多的国际责任和义务，因此，中国需要不断推进金融体系改革开放。

一、人民币将获得更加广泛的国际使用

中国经过多年的改革开放，尤其是中国人民银行近年来在汇率形成机制、国债收益率、银行间债券市场和外汇市场对外开放以及提高数据报送标准等方面的一系列努力，人民币达到了IMF制定的“可自由使用”标准，成功加入SDR，这标志着人民币获得了世界性认可，国际地位空前提高。可以预见，人民币今后在世界范围内将逐步得到更加广泛的使用，这主要因为：一是人民币正式取得储备货币地位。人民币加入SDR前，已有不少国家和地区的中央银行或货币当局持有人民币资产，但是因未得到国际权威机构的承认，并非视为当然的外汇储备，人民币加入SDR后，各国和地区中央银行或货币当局持有的人民币资产将无可争议地被统一认定为外汇储备。同时，IMF也相应修改了外汇储备币种构成调查（COFER）的统计报表，将之前统计的七种货币增加至八种，人民币被纳入并按惯例单独列出。参与COFER的各国和地区都需要向IMF报送官方持有人民币资产的情况，IMF也会定期公布各国和地区将人民币作为外汇储备的汇总统计。这无疑将推动各国和地区央行或货币当局增持人民币资产，事实上，入篮后的几个月，央行类合格机构投资者开户进入银行间债券市场的数量确实在不断增加。二是人民币成为IMF官方交易货币。入篮后，人民币成为IMF认定的五种“可自由使用”货币之一，根据IMF的规定，今后各成员国向IMF缴纳份额、IMF向成员国提供贷款和成员国向IMF还款、IMF向成员国支付利息等，均可选择人民币进行。三是伴随着中国作为世界第一贸易大国、GDP排名第二的经济大国和人民币储备货币地位，人民币在国际经贸支付、计价、投融资以及外汇交易等方面也将得到日益广泛的使用。

2016年以来，人民币的国际使用一定程度上不升反降，这主要是受了美元加息、汇率波动、英国“脱欧”等国际不确定性因素增大等的影响，但这并不会改变人民币入篮后使用范围扩大的长期趋势。

二、推动中国金融体系进一步改革开放

地位越高，责任越大，人民币入篮后，国际社会对人民币和中国金融体系的要求和标准也更高了，而且进入SDR货币

篮子也并非一劳永逸，因此人民币加入SDR既是压力也是动力，中国金融体系还需进一步改革开放。一是货币政策制定要求更高。人民币成为国际储备货币后，中国的货币政策、人民币的汇率和利率形成机制及其变化等不仅仅影响国内，还会影响其他国家及使用人民币的企业和个人，产生“外溢效应”。同时也需要有透明的、可预期的、市场化的人民币汇率和利率指标，便于国外政府和居民对人民币资产进行投资交易。二是资本项目和资本市场对外开放。人民币尽管已经加入SDR，但在IMF统计认定的“可自由使用”标准中，人民币在国际银行业负债币种构成、国际债务证券计价货币、货币的全球外汇交易量等指标上仍然较低，中国在跨境交易便利程度、金融市场开放等方面与美国、英国等其他储备货币发行国仍有不小差距。因此，中国将来还要继续有序推进资本市场双向开放，拓展人民币资产市场的广度和深度。三是提升金融监管能力。像中国经济融入全球一样，人民币入篮后中国金融体系也将融入全球，资金跨境流动频繁、境外人民币规模日益扩大、主要国家金融政策相互影响加剧、经济金融环境不确定性加大，必然对金融监管能力提出更高要求，中国金融监管要适应开放新形势，进一步提高监管标准、完善宏观审慎框架下的外债和跨境资本流动管理体系、提升与国际市场的政策沟通和预期引导能力，为人民币发挥储备货币功能提供信心支撑。

三、加快人民币国际化进程

推动人民币国际化进程的举措是多方面的，包括资本市场对外开放、汇率和利率走向市场化、贸易投资便利化以及人民币跨境清算等基础设施，人民币加入SDR提高了人民币的国际声誉，奠定了人民币的国际地位，当然也是人民币国际化的重要组成部分并与上述方面相互作用，共同推动人民币国际化进程。正如中国人民银行行长周小川所说，加入SDR使中国可以成为很多国际商品定价国，中国可以在国际资本市场以更低的成本借贷，人民币可以被更多的国家需求等。具体表现在：一是人民币资产自动配置需求会增加。国际货币基金组织、国际清算银行和世界银行等国际组织管理着以SDR计价的资产，人民币加入SDR后，SDR篮子的币种和权重进行了相应调整，这些机构需要根据SDR篮子货币权重进行资产配置，从而增加人民币资产需求。二是外国政府增持人民币官方储备。人民币加入SDR之前已有不少国家将人民币纳入储备，人民币正式获得国际储备货币地位后，各国将人民币纳入外汇储备的意愿将会进一步增强。三是各国企业和个人将更加广泛地使用人民币。首先是中国企业和个人会在国际交易中使用人民币进行支付结算，随着人民币的国际认知度逐步提高，市场对人民币信心日益增强，人民币将越来越广泛地出现在跨境贸易、投融资、旅游和留学等交易中，也会有越来越多的国家和地区可以运用人民币进行投资和支付，二者相辅相成，促进人民币国际使用范围和规模不断扩大。四是有助于推动人民币成为国际大宗商品定价结算货币。这是一国货币成长为国际货币的重要途径之一，20世纪70年代产生的“石油美元”就是美元国际地位的重要支撑点，所以人民币国际化之路应该充分借鉴这条经验。同时，上述几个方面都可能会产生人民币计价的债务，为对冲利率和汇率风险，境内外企业和个人也要在人民币在岸市场和离岸市场管理资产负债头寸，从而也会产生大量人民币交易需求。

货币国际化有一个比较长期的演进过程，不能“揠苗助长”。在中国国内经济转型尚未完全成功、有效供给不充分、金融体系不健全、利率汇率市场化机制尚在建设之中、资本市场不成熟、国际市场化不确定性增加等环境下，人民币国际化也不可操之过急，中间还会出现波折，练好内功，巧借入篮之力，自然会水到渠成。

四、促进国际货币体系更加完善

人民币是SDR自1969年首次发行以来第一个被纳入篮子的货币，也是SDR篮子货币中的第一个新兴市场经济体货币，这对于推动几十年来改革进程缓慢的国际货币体系加大改革力度，走向更加合理、均衡和公平意义重大。一是人民币入篮为加快国际货币体系改革开了个好头。数十年来，国际金融治理结构不尽合理，对发展中经济体和新兴市场经济体利益诉求反映不够，改革行动迟缓，此次人民币加入SDR一方面是中国经济实力和国际地位提升的结果，另一方面也是IMF积极努力的结果，可以说拉开了国际货币体系改革完善的序幕，可以预期，今后的国际货币体系将会逐步与各类经济体经济地位相适应。二是显著提升SDR的国际影响力。目前SDR使用范围小，仅能用于IMF与成员国之间的官方结算；规模也小，SDR在全球储备中所占份额不足4%；分配也不尽合理，严重阻碍了SDR的发展。人民币加入SDR，有助于重新吸引国际社会对SDR的关注，进而扩大SDR规模，拓宽SDR 在国际贸易、国际借贷、证券发行和资产计价等中的使用；也使得SDR 的代表性显著增强，人民币入篮后，SDR篮子货币发行国的GDP超过了全球的60%，出口量占世界的比重接近90%，从而助力SDR的发展。三是人民币加入SDR将使得国际货币体系更加稳定。SDR中的主要权重是美元，美元的波动对其影响较大，人民币加入且占权重约一成，将显著增强SDR价值和价格的稳定性。目前，全球主要的国际储备货币是美元，其货币政策的局限性和汇率大幅波动将显著影响各国汇率、国际资金流动和国际储备的稳定性，尤其是在爆发2008年全球金融危机和欧债危机后，反映得更加明显，这是一个主权货币作为国际储备货币的机制缺陷。SDR具备超主权储备的特征与潜力，应该进一步扩大SDR的发行，有助于解决一些国家外汇储备不足的问题，缓解所谓的“特里芬难题”。

专题六 外汇市场自律机制

近年来，随着外汇市场发展，各主要成熟外汇市场相继建立外汇市场委员会，在加强外汇市场沟通、推广外汇市场准则等方面发挥了重要作用。其中美国、英国、欧洲、日本、新加坡、中国香港、澳大利亚和加拿大等地的八家委员会在国际上影响力较大。为维护市场正当竞争秩序，促进外汇市场有序运作和健康发展，2016年6月我国外汇市场由银行间外汇市场成员在上海成立了全国外汇市场自律机制，在符合国家有关汇率政策和外汇管理规定的前提下，对人民币汇率中间价报价行为，以及银行间外汇市场交易和银行柜台结售汇与跨境人民币业务进行自律管理。

一、各外汇委员会主要职能

（一）组织讨论并提出建议

上述八家委员会均定期组织召开会议，组织成员就外汇市场重要问题展开讨论并提出建议。各委员会每年开会3~6次。以伦敦外汇联合常务委员会为例，其在2015年共召开5次会议，分别涉及英国大选对外汇市场的影响、英镑及其他货币汇率波动、新兴市场经济体外汇市场情况、中国“8·11汇改”及其影响、全球外汇市场准则推进情况等议题。2016年以来，该委员会已召开5次会议，其中2月、3月和4月的会议主要讨论BIS计划于当年5月公布的《全球外汇市场准则》并形成反馈意见。

（二）定期开展市场调研

除欧央行外汇联系小组[①]外，其余七家委员会均于每年4月和10月开展半年度外汇市场交易量调查，各委员会也会根据市场情况不时开展各类调研。如2009年，伦敦外汇联合常务委员会就金融危机期间英国外汇市场及其操作情况展开调查，并形成报告。香港财资市场公会于2015年对美元/港元和美元/人民币的即期汇率基准进行调研，并据此修订了市场交易情况在定价框架中的权重。

（三）开展研究并发表成果

各委员会一般就市场重点问题撰写工作论文或编辑出版刊物。如2009年，伦敦外汇联合常务委员会就金融危机期间英国外汇市场及其操作情况展开调查，调查结果形成单独报告[②]在英国央行网站公布。香港财资市场公会每年也发布多次时事通讯，介绍委员会举办的论坛和研讨会等情况。

（四）制定并推广市场规范性文件

各委员会的主要职责之一是制定市场行为准则和市场最佳实践等规范性文件并向市场进行推广。目前，八家委员会中，中国香港、英国、美国、新加坡和日本已经建立了自己的市场准则和规范[③]，澳大利亚和欧洲使用了金融市场协会（ACI）市场准则[④]。

---

① 欧元区各国的半年度外汇市场交易量调查由各国相关机构单独开展。

② http://www.bankofengland.co.uk/markets/Documents/forex/fxjsc/fxpaper090923.pdf。

③ 香港财资市场公会，*Code of Conduct and Practice*；伦敦外汇联合常务委员会，*The Non-Investment Products Code*；纽约外汇市场委员会，*Guidelines for Foreign Exchange Trading Activities*, *Management of Operational Risk in Foreign Exchange*；新加坡外汇市场协会，*The Singapore Guide to Conduct and Market Practices for Treasury Activities*；东京外汇市场委员会，*Tokyo Code of Conduct*。

④ The Financial Markets Association ，*ACI Model Code*。

（五）沟通市场成员与金融监管机构

八家委员会都与金融监管机构保持着密切联系。首先，八家委员会成员中均有来自金融监管机构的代表。其中，美国、英国、欧洲、中国香港、澳大利亚、加拿大等六家委员会的主席均由金融监管机构官员担任，东京外汇市场委员会的秘书由央行人员担任。其次，上述委员会多由央行主管或定期向央行报告工作。例如英国、欧洲、澳大利亚等委员会由央行直接设立或主管，澳大利亚央行对其外汇市场委员会的成员有提名和决定权。香港财资市场公会也定期就市场基准等业务向金管局提交报告。

（六）开展国际交流与合作

各委员会的重要工作之一是推广全球统一的外汇市场准则。2013年5月，八家委员会联合起草发布了《最佳市场实践准则和共享的全球性原则》，表示八家委员会将共同合作，加强沟通与协调，就全球外汇市场发展交流意见，并提出一些可共享的高标准原则，使各国自身的外汇市场准则更为稳健。从2014年起，八家委员会每年召开一次会议，截至2016年末已召开三次会议，会议议题围绕外汇市场发展变化、行为准则与最佳市场实践等。2015年的会议审议通过并联合发布了新的声明《全球序言：最佳市场实践准则和共享的全球性原则①》。

（七）其他职能

除上述几点外，部分委员会还承担其他职能。例如伦敦外汇联合常务委员会的职能包括制订外汇市场应急方案，在市场紊乱时发挥协调作用等；新加坡外汇市场协会承担调解市场参与者之间纠纷的职能等；香港财资市场公会的职能包括组织会员专业培训以提升市场从业人员的专业水平、发布基准定价和参考报价等。

二、各国外汇市场委员会发挥的作用

一是建立全球统一的市场规范体系。八家委员会参照或直接采用ACI市场准则，在各成熟外汇市场上建立了统一的市场规范体系；八家委员会于2015年通过并发布的《全球序言：最佳市场实践准则和共享的全球性原则》，为推广全球统一的外汇市场准则做好了准备。

二是向央行等监管机构提供市场情况和建议。半年一度的调查报告为央行等监管机构提供了市场情况，便于其制定和执行宏观经济政策，委员会组织的调研和会议为监管机构提供了市场人士建议。

三是帮助成员解读最新监管政策和动向。如伦敦外汇联合常务委员会每次会议上，都有来自监管部门的官员介绍涉及外汇市场的最新监管进展。2016年5月的会议上，金融市场行为监管局（FCA）的官员介绍了以下情况：其一是欧洲监管当局（ESA）对保证金规则监管技术标准的更新情况，其二是欧盟基准指标监管规则总体情况，其三是市场滥用行为监管规则（MAR）的更新情况。

四是在2008年全球金融危机后，各委员会组织成员开展调研和讨论。如东京外汇市场委员会于2008年10月与日本央行共

① Global Preamble: Codes of Best Market Practice and Shared Global Principles。

同举办“全球运营经理大会[①]”，讨论金融危机中外汇等市场面临的挑战；伦敦外汇联合常务委员会在2009年上半年成立专门工作小组开展了一项调查，检视金融危机期间英国外汇市场及其操作情况并形成报告；加拿大外汇委员会也于2009年组织成员进行讨论，提出针对金融危机的监管措施需考虑外汇市场的特殊性。

五是对国际热点问题予以快速反应。各委员会均针对国际热点问题组织热点讨论并提出观点。如欧央行外汇联系小组在2010年3月的会议上讨论央行退出超宽松货币政策的策略对外汇市场的影响；在2011年2月和2012年9月的会议上，成员分别讨论了美国多德—弗兰克法案和沃克尔规则出台后对外汇市场的影响；在2016年6月的会议上，成员讨论了英国“脱欧”公投后外汇市场和全球经济的前景等。

三、我国外汇市场自律机制

在借鉴国际经验的基础上，结合我国外汇市场特点，2016年6月由银行间外汇市场成员在上海成立了全国外汇市场自律机制。

全国外汇市场自律机制（以下简称自律机制）是由银行间外汇市场会员组成的市场自律和协调机制。自律机制在符合国家有关汇率政策和外汇管理规定的前提下，对人民币汇率中间价报价行为，以及银行间市场和银行柜台市场交易行为进行自律管理，维护市场正当竞争秩序，促进外汇市场有序运作和健康发展。

自律机制接受中国人民银行和国家外汇管理局的指导和监督管理，履行以下主要职责：制定工作指引；规范人民币汇率中间价报价行为；制定银行间市场交易行为及银行柜台市场交易准则和业务规范，并负责督促落实；处理市场成员之间的交易纠纷；开展国际合作；中国人民银行和国家外汇管理局赋予的其他职责。

目前，我国外汇市场建立的相关自律机制包括：建立了工作简报等信息沟通渠道，并设立了专门网页披露信息；逐步搭建覆盖外汇和跨境人民币、批发和零售市场业务人员的培训体系。同时，将在各主要外汇市场委员会涉足不多的领域进行积极探索，一是逐步建立监测体系，跟踪市场变动；二是探索建立自律行为评估体系，定期评估成员自律规范遵守情况，并将部分结果纳入宏观审慎评估（MPA）体系，增强约束力。

自律机制分为核心成员、基础成员和观察成员三层，不同的成员享有不同的权利和义务。其中，核心成员共14家，是指在外汇方面系统重要性程度高、市场影响力大、业务流程规范、内控机制完善、综合实力比较显著的金融机构。核心成员享有自律规则制定权，优先获取外汇市场新产品、新交易方式等市场创新先行先试的权利以及更大的跨境融资空间；同时，履行核心成员的义务，积极参与外汇自律机制的建设，协助推动外汇市场的发展、包括产品创新、手段丰富等。

① Global Operations Managers’ Conference。

自律机制成立初期，下设三个工作小组，分别为汇率工作小组、银行间市场交易规范工作小组、外汇和跨境人民币展业工作小组。未来根据履职需要，可增设其他专门工作小组。下一步，自律机制将在业务指导司局领导下，组织自律机制成员行努力推进外汇自律管理各项工作，提高我国外汇市场自律管理水平，为我国外汇市场的健康有序发展打下坚实基础。

自律机制的成立标志着中国外汇市场正在由过去的以他律为主转向他律和自律并重，对中国外汇市场改革和发展具有重大意义。一是适应外汇市场发展的必然要求。2015年以来中国人民银行进一步完善了人民币汇率形成机制，更加具有规则性、透明性和市场化的人民币兑美元汇率中间价形成机制在稳定市场预期方面发挥了积极作用。随着汇率市场化改革的继续推进，市场将在汇率形成中发挥更加重要的作用，建立外汇自律机制有助于以更低的社会成本、更有效的管理方式来维护市场秩序。二是自律机制是在国内外成熟经验基础上发展和完善的。一方面，目前全球主要八大交易市场（英国、美国、新加坡、中国香港、日本等）均成立外汇自律组织，隶属于全球外汇市场委员会，该委员会正在考虑进一步扩充成员。建立自律机制是与国际接轨、适应国际形势和国际潮流的需要，有助于更好地参与相关国际规范的制定，使我们在国际外汇市场上有更多的话语权。另一方面，国内利率定价自律机制的运行发展也提供了良好的经验借鉴。利率定价自律机制于2013年成立，从过去三年的运营情况来看，该机制在进一步推动利率市场化、激励和约束成员行为、规范同业业务、维护公平有序的市场秩序等方面发挥了重要作用，为外汇自律机制的建立提供了良好的经验借鉴。三是自律机制是对现有政策资源的整合和全覆盖。成立自律机制，对批发和零售外汇市场、本币和外币进行全覆盖，可避免自律重叠和空白，避免监管套利。

第六章　黄金市场

2016年国际金价呈先扬后抑的“倒V”形走势，全年上涨9.13%。全球黄金市场交易规模普遍增长，黄金投资基金持仓量有所回升，新兴市场国家增持黄金的步伐继续加快。中国黄金市场保持活跃，场内、场外交易量均维持高速增长态势。随着中国黄金市场创新和对外开放进程加快，“上海金”人民币黄金定价机制启动，银行间黄金市场做市商制度推出，黄金市场交易机制不断完善，黄金市场服务功能日益加强，中国黄金市场金融化、国际化程度持续提升。

一、黄金市场的运行情况

（一）黄金现货市场

1. 交易规模大幅增长，现货金价先涨后跌

2016年，上海黄金交易所交易规模持续快速增长，黄金累计成交4.87万吨，成交金额13.02万亿元，同比分别增长42.88%和62.63%。国内现货黄金价格跟随国际金价先涨后跌，呈现“倒V”形走势，黄金现货主力合约Au99.99年初开盘价222.86元/克，最高价300元/克，最低价181.2元/克，年末收盘价263.9元/克，较上年末收盘价上涨18.42%。

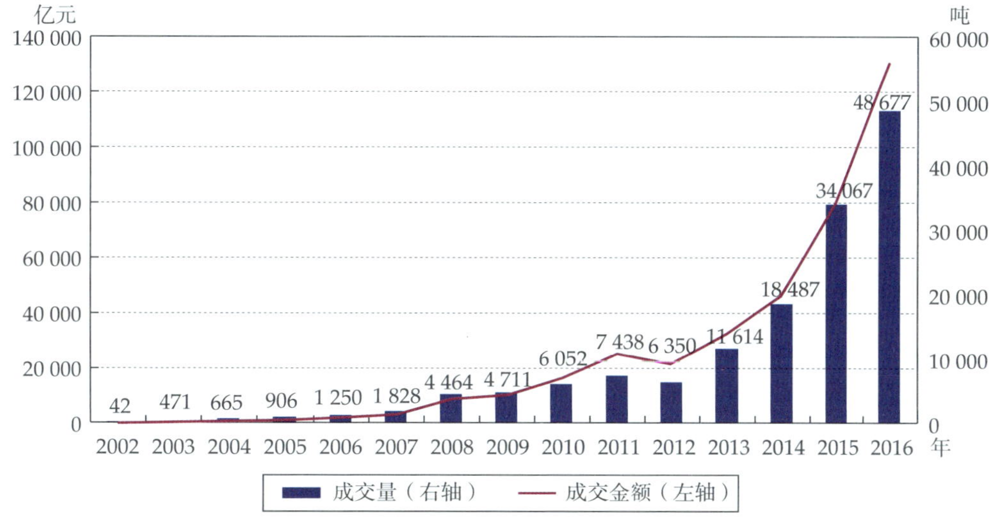

数据来源：上海黄金交易所。

图6-1　2002—2016年上海黄金交易所黄金成交量和成交金额

2. 竞价、询价、定价三大市场初步形成，市场结构趋于均衡

“上海金”人民币集中定价业务的推出，进一步补充完善了产品体系，在交易方式上形成了竞价方式、定价方式、询价方式三大市场架构，各市场业务互为补充协调发展，增强了上海黄金交易所市场服务功能。2016年，以竞价方式、询价方式、定价方式的成交量分别为3.04万吨、1.769万吨和0.0569万吨，竞价方式成交量占据了62.48%的市场份额，为主要成交方式，但询价方式成交量同比增速最快。

表6-1 2016年上海黄金交易所黄金竞价、询价和定价三种方式成交情况

	成交量（吨）	同比增长（%）	成交量占比（%）	成交金额（万亿元）	同比增长（%）
竞价	30 415	27.63	62.48	8.15	45.56
其中：现货	6 829	-26.21	14.03	1.81	-17.48
延期	23 586	61.81	48.45	6.34	86.01
询价	17 692	72.83	36.35	4.72	95.83
上海金（定价）	569	—	1.16	0.16	—
总计	48 677	42.88	100.00	13.02	62.63

数据来源：上海黄金交易所。

3. 清算、交割安全顺畅，主板黄金出入库规模有所下降

交易规模的大幅增长带动资金清算量进一步增长，2016年资金清算额达到35 072亿元，同比增长28.35%。受实物需求减少影响，实物出入库量有明显下降。主板黄金出库量1 970.37吨，同比下降23.68%；入库量2 060.16吨，同比下降22.72%。国际板黄金出库量27.85吨，同比增长91.41%；入库量126.75吨，同比增长308.21%。

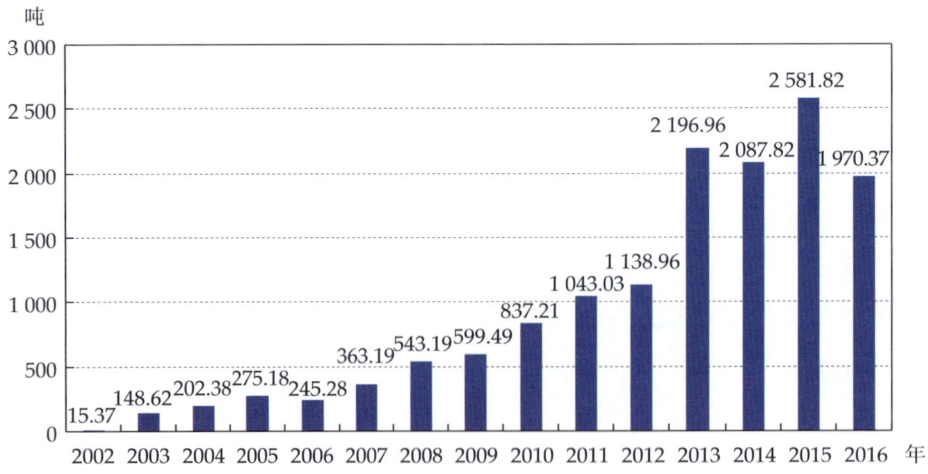

数据来源：上海黄金交易所。

图6-2 2002—2016年上海黄金交易所主板黄金出库量

4. 机构仍是市场交易主体，个人业务快速增长

2016年，机构黄金交易量3.98万吨，同比增长31.65%，占比81.71%，市场份额下降近7个百分点。机构交易规模在竞价市场和询价市场均保持平稳快速增长，占黄金业务的主体地位，但市场份额略有下降。个人交易表现更趋活跃，黄金交易量累计8 903.33吨，同比增长130.88%，占总交易量的18.29%，同比提高近7个百分点。

（二）黄金期货市场

1. 市场交易规模稳步扩大

按单边统计，2016年上海期货交易所黄金期货累计成交3 475.95万手（合34 759.5吨），同比增长37.30%；累计成交金额9.34万亿元，同比增长55.92%，占上海期货交易所所有品种总成交金额的10.99%。黄金期货连续交易持续活跃，月均成交量165.96万手，占同期黄金期货成交量的57.29%。

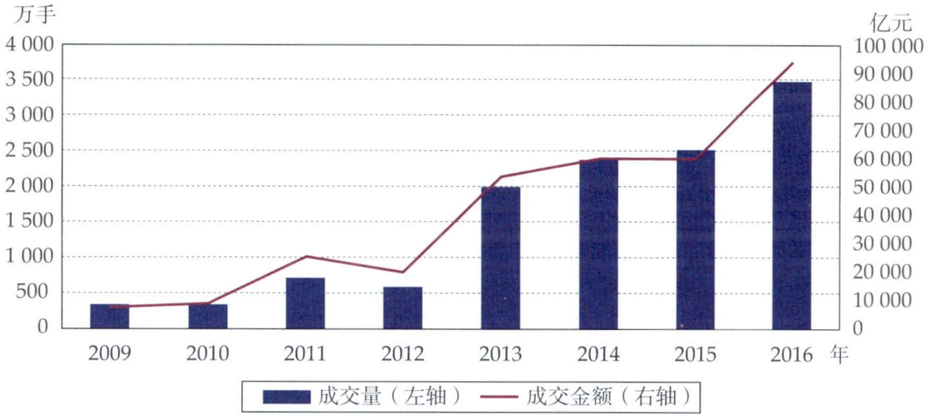

数据来源：中国期货业协会。

图 6-3 2009—2016年黄金期货成交量与成交金额

2. 市场持仓量持续增长

2016年，上海期货交易所黄金期货平均月末持仓量16.71万手（合167吨），同比增长47.11%。连续交易时段成交量持续增大，黄金期货价格连续性得到提高，投资者持仓规模持续提升。

3. 期现价差和内外盘价差较上年有所缩小

国内、国际黄金期货市场价差以及国内黄金期货、现货市场之间黄金价差较往年有所缩小。一方面，国内外黄金期货市场价差显著下降。上海期货交易所黄金期货与纽约COMEX黄金期货的平均价差从上年同期的5.18元/克降至2.70元/克，降幅为47.88%。另一方面，国内黄金市场的期现价差有所缩小。上海期货交易所黄金期货与上海黄金交易所Au（T+D）的平均价差由上年同期的2.22元/克降至1.70元/克，降幅为23.42%。

4. 商业银行黄金期货业务参与度提升

截至2016年末，有17家商业银行成为上海期货交易所会员，累计开展黄金期货自营交易1 327.11吨，同比增长34.47%，占上海期货交易所黄金期货交易总量的1.91%。

（三）商业银行黄金业务

1. 场内黄金现货业务快速增长

2016年，商业银行在上海黄金交易所的自营和代理黄金交易总量达37 576.17吨，成交10.05万亿元，增幅分别达到48.53%和69.04%，交易占比由上年的74.26%增至77.2%。自营黄金成交量25 966吨，同比增长42.53%，占交易所黄金交易规模的53.34%。代理机构和个人累计交易黄金11 610.17吨，同比增长63.98%。其中，代理机构交易黄金2 745.53吨，同比下降15.45%；代理个人交易黄金8 864.64吨，同比增长131.28%。

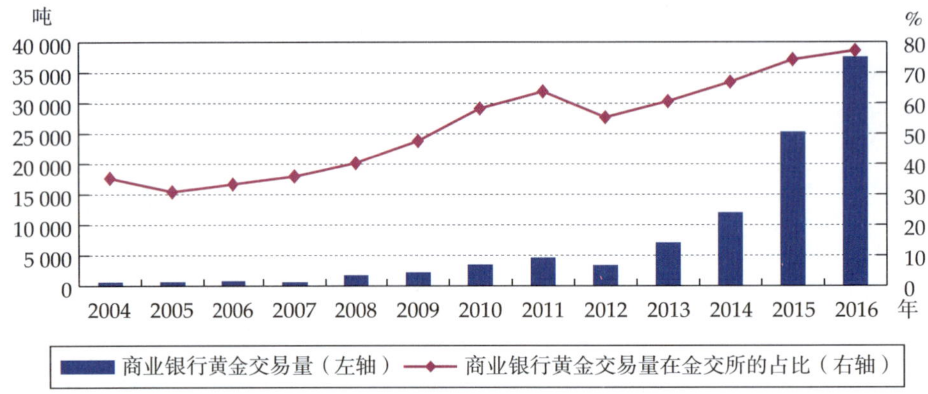

数据来源：中国黄金市场监测分析系统数据库。

图6–4 商业银行在金交所的黄金交易总量和占比情况

2. 境内自有黄金业务总体保持增长

2016年，商业银行在境内开展的各项场外黄金业务累计成交7 655.13吨，同比增长15.34%，其中账户金业务、黄金租借业务增长较快，实物金销售、场外黄金衍生品交易有所回落。

（1）实物黄金销售量有所下降。

2016年，商业银行累计销售实物黄金377.32吨，同比减少10.03%，销售金额1 070.0亿元，同比增加5.83%。其中，自营品牌金销售113.51吨，同比增长3%，代理品牌金销售23.08吨，同比下降9.33%；黄金积存（定投）销售240.71吨，同比下降15.17%。实物黄金销售量总体保持稳定。

（2）账户金交易量显著增长。

2016年，商业银行账户金累计交易2 102.61吨，交易金额5 638.18亿元，同比分别增长71.34%和95.57% 。其中，美元账户金和人民币账户金分别交易213.07吨和1 889.54吨，同比分别增长81.54%和70.26%。账户金交易需求有所提升。

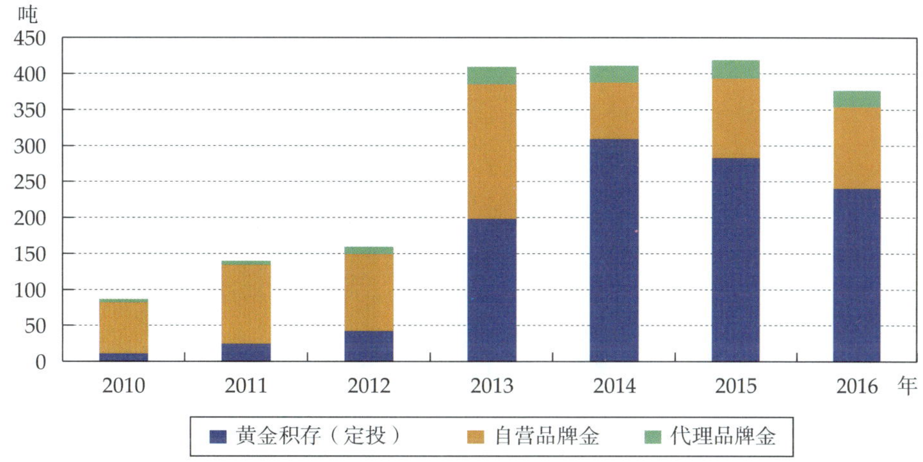

数据来源：中国黄金市场监测分析系统数据库。

图6-5　2010—2016年商业银行实物黄金销售量

数据来源：中国黄金市场监测分析系统数据库。

图6-6　2010—2016年商业银行账户金成交量

（3）黄金租借业务保持增长。

2016年，商业银行累计租出黄金3 070.38吨，同比增长26.15%，名义成交金额8 175.36亿元，同比增长42.1%。其中，商业银行对客黄金租赁1 827.78吨，较上年增长15.35%；同业之间累计拆出黄金1 242.59吨，同比增长46.32%。黄金租借业务增幅收窄，市场融资需求逐步满足。

（4）黄金质押业务同比降低。

2016年，商业银行累计接收质押黄金3.42吨，发放黄金质押贷款6.00亿元，同比分别减少87.55%和48.89%。

（5）黄金理财业务销售量略有回升。

2016年，商业银行出售各类挂钩黄金的理财产品名义本金额达5 849.27亿元，同比增加5.07%；到期赎回5 136.64亿元，同比减少17.75%。

（6）境内场外黄金衍生品交易同比下降。

2016年，境内场外黄金衍生品业务累计

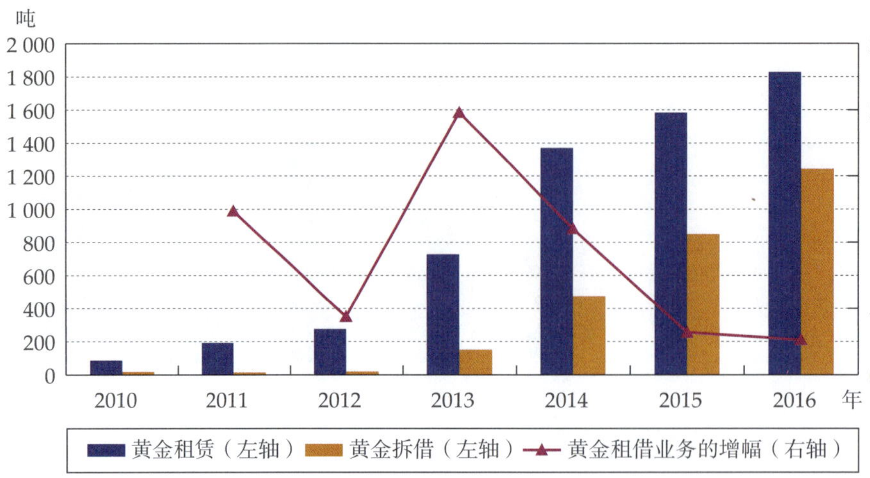

数据来源：中国黄金市场监测分析系统数据库。

图6-7　2010—2016年黄金租赁、黄金拆借业务量及增长情况

交易1 834.39吨，同比下降17.25%。其中，黄金远期成交1 222.07吨，同比减少17.92%；黄金掉期成交596.52吨，同比减少17.01%；黄金期权成交15.79吨，同比增加70.70%。从分币种的黄金衍生品交易情况看，以人民币报价的黄金衍生品累计成交831.35吨，同比下降20.67%；以美元报价的黄金衍生品累计成交1 003.04吨，同比减少14.19%。

3. 境外黄金交易以衍生品业务为主

2016年，商业银行各类境外黄金交易累计成交15 800.46吨，成交金额6 339.4亿美元，同比分别增长13.23%和22.33%。其中，境外黄金掉期累计成交10 423.76吨，同比增长24.35%；境外黄金远期成交1 563.8吨，同比减少20.25%；境外黄金期货成交148.13吨，同比增长8.43%；境外黄金期权成交2.07吨，同比增长4.18%；境外黄金即期成交3 662.71吨，同比增长5.49%。从交易结构看，黄金远期和黄金掉期分别占商业银行境外交易黄金衍生品的9.9%和65.97%。境外黄金即期的交易占比为23.18%，与上年同期基本持平，衍生品业务占比超过七成。

二、黄金市场运行的主要特点

（一）中国黄金市场增速领先，国内外现货价差有所扩大

2016年上海黄金交易所黄金产品、上海期货交易所黄金期货交易量同比分别增长42.88%和37.30%。同期，美国黄金期货交易量增长37.65%，伦敦黄金市场清算量增长11.27%，国内黄金市场增速领先国际主要黄金市场。

2016年国内外市场价差出现较大波动，全年国内较国际现货金价平均高1.46元/克，同比增长89.61%。前10个月国内外价差相对平稳，11~12月价差幅度迅速扩大，国内较国际现货金价价差一度高达8元/克左右，年末价差回落至5元/克左右。其影响因素主要有：一是临近年末传统用金高峰期，黄金供给增加有限的情况下市场存在价差扩大的预期。二是市场价格结构性波动导致价差进一步扩大。第四季度以来金价大跌导致境外价格相较境内价格下探幅度更大，促使价差进一步扩大。三是国内黄金市场深度和承接力度有

所增强，黄金主力品种日交易量均较前几年大幅增长，商业银行在日内的进口抛盘对价差收缩的作用并不显著。四是人民币兑美元汇率走低，一定程度上促进了境内外黄金价差的扩大。

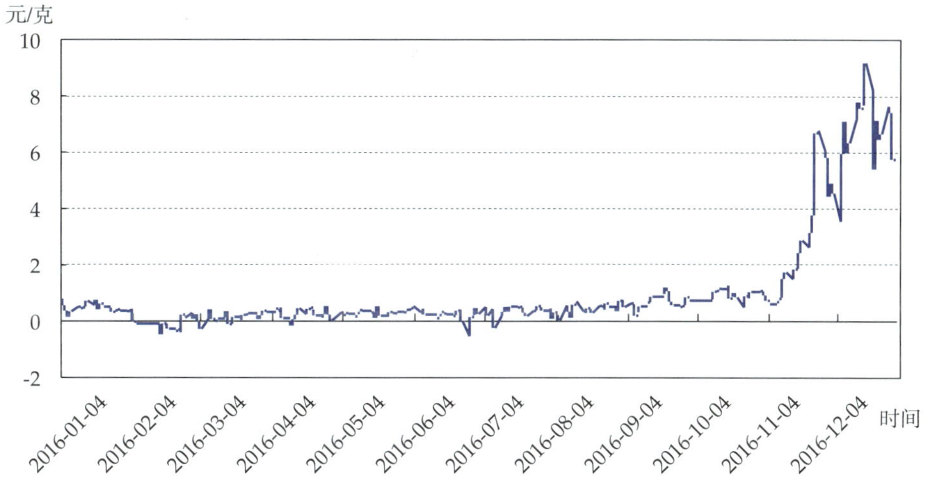

数据来源：上海黄金交易所、路透数据库。

图6-8　2016年国内外黄金现货价差波动情况

（二）市场产品结构日趋均衡，延期与询价交易大增

2016年，上海黄金交易所黄金延期产品、黄金现货实盘产品和黄金询价产品三分市场，互为补充，市场产品结构不断优化。受黄金市场价格波动较大的影响，市场交易性需求上升，黄金延期交易产品交易量大涨。黄金投资性需求不断提升，询价交易发展较快。2016年，上海黄金交易所黄金现货实盘产品累计成交6 828.84吨，较上年下降26.21%，占黄金成交总量的14.03%，交易占比较上年大幅减少13.13个百分点。各类黄金延期产品累计成交23 586.32吨，同比增长61.81%，交易占比为48.46%，较上年增加5.67个百分点。询价交易累计成交17 692.17吨，交易占比提升至36.35%，其中询价Au9999合约成交14 159.32吨，较上年增长100.33%。

（三）商业银行引领场内黄金市场，自营、代理业务全面增长

商业银行在上海黄金交易所各类黄金业务交易量占比近八成，仍是场内黄金交易主力军。2016年，商业银行在上海黄金交易所的自营和代理黄金交易量和交易额同比分别增长48.53%和69.04%。商业银行在上海黄金交易所的黄金交易占比达77.2%。商业银行自营黄金成交量同比增长42.53%，占交易所黄金交易规模的53.34%。代理机构和个人在上海黄金交易所黄金交易同比增长63.98%。2016年，商业银行总体自营交易规模增速较快，从细分业务看，询价交易量1.56万吨，同比增长79.39%；竞价成交量0.98万吨，同比增长3.10%。在目前黄金市场日趋多元化的竞争格局下，商业银行询价业务发展速度快于竞价业务。

三、黄金市场的制度与基础设施建设

（一）规范市场交易行为，加强风险防控管理

2016年5月，中国人民银行发布《关于规范银行业金融机构账户黄金业务有关事项的通知》（银办发〔2016〕94号），明确了银行业金融机构开办账户黄金业务应具备的条件，以及业务备案管理、定期报告制度。同时，要求银行开办账户黄金业务不得开展杠杆交易，并建立账户黄金实物备付制度，加强投资者准入管理，进一步规范了金融机构黄金业务行为，防范黄金市场交易风险。

（二）推进市场机制建设，助力黄金市场深化发展

一是建立“上海金”人民币基准价定价机制。上海黄金交易所于2016年4月19日推出“上海金”人民币基准价定价机制，为全球黄金市场提供公允、可交易、可信赖的人民币黄金基准价格，丰富了以黄金为标的的风险管理工具和创新工具，对人民币黄金市场的价格形成机制与加快中国黄金市场国际化进程起到推动作用。同步推出挂钩“上海金”基准价的系列衍生产品，推动“上海金”在人民币黄金场外衍生品市场发挥基准作用。

二是建立银行间黄金询价市场做市商制度。2016年1月，上海黄金交易所会同中国外汇交易中心启动银行间黄金询价市场做市商制度，由10家正式做市商和6家尝试做市商承担在市场连续提供买卖双边价格的做市业务。做市商制度提高了银行间黄金询价交易流动性，提升了机构投资者询价交易效率，促进价格发现机制，黄金市场交易模式更加丰富。12月，上海黄金交易所正式发布人民币黄金远期价格曲线。

（三）加强基础设施建设，提升市场服务功能

一是上海黄金交易所加快推进新一代技术系统自主开发建设进程。成功上线“上海金”集中定价系统、数据服务平台、易金通APP等自主开发重点项目，完善风险监控系统，加强网络安全运维，确保市场平稳运行。

二是上海黄金交易所首款移动互联网产品“易金通”上线。“易金通”是上海黄金交易所发挥移动互联网技术优势，结合市场需求、联合各会员单位共同推出的黄金市场“互联网+”产品。“易金通”完成了黄金交易从桌面向手机的迁移，为投资者通过手机等多种终端参与交易提供便利，有利于打造惠及群众的“百姓金”平台，更好地推动黄金投资实现便利普惠。

三是国际板正式上线债券充抵保证金业务。国际会员可利用其托管在中央国债登记结算有限责任公司等境内指定债券托管机构的合格债券作为信用担保，用于开展上海黄金交易所延期类保证金产品的交易，从而减少国际会员人民币资金的实际占用成本，国内债券市场和黄金市场的跨市场合作进一步深化了市场服务功能。

四、黄金市场对外开放情况

（一）国际板业务发展不断深化

2016年，国际板黄金成交量3 991.84吨，成交金额10 870.72亿元。截至2016年12月底，上海黄金交易所国际会员共67家，较

成立之初新增了27家，国际会员代理的国际客户数达67家。黄金实物库存充抵保证金和债券充抵保证金业务的陆续推出，使得国际投资者可以以黄金实物或债券充抵交易保证金，参与国际板交易，有效扩大了国际会员资金来源；同时在会员管理、资金清算、实物交割、风险管理和技术系统等多个方面进行了一系列创新与突破，进一步便利了境外投资者交易，提高了市场运行效率。国际板业务整体发展良好，人民币计价黄金的投资意愿不断增强，黄金市场对外开放程度进一步提升。

（二）对外跨市场合作进一步扩大

上海黄金交易所与包括美国芝加哥商品交易所、迪拜黄金与商品交易所、香港交易及结算所等在内的多家境外同业机构探索建立长效合作机制，积极开展跨市场合作，为境内外投资者开辟多元化的投资渠道。如上海黄金交易所与迪拜黄金与商品交易所签署《上海金基准价授权使用协议》，授权迪拜黄金与商品交易所在其开发的以离岸人民币计价的黄金期货合约中，使用“上海金”基准价作为该合约的现金结算价，“上海金”基准价首次应用在国际金融市场。另外与香港交易所集团签署了合作备忘录，积极探讨在黄金及贵金属产品研发、跨市场互联互通机制设计等多个领域的合作可能性，进一步促进内地与香港黄金市场的联系。

（三）商业银行积极参与国际黄金市场

商业银行境外黄金业务不断拓展，境外市场交易量连年增长。2016年，商业银行各类境外黄金交易累计成交量和成交金额较上年分别增长13.23%和22.33%。此外，我国国有大型商业银行不断开拓国际黄金市场，参与国际黄金定盘交易，争取国际黄金市场话语权。继2015年中国建设银行、中国银行加入伦敦金银市场协会（LBMA）黄金价格机制后，2016年，中国工商银行和交通银行相继获准加入该机制，成为LBMA黄金定盘商，参与伦敦黄金定盘价报价。国内商业银行在全球黄金市场中的作用和影响力不断提升。

五、黄金市场发展展望

2017年，中国黄金市场将坚持改革创新和风险防范并重，促进黄金市场规范协调发展。

一是完善黄金市场产品体系，发挥黄金租借、质押、远期、掉期等业务的投融资功能和套期保值功能，切实发挥黄金市场支持实体经济作用，支持黄金产业健康发展。

二是健全黄金市场制度和基础设施建设，完善询价市场做市商制度，构建中远期黄金基准价格体系，推动建立中央对手方清算机制，加强黄金市场技术系统建设和安全运维，进一步提升我国黄金市场服务效率和服务水平。

三是继续推进黄金市场对外开放战略，进一步完善上海黄金交易所国际业务板块，积极发挥上海金人民币黄金定盘价机制作用，提高我国在国际黄金市场的影响力和话语权。

四是切实加强黄金市场监督管理，开展市场动态监测分析，确保黄金市场平稳运行。推动健全金融机构黄金市场业务风险管控制度，防范市场风险。加强黄金市场宣传教育工作，引导投资者通过合法渠道参与黄金市场投资。

专题七　“上海金”成功推出

“上海金”人民币集中定价交易业务于2016年4月19日正式启动。上海金集中定价交易是指市场参与者在上海黄金交易所平台上，按照以价询量、数量撮合的集中交易方式，在达到市场量价相对平衡后，最终形成上海金人民币基准价的交易。运行半年多以来，上海金定价交易业务交易、清算、交割和风险控制等各个环节平稳运行，价格形成机制公开透明，基准价格合理公允，“上海金”基准作用显现，市场参与度不断提高，对国内外黄金市场的影响力正在逐步显现。

一、“上海金”定价交易业务运行情况

（一）交易、交割和清算安全顺畅，业务发展稳健

截至2016年底，上海金定价交易累计成交量为569.19吨，成交金额为1 552.75亿元，日均成交量与伦敦金定价成交量的差距正在缩小。上海金定价机制运转已初具市场规模。

（二）价格形成机制公开透明，基准价格合理公允

根据运行监测，每场次“上海金基准价”通过最少1轮、最多16轮的“以价询量”的交易过程产生，这与伦敦金定价一般在15轮次以内交易产生的情况相似。每场次上海金定价交易均能产生“上海金基准价”，且该基准价符合当时市场的实际情况。

（三）风险管理和资源调配的市场功能显现

在每个定价交易时段，以“上海金基准价”成交的定价交易量均在1吨以上。上海金定价为市场提供了以“上海金基准价”公允市价进行交易的大宗交易服务平台，规避了竞价交易时间短、交易量大而带来的流动性风险和市场风险，有利于市场参与者提高交易效率，调配资源。

（四）定价主体开放多元，具有广泛代表性

为使价格充分反映人民币黄金市场产用金和投资链的供需均衡，上海黄金交易所选择了12家定价成员和6家提供参考价成员共同报价，包括了商业银行、产用金企业等多元化市场主体，地域上包括境内会员和国际会员，范围广泛丰富，体现了人民币黄金市场多元化特点，价格能够真实反映各方供需诉求。在上海金定价交易过程中，每个场次核心定价成员均参与初始价参考报价，所有定价成员都要求履行量差分担的义务，并负责任地进行补充申报，有效提高了市场定价效率。

（五）定价管理严格规范，有效维护交易市场各方合法权益

黄金集中定价的交易、清算和交割，交易双方不需相互授信，既降低了违约风险，也有助于提高清算和交割效率。上海黄金交易所加强市场监管，严控风险，通过多项措施，严格防范任何操纵价格等扰乱市场、具有误导性和欺诈性的交易行为。同时，为进一步保证定价机制的公正性，上海黄金交易所组织筹建由市场主要参与者、上海黄金交易所、行业协会等机

构专业人士共同组成的上海金集中定价交易监督管理委员会，负责对上海金集中定价交易业务的合规性进行监督管理。

二、“上海金”基准作用显现

上海金人民币基准价的推出，进一步完善了中国黄金市场的价格形成机制，为黄金相关衍生品提供定价基准，有助于促进黄金市场产品创新，为市场参与者提供更丰富的风险管理工具，从而更好地发挥市场服务实体经济的功能。

（一）作为黄金企业套期保值交易贸易结算的基准

“上海金基准价”为黄金生产链企业在签订黄金、黄金原料等贵金属贸易和交易合约时，提供了除以美元标价的伦敦金、纽约金之外亚洲时区黄金基准价格的选择。以“上海金基准价”为价格锚签订黄金相关的贵金属资源、原料和成品的国际套期保值交易、进出口贸易合约，有利于降低我国黄金企业的汇率风险，增强在国际贵金属市场中的资源调配能力以及人民币的计价和结算能力。目前，已经有部分产金企业正在研究在进口铜金矿等黄金原料和黄金成品等贸易中运用以人民币计价的“上海金基准价”的可行性和应用范围。

（二）作为黄金租赁、抵押等黄金资金融通的计价依据

目前交通银行、中国建设银行、中信银行、上海银行、渣打银行等多家商业银行在与客户进行黄金租赁业务时，已经将“上海金基准价”作为黄金租赁合同的价格计算基准。在商业银行之间以及商业银行与客户之间进行黄金租赁、抵押等业务时，“上海金基准价”公允合理的合同价格在保护交易双方合理权益方面发挥了重要作用。

（三）作为银行间询价市场中黄金即期、远期、期货、期权等黄金衍生产品现金结算价

“上海金”上市首日，上海黄金交易所询价平台同步推出挂钩“上海金基准价”的现金结算型询价合约，构建“上海金基准价”在人民币黄金询价衍生品市场的应用场景。截至2016年底，以“上海金基准价”为参考价格的现金结算型询价交易，累计成交量为2 489吨。

（四）金融机构设计产品的锚定价格

“上海金基准价”为商业银行黄金理财产品提供了可供交易的基准价格，使理财产品的估值更加准确和合规。中国银行已经发行了以“上海金基准价”作为其锚定价格的黄金积存理财产品。交通银行、招商银行、平安银行等也正在推进发行以“上海金基准价”为基准的黄金积存、黄金期权等黄金衍生产品的相关工作。中信证券、国泰君安证券已经推出了以“上海金基准价”为标的的金融产品，并通过上海黄金交易所定价交易平台进行头寸管理。

三、“上海金”国际影响力逐步扩大

上海金人民币基准价的发布，凸显了中国作为黄金生产和消费大国的定价影响力，具有风向标的作用。“上海金”与“伦敦金”和“纽约金”一起为国际市场参与者提供更为全面和客观的不同时区的黄金价格。国内外投资者对“上海金基准价”的关注提升了国内黄金市场的国际影

响力。同时，上海黄金交易所通过与迪拜黄金与商品交易所签署《上海金基准价授权使用协议》，授权其使用“上海金基准价”并开发与“上海金基准价”挂钩的人民币交易产品，将“上海金基准价”首次应用于国际金融市场。“上海金基准价”的国际影响力逐步扩大，加快了国内黄金市场国际化推进进程。

第七章 期货市场

2016年，中国商品期货市场规模进一步放大，过半数商品期货品种运行呈现价量齐升。金融期货中，国债期货市场运行有序，成交、持仓稳步增长；股指期货成交、持仓同比大幅下降，期现货价格依然高度相关。《期货交易管理条例》等多项条款修正出台，“保险+期货”试点力度加大，期货市场监管更趋严格。总体来看，期货市场价格发现、资源配置功能得到有效发挥，服务实体经济的能力继续增强。

一、期货市场的运行情况

（一）商品期货市场

2016年，全国商品期货累计成交量为41.19亿手（以下数据均按单边计算），累计成交额为177.41万亿元，同比分别增长27.26%和30.00%。

分交易所来看，2016年上海期货交易所累计成交量为16.81亿手，累计成交额为84.98万亿元，同比分别增长59.99%和33.71%，分别占全国商品期货市场的40.80%和47.90%，较上年占比有所上升；郑州商品交易所累计成交量为9.01亿手，累计成交额为31.03万亿元，同比分别下降15.79%和增长0.16%，分别占全国商品期货市场的21.88%和17.49%，占比略有上升；大连商品交易所累计成交量为15.37亿手，累计成交额为61.41万亿元，同比分别增长37.73%和46.43%，分别占全国商品期货市场的37.32%和34.61%，占比有所下降。

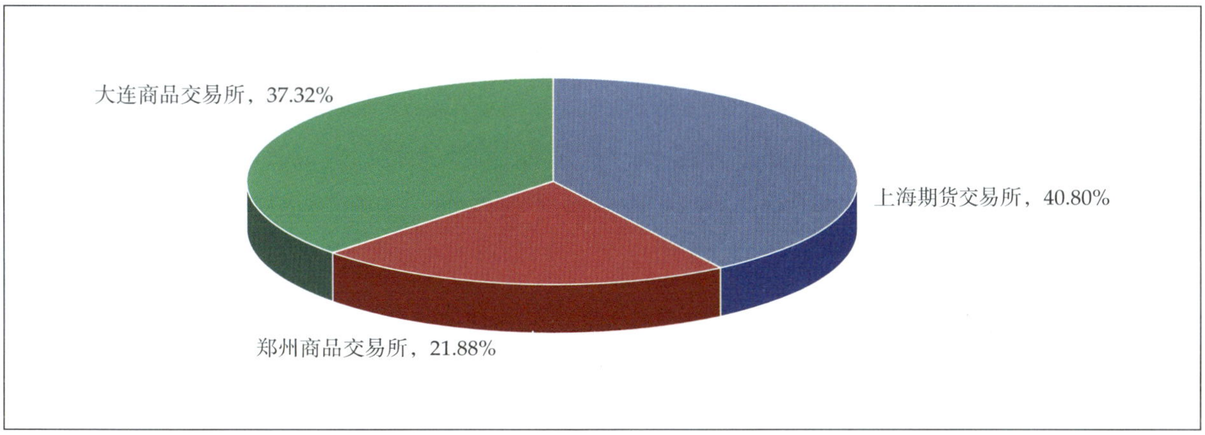

数据来源：中国期货业协会。

图7-1 2016年各商品期货交易所成交量占比

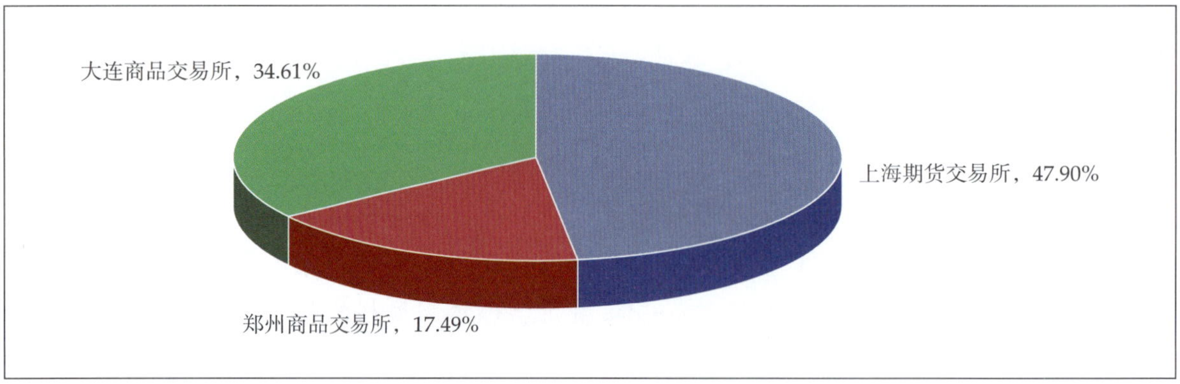

数据来源：中国期货业协会。

图7-2 2016年各商品期货交易所成交额占比

从成交活跃程度来看，2016年商品期货成交量前十大品种依次为螺纹钢、豆粕、铁矿石、菜籽粕、石油沥青、PTA、棕榈油、甲醇、聚丙烯和玉米，合计成交量为27.93亿手，占全部商品期货成交总量的67.80%；成交额前十大品种依次为螺纹钢、铁矿石、铜、天然橡胶、豆粕、黄金、镍、棕榈油、白糖和锌，合计成交额为111.62万亿元，占全部商品期货成交总额的62.91%。

根据美国期货业协会（FIA）统计的2016年成交量数据，上海期货交易所排名第6位，比2015年上升5位；大连商品交易所排名第8位，比2015年上升1位；郑州商品交易所排名第11位，比2015年下降1位。如果仅按商品类期货与期权成交量计算，上海期货交易所排名第1位，大连商品交易所排名第2位，郑州商品交易所排名第4位。

（二）金融期货市场

2016年，我国金融期货市场总成交量0.18亿手，累计成交金额18.22万亿元，同比分别减少94.62%和95.64%，分别占全国市场的0.44%和9.31%。截至2016年末，金融期货市场开户人数达到35.67万户，其中自然人32.15万户，特殊法人（持牌金融机构）2.63万户，一般法人0.56万户，期货资管客户0.33万户，各类市场机构有序参与交易，金融期货市场稳步发展。

1. 国债期货市场运行有序，成交、持仓稳步增长

总体来看，2016年国债期货成交、持仓稳步增长，期现货联动性增强，交割业务平稳顺畅。国债期货全年累计成交893.40万手，日均成交3.66万手，较2015年增长46.76%；累计成交金额8.90万亿元，日均成交金额364.81亿元，较2015年增长48.09%。截至12月31日，国债期货总持仓8.03万手，较2015年底增长37.04%，其中5年期国债期货持仓1.91万手，10年期国债期货持仓6.12万手。2016年国债期货价格波动总体较小，期现货联动紧密。5年期国债期货主力合约日均波动0.12%，平均基差0.74元；10年期国债期货主力合约日均波动0.20%，平均基差0.95元；5年期国债期货和10年期国债期货主力合约与现货的价格相关性分别为98.90%和99.13%。2016年以来，国债期货顺利完成8个合约的交割，总交割量为5 012手，平均交割率为1.76%，交割平稳顺畅，投资者交割行为理性。

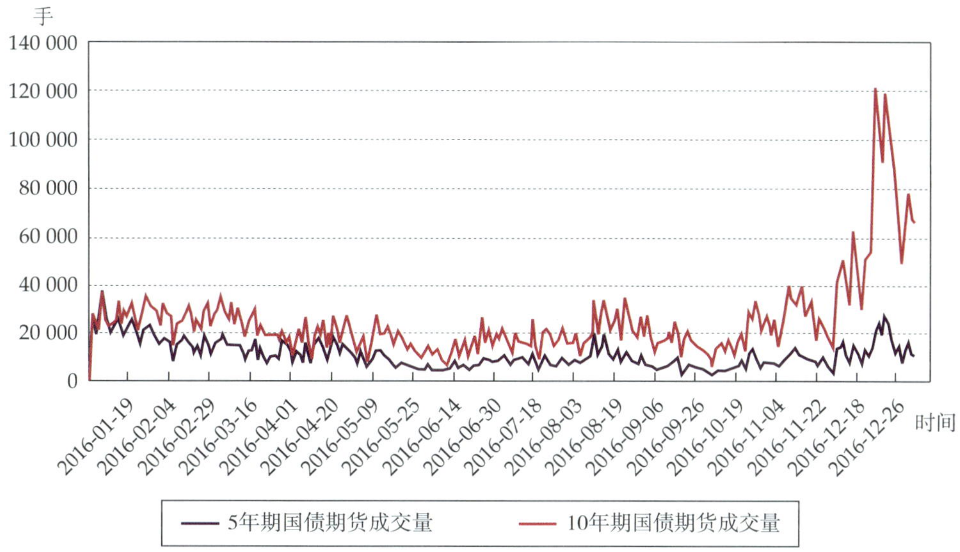

数据来源：中金所。

图7-3　2016年国债期货每日成交量

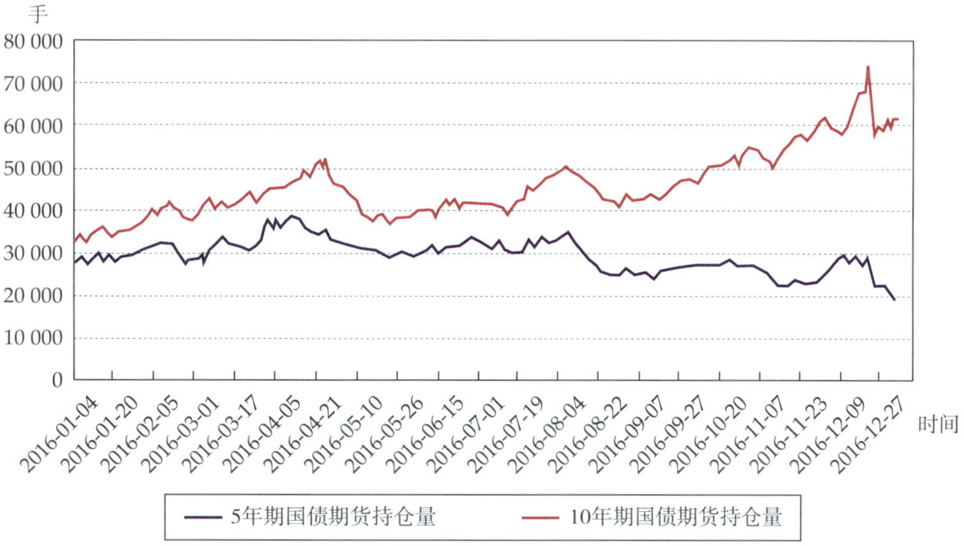

数据来源：中金所。

图7-4　2016年国债期货每日持仓量

2. 股指期货成交、持仓同比大幅下降，期现货价格依然高度相关

2016年，我国股指期货市场总体运行平稳，股指期货成交量和持仓量较上年大幅下降，期现货价格相关性依然较高。股指期货三个产品总成交量940.18万手，总成交金额9.32万亿元，分别同比下降97.19%和97.74%；日均成交量和日均持仓量分别为3.85万手和9.46万手，同比减少97.19%和47.39%；日均成交持仓比为0.41，同比降低93.76%。股指期货三个产品期现货价格相关性较高，沪深300、上证50和中证500股指期货主力合约收盘价和对应现货指数收盘价的价格相关系数分别为99.22%、99.65%和98.28%。

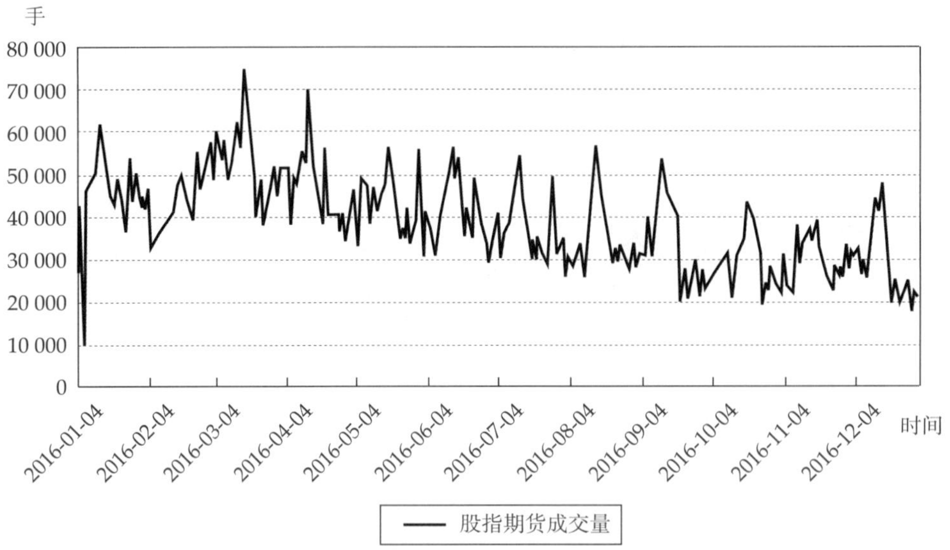

数据来源：中金所。

图7-5 2016年股指期货每日成交量

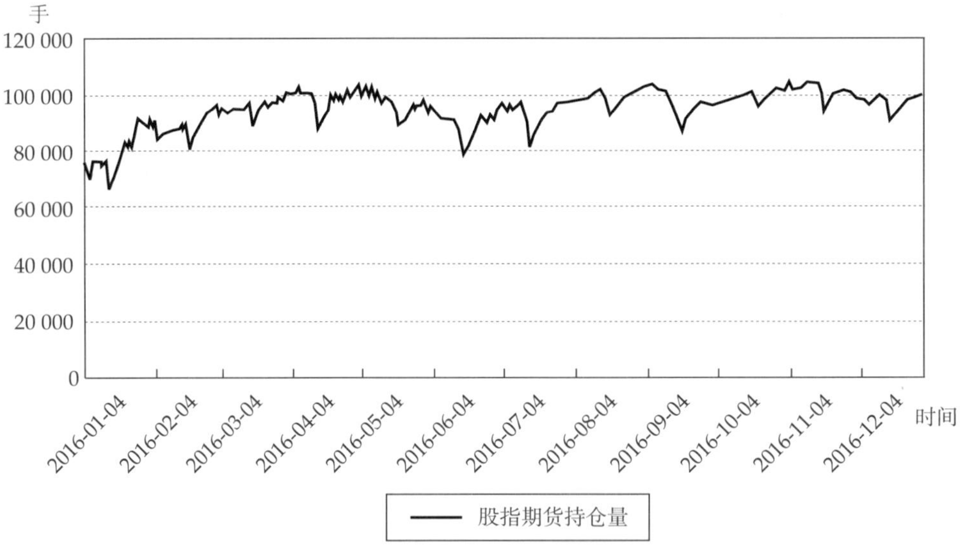

数据来源：中金所。

图7-6 2016年股指期货每日持仓量

二、期货市场运行的主要特点

（一）商品期货市场规模持续增长

2016年，全国商品期货累计成交量为41.19亿手（以下数据均按单边计算），累计成交额为177.41万亿元，同比分别增长27.26%和30.00%，创历史新高。

按商品大类来看，主要能源化工期货品种中，动力煤、聚氯乙烯、石油沥青、焦炭和焦煤的成交量同比大幅上升，增长率分别为1 796.88%、617.68%、476.63%、222.18%和161.53%；玻璃的成交量同比上升超过60%；天然橡胶和聚丙烯的成交量略有增加；聚乙烯、燃料油和PTA的成交量有所下降；纤维板、胶合板和甲醇的成交量下降幅度超过50%。

主要金属类品种方面，锰硅、热轧卷板、硅铁、锡和铅的成交量大幅上升，同比增长分别为2 605.30%、2 050.79%、1 573.56%、514.27%和248.16%；铝、螺纹钢、锌、镍、黄金和铁矿石的成交量同比上升均超过30%；铜和白银的成交量有所回落；线材的成交量下降幅度超过80%。

主要农产品类品种方面，一号棉、菜籽油、粳稻、玉米和玉米淀粉的成交量大幅上升，分别同比增长256.12%、251.25%、245.45%、190.72%和149.30%；黄大豆一号、鸡蛋和豆粕的成交量增长超过30%；棕榈油、强麦和豆油的成交量略有增加；菜籽粕、白糖和早籼稻的成交量则有所下降；普麦、晚籼稻、黄大豆二号和油菜籽的成交量下降幅度超过50%。

（二）全国多数商品期货品种呈现量价齐升

2016年，全国过半商品期货品种呈现量价齐升。

1. 有色金属：除铜外，其他有色金属期货价升量增

铜期货累计成交7 239.49万手，同比减少18.03%；年末持仓24.04万手，同比减少37.82%。铜期货主力合约收盘价45 500元/吨，较年初上涨26.49%。铝期货累计成交4 439.18万手，同比增长93.84%；年末持仓33.29万手，同比下降4.52%。铝期货主力合约收盘价12 795元/吨，较年初上涨20.37%。锌期货累计成交7 306.59万手，同比增加61.52%；年末持仓20.65万手，同比增加0.47%。锌期货主力合约收盘价21 045元/吨，较年初上涨59.86%。铅期货累计成交456.12万手，同比增加2.5倍；年末持仓4.10万手，同比增加1.4倍。铅期货主力合约收盘价17 665元/吨，较年初上涨34.39%。锡期货累计成交量316.83万手，同比增长5.1倍；

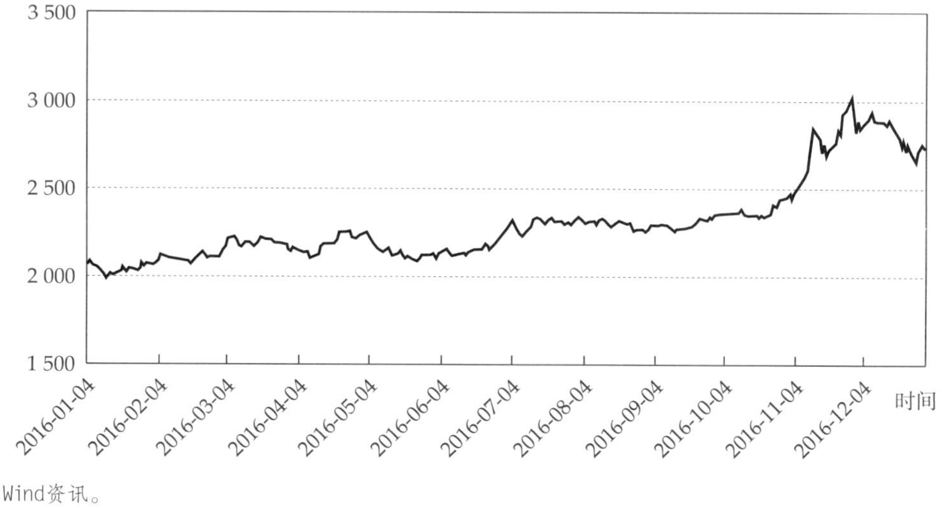

数据来源：Wind资讯。

图7-7 2016年上海期货交易所有色金属指数走势

年末持仓0.70万手，同比增长1.1倍。锡期货主力合约收盘价146 820元/吨，较年初上涨60.09%。镍期货累计成交10 024.99万手，同比增加57.65%；年末持仓30.76万手，同比增加14.27%。镍期货主力合约收盘价85 560元/吨，较年初上涨24.13%。

2. 钢铁：钢材与铁矿石价升量增

螺纹钢期货累计成交量为93 414.84万手，同比增加72.66%；年末持仓量为133.50万手，同比下降29.57%。螺纹钢期货主力合约收盘价2 867元/吨，较年初上涨61.34%。热轧卷板期货累计成交量为4 328.18万手，同比增加20.5倍；年末持仓量为18.42万手，同比增长2.7倍。热轧卷板期货主力合约收盘价3 305元/吨，较年初上涨71.33%。铁矿石期货累计成交量为34 226.53万手，同比增加31.86%；年末持仓量为55.07万手，同比下降41.36%。铁矿石期货主力合约收盘价548元/吨，较年初上涨70.45%。

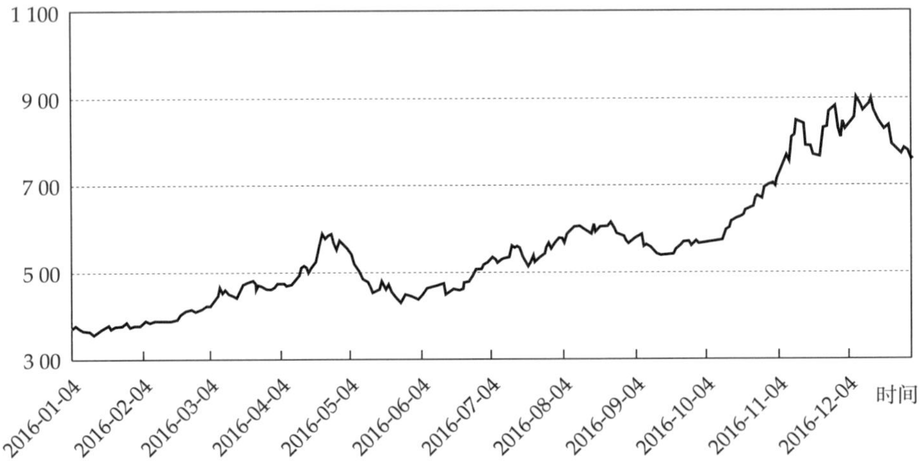

数据来源：Wind资讯。

图7-8 2016年中国期货市场监控中心钢铁期货指数走势

3. 能化：过半品种价升量增

动力煤、PVC、沥青、焦炭、焦煤、玻璃、天然橡胶和聚丙烯价升量增，其累计成交量同比分别增加1 796.88%、617.68%、476.63%、222.18%、161.53%、62.82%、17.22%和15.12%，年末收盘价较年初分别上涨64.39%、28.84%、51.27%、138.68%、112.07%、48.48%、80.61%和51.93%；聚乙烯、燃料油、PTA、甲醇和纤维板价升量减，其累计成交量同比分别下降15.79%、24.59%、25.42%、56.56%和98.96%，年末收盘价较年初分别上涨23.04%、86.88%、22.88%、58.78%和42.15%；胶合板价量齐减，其累计成交量同比下降95.54%，年末收盘价较年初下降1.21%。

数据来源：Wind资讯。

图7-9 2016年中国期货市场监控中心能化期货指数走势

4. 农产品：近半品种价升量增

一号棉、菜籽油、黄大豆一号、鸡蛋、豆粕、棕榈油、强麦和豆油价升量增，其累计成交量同比分别增加256.12%、251.25%、73.15%、52.69%、34.35%、24.79%、9.21%和2.44%，年末收盘价较年初分别上涨33.24%、27.83%、18.76%、5.87%、20.51%、29.10%、4.08%和23.37%；菜籽粕和白糖价升量减，其累计成交量同比分别下降57.56%和62.84%，年末收盘价较年初分别上涨26.93%和20.31%；玉米和玉米淀粉价减量增，其累计成交量同比分别增加190.72%和149.30%，年末收盘价较年初分别下降19.76%和12.88%。

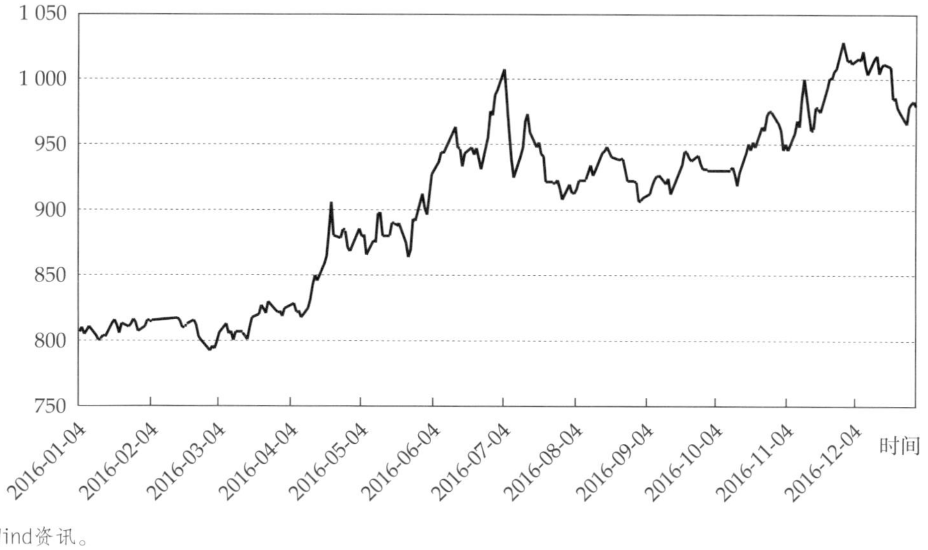

数据来源：Wind资讯。

图7-10 2016年中国期货市场监控中心农产品期货指数走势

（三）国债期货市场机构投资者参与程度不断提高

2016年，国债期货市场规模稳步提升，市场功能受到广泛认可，机构投资者参与程度不断提高。在自营机构参与方面，具有国债承销团成员资格的证券公司均已入市，证券公司自营成为国债期货市场最主要的机构投资者。2016年，证券公司自营在国债期货市场的日均成交量、持仓量占比分别为15%和34%，综合排名靠前。在资管机构参与方面，证券公司、公募基金、私募基金、期货公司等机构资产管理产品的交易规模增长迅速，已经成为国债期货市场最大的持仓主体。2016年，全部资产管理产品在国债期货市场的日均成交量、持仓量占比分别为23%和37%。

（四）股指期货市场流动性大幅下降

2015年实施的临时管控措施，有效抑制了市场过度投机，同时客观上股指期货市场运行质量也大幅下降。2016年，股指期货市场成交量和持仓量同比大幅降低，最优买卖价差明显扩大，市场厚度显著下降，市场流动性大幅下降，套期保值交易因缺乏对手方，无法有效开展。其中，沪深300股指期货的累计成交量为422.56万手，累计成交额为4.01万亿元，同比分别下降98.48%和98.83%。上证50股指期货累计成交量为162.44万手，累计成交额为1.05万亿元，同比分别下降95.42%和96.59%。中证500股指期货的累计成交量为355.19万手，累计成交额为4.26万亿元，同比分别下降84.00%和89.13%。

三、期货市场创新

（一）"保险+期货"写入中央一号文件

全球期货市场最先萌芽于美国芝加哥农产品市场，用于应对价格波动风险、农产品保存和运输中的各种风险，农产品成为美国和全球期货市场的重要组成部分，在农产品生产、贸易、运输等各环节的风险对冲上发挥着不可替代的作用。而我国农业长期以来有靠天吃饭的说法，虽然近年来在农业科技和产业技术上有较大的提升，但是在面对价格波动风险上，广大农民和企业依然处于被动地位。鉴于此，2016年中央一号文件《关于落实发展新理念加快农业现代化实现全面小康目标的若干意见》中，在"完善农业保险制度"一款明确提出，要稳步扩大"保险+期货"试点，通过"保险+期货"的形式，由保险公司和期货公司的专业人员帮助锁定农产品的最终价格，对冲价格大幅波动带来的风险和损失，让农业企业和个人获得稳定的收益，从而更加专注于农业技术和相关产业技术升级，从而有力地保障我国农业供给侧结构性改革。在农业供给侧结构性改革的推进过程中，农产品衍生品市场具有不可替代的作用。

为落实中央一号文件精神，农业部、证监会、保监会指导期货交易所、保险机构、期货经营机构以及涉农企业加大了"保险+期货"试点力度。大连商品交易所以玉米和大豆为试点品种，开展了12个"保险+期货"试点项目，试点的现货量是2015年试点的54倍，其中8个试点项目发生理赔，共计理赔

481.79万元，有效地规避了价格下跌风险；郑州商品交易所以棉花和白糖为试点品种，也首次启动“保险+期货”试点，确定了10个试点项目，涵盖了8个省区；上海期货交易所的天然橡胶“保险+期货”试点也正在积极推进之中，2016年11月，上海期货交易所在海南举行海南“保险+期货”与精准扶贫座谈会，就“保险+期货”项目试点进行了讨论，明确了试点的实施进度和工作安排。2016年期货市场服务实体经济特别是服务“三农”工作得到进一步深化。

（二）白糖、豆粕期权获批上市

2016年12月16日，证监会宣布已批准郑州商品交易所、大连商品交易所分别开展白糖、豆粕期权交易。同日，郑州商品交易所、大连商品交易所分别就白糖、豆粕期权合约及相关规则公开征求意见。根据征求意见稿，白糖、豆粕期权将实施做市商制度，自然人投资者的参与门槛为10万元。这标志着我国商品期货市场将步入期权时代，涉农企业风险管理工具将进一步丰富和灵活。待白糖、豆粕期权推出后，在涉农企业中积极推进的“保险+期货”试点，还可以积极尝试“保险+期权”的模式。以期货价格为重要参考指标、以期货市场为重要风险分散场所的“保险+期货”模式，以及对农户来说既能保证收益又无额外损失的农产品期权将成为支持农业市场化改革的重要工具。积极引导涉农企业利用期货、期权管理市场风险，将不断增强期货市场服务“三农”的能力，提升期货市场服务农业实体经济的有效性。

（三）首家期货公司发起设立公募基金

2016年10月18日，证监会发布《关于核准设立南华基金管理有限公司的批复》，南华期货正式获批设立公募基金，这是国内期货业的首张公募牌照。南华基金管理有限公司由南华期货股份有限公司全资控股，注册资本为1.5亿元人民币，公司注册地为浙江省宁波市。公司经营范围为基金募集、基金销售、资产管理、特定客户资产管理和中国证监会许可的其他业务。从2016年1月申请材料被证监会接收，到正式受理，再到10月18日证监会核准南华期货发起设立南华基金管理有限公司的申请，历经190个工作日。期货公司试水公募行业不仅反映出金融机构的混业经营趋势，同时也标志着衍生品性质理财产品种类将得以拓宽。

四、期货市场制度和基础设施建设

（一）《期货交易管理条例》修订

国务院于2016年2月6日颁布了《国务院关于修改部分行政法规的决定》（国务院令第666号）。其中，对《期货交易管理条例》多项条款作了修改。此次修改充分体现了简政放权、放管结合、优化服务的改革精神，取消需国务院期货监督管理机构批准的事项，同时放宽了期货公司及其他期货经营机构的高管资格管理制度，以及对其非合规经营的处罚措施。《期货交易管理条例》的修订，有利于促进政府由事前审批向事中事后监管的转型，并进一步激发期货市场参与机构的活力。

（二）期货资管业务监管趋严

据中国基金业协会最新数据显示，截至2016年12月底，全国期货公司资管业务总规模为2 792亿元，同比增长167.17%。随着期货资管规模迅速扩大，监管机构对期货资管业务的监管逐步趋严。

2016年5月，中国期货业协会向多家期货公司下发“关于征求《期货公司资产管理子公司管理规则（征求意见稿）》意见的通知”，意见稿规定期货公司设立资管子公司为事后备案事项，但同时也指出子公司应当满足相应要求，列明了“子公司与母公司及关联子公司之间不得存在有利益冲突的同类业务”等负面行为清单。7月14日，证监会又发布了《证券期货经营机构私募资产管理业务运作管理暂行规定》，被称作资管新“八条底线”，重点加强对资管计划杠杆管理、结构化资管产品、开展或参与“资金池”业务、实施过度激励等的规范。此规定对于期货公司发行资管产品的影响较大，2016年1~7月期货公司月平均发行资管产品306个，8~12月跌至97个，较1~7月下降68.3%。另外，鉴于当下期货公司集合资产管理业务放开后，期货资管产品种类增多，风险特征各异，现行风险计算方式无法准确反映期货资管业务风险状况，证监会就2007年出台的《期货公司风险监管指标管理办法》进行了修订，并制定了《期货公司风险监管报表编制与报送指引》作为实施该规章的配套文件，证监会已于2016年10月就以上文件向社会公开征求意见。

（三）金融期货市场实施跨市场账户连通

为进一步夯实跨市场联动监管的基础，更好地提升跨市场监管协作的效率，证监会组织相关单位大力推进跨期现一码通账户体系的建设工作。2016年7月底，跨期现一码通账户技术系统正式上线。跨期现一码通账户体系实现了金融期货账户与现货账户连接，要求参与证券、期货市场的投资者统一开立一码通账户。一码通账户既包括期货账户信息，也包括A、B股等证券账户信息，可以实现投资者身份信息的统一识别和管理，有利于开展期现货市场的联动监管，及时发现跨市场交易异常客户，防范跨市场交易风险。

此外，中国金融期货交易所与中央国债登记结算有限责任公司就国债期货券款对付（DVP）交割业务达成合作协议，能够在指定交割日实现买卖双方债券和资金的同步交收。双方将进一步加强债券期现货市场互联互通，研究完善跨市场风险监测协作机制，共同促进国债期货市场健康发展。

（四）商品期货的市场风险管理加强

2016年4月及9~11月，以黑色系品种为代表的大宗商品价格先后出现两波强势上涨行情，铁矿石、焦煤、焦炭、螺纹钢、热轧卷板等品种经历了过山车行情。其中，焦煤、焦炭期货年度涨幅分别为108%和136%，黑色系品种涨幅普遍超过60%。部分品种交易量快速增长。为配合政府调控，维护期货市场平稳运行，抑制市场过度投机，在证监会指导下，相关期货交易所对部分品种的交易手续费、保证金标准和涨跌停板幅度进行调整，要求会员单位做好风险防范工作，提醒投资者理性投资，并推动资管产品账户信息报备。随着政策“组合拳”作用的显现，相关品种交易热度下降，市场运行逐渐平稳。

（五）期货市场对外开放稳步推进

金融期货市场的国际化有序推进，在跨境业务、国际组织、国际研究等方面取得积极进展。一是中国金融期货交易所（以下简称中金所）与上海证券交易所、深圳证券交易所、中巴投资有限责任公司及巴基斯坦哈比银行组成联合体，成功竞得巴基斯坦证券交易所40%的股权，进一步落实“一带一路”倡议和中巴经济走廊建设规划。二是积极支持中欧国际交易所（以下简称中欧所）的建设与发展。中欧所成立一年多以来，总体运行平稳，交易额稳定增长。截至2016年12月31日，中欧所共有133只产品挂牌交易，总交易额合计46.57亿元人民币，人民币计价产品交易额约占总交易额的7%。三是中金所于2016年7月正式加入国际掉期与衍生品协会（ISDA），研究和探索场内外业务协同发展及配套服务模式。

五、期货市场发展展望

2017年，我国期货市场将坚持稳中求进，依法从严全面监管，不断提高市场监管效能，防控金融风险，切实推进和服务供给侧结构性改革，提升期货市场服务实体经济和社会发展的能力。商品期货方面，将继续立足于满足实体经济的发展要求，积极稳妥地开发上市更多符合实体经济需要、市场条件具备的期货新品种，包括豆粕、白糖等农产品期权和原油期货等；将紧贴“一带一路”战略，提升期货市场对外开放度；将加强对市场的一线监管，筑牢防范风险防线，全面从严依法监管，维护市场平稳运行。金融期货方面，将扎实做好产品业务储备，继续推进技术先行战略，持续优化市场宣传教育，进一步完善国债期货投资者结构，积极拓展国际合作，全面推动金融期货市场发展，更好地满足风险管理需要。

第八章　金融衍生品市场

2016年我国金融衍生品市场继续平稳健康发展，市场规模稳步增长，交易保持活跃。利率互换市场创新继续深化，互换利率总体震荡上行，集中清算成为利率互换的主要清算方式。信用衍生品市场新添产品。汇率衍生品交易量增加，外汇远期交易量和集中清算量大幅增长，市场创新和制度建设进一步推进。场外大宗商品金融衍生品市场产品种类不断丰富，集中清算业务出现高速增长。

一、人民币利率衍生品市场

（一）人民币利率衍生品市场运行情况

2016年，人民币利率衍生品市场成交9.93万亿元，同比增长12.7%。其中，普通利率互换成交9.93万亿元，标准利率互换成交8亿元，债券远期成交14.86亿元，标准债券远期成交1亿元，远期利率协议成交1亿元。截至年末，利率互换市场名义未平仓余额为8.26万亿元（单边计），同比增长27.6%。

普通利率互换中，从期限结构看，1年及1年以下品种成交占比为79.34%，1~3年和3~5年品种成交占比分别为4.74%和15.92%；从参考利率看，以FR007为浮动端参考利率的互换交易占比为85.93%，以ShiborO/N和Shibor3M为浮动端参考利率的互换交易占比分别为2.73%和11.11%。

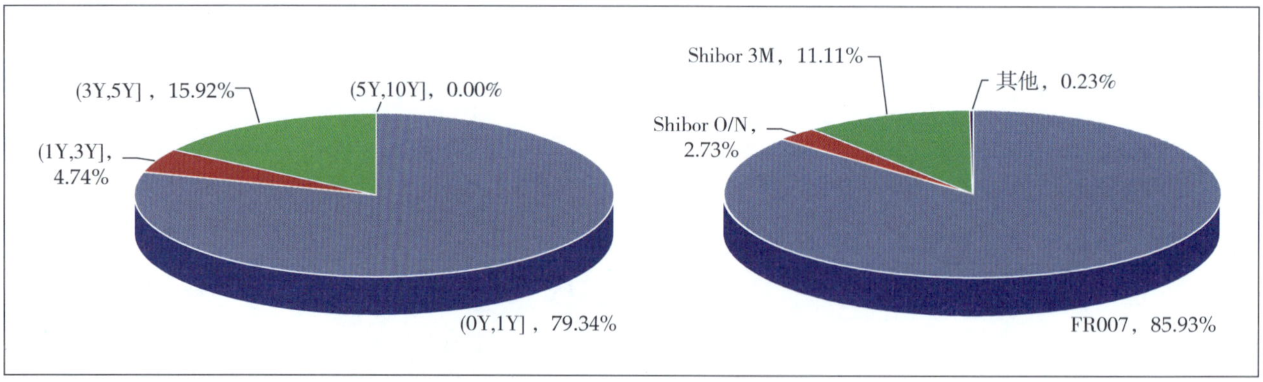

数据来源：中国外汇交易中心。

图8-1　2016年普通利率互换期限结构及参考利率结构

2016年，利率互换市场成员规模不断增长，类型逐步丰富。截至年末，利率互换市场参与机构（含产品）205家，包括银行类金融机构、证券公司、保险公司、非法人产品等类型；利率互换市场制度备案机构（含产品）197家；承诺使用利率互换交易确认功能的机构（含产品）148家。

（二）人民币利率衍生品市场运行的特点

1. 利率互换市场保持平稳发展

利率互换交易规模稳步增长。2016年度各月利率互换新增交易结构与上年基本一致，但交易金额较上年各月有不同程度的上升。尤其在2016年底，其中11月、12月交易名义本金持续突破历史高值，分别达到1.07万亿元和1.14万亿元。

X-Swap交易占比不断提高。2016年双边授信点击的交易平台X-Swap成交利率互换2.40万笔，名义本金3.54万亿元，市场占比35.4%，较上年提高10个百分点。交易压缩业务稳步推进。2016年交易中心组织了13场利率互换多边冲销，73场利率互换双边冲销，合计提前终止合约2.13万笔，名义本金1.63万亿元。

2. 利率互换期限结构仍以1年期及以下为主

从期限结构上看，2016年利率互换仍以1年期及以下合约交易为主，但期限结构呈现向长端移动的趋势。全年交易合约中，1月期及以内交易名义本金额占总成交量的2.8%；1月至1年期交易名义本金额达7.59万亿元，占比76.5%；2年至5年期交易名义本金额达2.05亿元，占比20.7%。

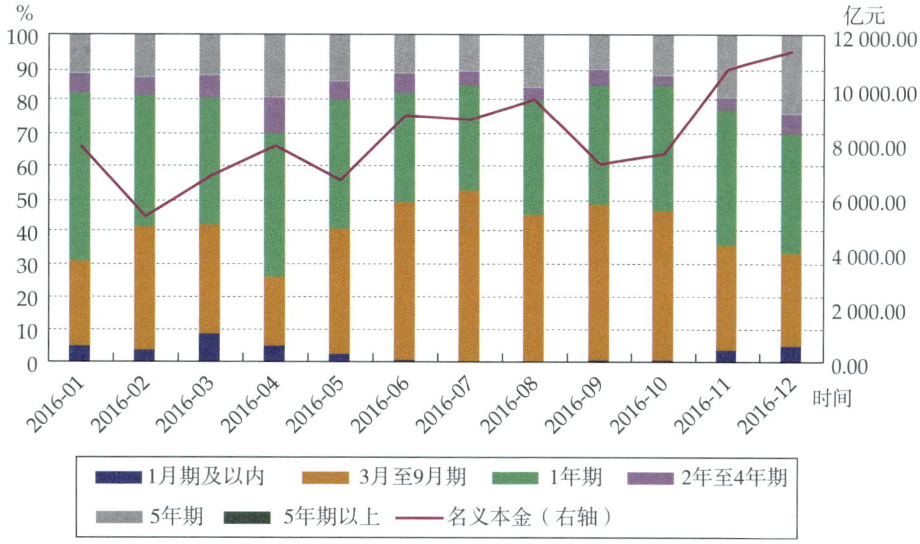

数据来源：中国外汇交易中心。

图8-2 2016年利率互换交易期限结构

从挂钩标的利率来看，浮动端依然以挂钩七天回购定盘利率（FR007）为主，但挂钩其他标的互换交易占比有所上升，其中以3个月Shibor利率为主。2016年全年FR007互换交易名义本金总计8.52万亿元，成交占比为85.9%，较上年下降4个百分点左右；挂钩Shibor利率（包括隔夜和3个月Shibor利率）者交易成交占比为13.8%，较上年上升5个百分点左右；挂钩其他利率交易占比为0.3%。

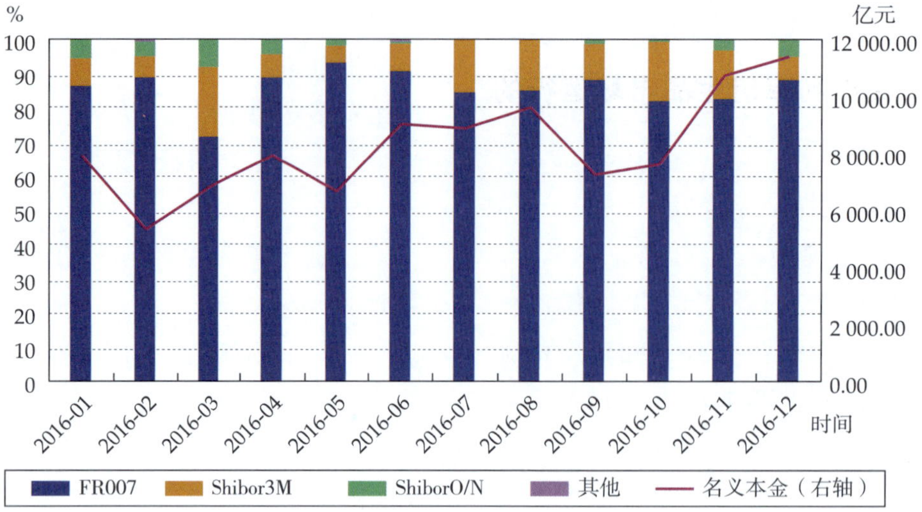

数据来源：中国外汇交易中心。

图8-3　2016年利率互换交易标的结构

3. 利率互换价格总体震荡上升

2016年初至3月中上旬，受货币市场短期利率总体平稳、Shibor3M等货币市场中长期利率震荡下行、部分指标显示经济下行压力较大等因素影响，FR007品种互换利率小幅波动，Shibor3M品种互换利率震荡下行。3月下旬以后，伴随着部分经济指标好转、Shibor3M等货币市场中长期利率上行、政策预期变化等因素，加之信用事件等因素引发债券收益率总体上行，互换利率持续上升，4月底以后逐步回落并维持震荡。

8月底以后，受货币市场利率走高、货币政策预期转变、通胀水平上升、部分经济指标向好等因素影响，互换利率稳步上升，并且随着债券市场的大幅调整，在10月底以后加速上行，波动显著扩大，年末有所回落。

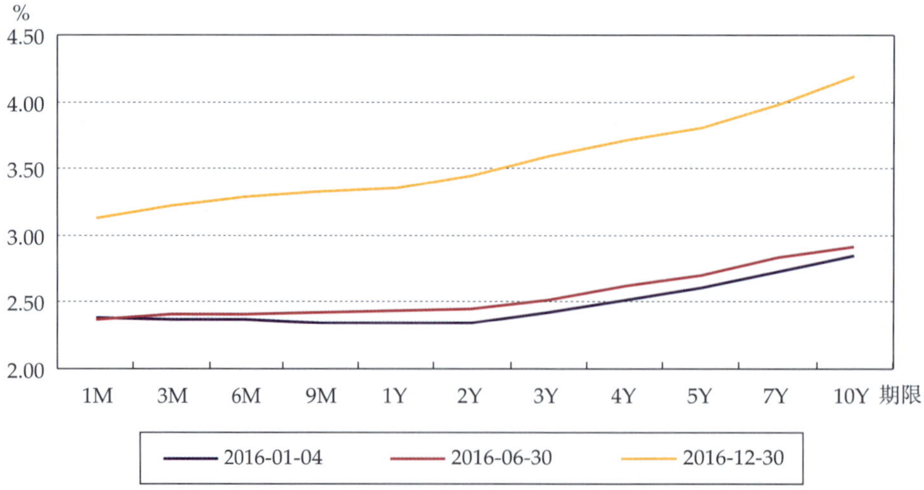

数据来源：中国外汇交易中心。

图8-4　IRS-FR007收盘曲线走势图

在此期间，1年期FR007利率互换收盘曲线利率最高升至3.52%，年末为3.35%，较年初上升101个基点；5年期Shibor3M利率互换收盘曲线利率最高升至4.51%，年末为4.40%，较年初上升114个基点。

4. 利率互换集中清算成为主要清算方式

2016年上海清算所人民币利率互换强制集中清算业务良好运转，利率估值服务平稳运行。全年清算共计8.72万笔，名义本金总计9.82万亿元，占同期所有交易金额的99.0%，集中清算已稳定成为普通利率互换的主要清算方式。

上海清算所继续深化人民币利率互换分层清算会员体系建设，截至12月底，共有122家业务参与者，同比增加27家；全部参与者包括5家综合清算会员、42家普通清算会员、75家代理客户。分层清算会员体系建设与参与者类型、数量的扩充二者相互促进，形成良性循环。

（三）市场创新

1. 利率互换市场投资者类型进一步丰富

2016年，利率互换市场的参与者规模继续增长，投资者结构更加多元化。一是开放非法人产品进入利率互换市场取得积极进展。全年共有58只非法人产品完成入市备案，包括公募基金专户、私募基金、银行理财产品、证券公司资管计划以及保险资管计划等类型。二是7月27日，新开发银行达成人民币利率互换交易，成为首家完成银行间市场人民币利率互换交易的国际金融组织。不同类型的投资者交易目的不同、交易策略多样，有利于利率互换市场活跃度的进一步提高，更好地发挥利率互换市场价格发现、风险管理等功能。

2. 中国（上海）自由贸易试验区达成首笔利率互换交易

2016年4月8日，兴业银行资金中心与星展银行通过全国银行间同业拆借中心国际金融资产交易平台达成自贸区首笔利率互换交易（NDIRS）。该笔交易以FR007为浮动端参考利率，名义本金1亿元人民币，采用双边清算方式，每期交割金额以美元支付。NDIRS交易与在岸IRS主要有以下差别：一是交割币种，NDIRS由双方机构协商确定交割币种，一般以美元为主；二是清算方式，NDIRS目前主要采用双边清算方式，在岸普通IRS已基本实现集中清算；三是参与机构，NDIRS参与机构主要为香港地区机构，客盘以香港及海外对冲基金为主。目前，FT账户NDIRS的交易机构是所有获得FT牌照且为人民币利率互换市场成员的机构。首笔自贸区利率互换交易的达成，是上海自贸区金融创新的又一重要突破，也为日后境外机构参与人民币利率互换业务提供了有益经验。

二、人民币信用衍生品市场

（一）人民币信用衍生品市场运行情况

银行间市场信用风险缓释工具（Credit Risk Mitigation，CRM）产品包括信用风险缓释合约（Credit Risk Mitigation Agreement，CRMA)和信用违约互换（Credit Default Swap，CDS）两个合约类产品，以及信用风险缓释凭证（Credit Risk Mitigation Warrant，CRMW）和信用联结票据（Credit-Linked Notes，CLN）两个凭证类产品，其中，CRMA和CRMW为盯住参考债项的产品，CDS和CLN为盯住参考实体的产品。2016年10月31日，工商银行、农业银行、中国银行、建设银行、交通银行、民生银行、兴业银行、浙商银行、上海银行、中债信用增进10家机构开展了银行间市场首批CDS交易。截至2016年底，银行间市场共开展CDS交易19笔，合计名义本金3.7亿元。交易参考实体涉及石油天然气、电力、水务、煤炭、电信、食品、航空等行业。交易期限以短期限为主，其中，1年及以下的交易17笔，1年至2年的交易2笔。2016年，银行间市场共创设CRMW产品1只，名义本金8亿元，是由中信建投证券创设的首单将不良资产ABS优先档证券作为参考债务的CRMW产品。

各类市场参与者按照新的规则指引的要求，向交易商协会备案相关资质。截至2016年底，共有17家CRM核心交易商、7家一般交易商、11家CRMW创设机构和11家CLN创设机构完成相关备案工作。

（二）修订信用风险缓释工具业务规则

为进一步发挥金融对实体经济的支持作用，丰富市场参与者风险管理手段，完善市场信用风险分散、分担机制，交易商协会组织市场专家，按照“推产品、降门槛、简流程、调框架”的工作思路，分别在丰富CRM产品种类、优化参与者层级结构、简化凭证类产品创设流程、调整相关制度文件框架等方面对原有CRM相关制度进行了调整。经中国人民银行备案同意后，交易商协会于2016年9月23日正式发布修订后的《银行间市场信用风险缓释工具试点业务规则》（以下简称《业务规则》）及相关产品指引，还同步发布《中国场外信用衍生产品交易基本术语与适用规则（2016年版）》。此次CRM创新进一步满足了市场参与者主动管理信用风险的需求，有助于促进债券市场发展，充分发挥金融衍生品服务实体经济的作用。

1. 在原有的CRMA、CRMW两类产品的基础上，同时推出CDS和CLN两项新的CRM产品

CDS是盯住参考实体债券、贷款等债务的信用风险，由卖方为买方提供风险损失保护的双边合约；CLN是附有现金担保的CDS产品，投资者购买CLN，在未发生信用事件时取得本金的利息和CDS保费的双重收益，在发生信用事件时用认购的本金向发行主体进行担保赔付。

2. 在控制风险的前提下，放宽市场进入门槛

《业务规则》将原有CRM参与者的资质门槛要求调整为核心交易商和一般交易商两类，核心交易商包括金融机构、合格信用增进机构等。一般交易商包括非法人产品和其他非金融机构等。核心交易商可与所有参与者进行CRM交易，一般交易商只能与核心交易商进行CRM交易。

3. 保留凭证类产品的资质要求，同时简化创设流程

《业务规则》对于CRMW和CLN等凭证类CRM产品，保留原有的创设机构资质要求，同时简化创设流程，由创设机构自主创设产品，交易商协会对创设产品的披露信息进行形式审核后，由投资者自行认购并在二级市场交易流通。

4. 建立CRM业务管理“大规则+子指引”的伞形框架

修订后的《银行间市场信用风险缓释工具试点业务规则》，将原“指引”名称修订为“规则”，沿用原指引的章节设置，明确CRM业务大的管理框架，再以CRMA、CRMW、CDS和CLN等每个产品发布子指引的方式明确具体产品的规则要求。

三、人民币汇率衍生品市场

（一）人民币汇率衍生品市场运行情况

2016 年，银行间人民币汇率衍生品市场交投活跃。全年银行间人民币汇率衍生品累计成交10.92万亿美元，同比增长25.7%。其中，人民币外汇远期累计成交 1 529.03亿美元，同比增长 3.1倍；人民币外汇掉期累计成交10.00万亿美元，同比增长19.8%；人民币外汇期权累计成交7 470.85亿美元，同比增长1.6倍。

2016年，人民币汇率衍生品中央对手清算量大幅增加，达到3.79万亿美元。其中，人民币外汇和货币掉期清算量为3.65万亿美元，占银行间市场外汇和货币掉期交易量的36.4%，比上年提升了11.3个百分点；人民币外汇远期清算量为1 038.83亿美元，占银行间市场外汇远期交易量的67.9%，比上年提升了27.5个百分点。

2016年，人民币汇率衍生品市场会员进一步扩大。其中，人民币外汇远期会员154家（其中中央对手清算参与者29家），人民币外汇掉期会员154家（其中中央对手清算参与者29家），人民币外汇货币掉期会员127家，人民币外汇期权会员87家（8月上海清算所开展场外外汇期权业务后，新增外汇期权中央对手清算参与者20家）。

（二）人民币汇率衍生品市场运行的特点

1. 汇率衍生品成交增速继续领先即期交易

2016年银行间外汇市场人民币汇率衍生品市场成交10.92万亿美元，同比增长25.7%。人民币外汇即期市场成交5.93万亿美元，同比增长21.9%。自2009年以来，人民币汇率衍生品市场增幅始终快于即期交易，汇率衍生品占比进一步上升。2016年，人民币汇率衍生品成交在整个银行间外汇市场中的占比（不含外币拆借）从上年的63.9%提升至64.6%，连续八年增长，该比例已非常接近国际清算银行发布的国际外汇市场即期与衍生品市场的基本格局33：67。

2. 外汇远期交易量呈现爆发式增长

2016年，银行间市场人民币外汇远期交易量为1 529.03亿美元，同比增长311%。其

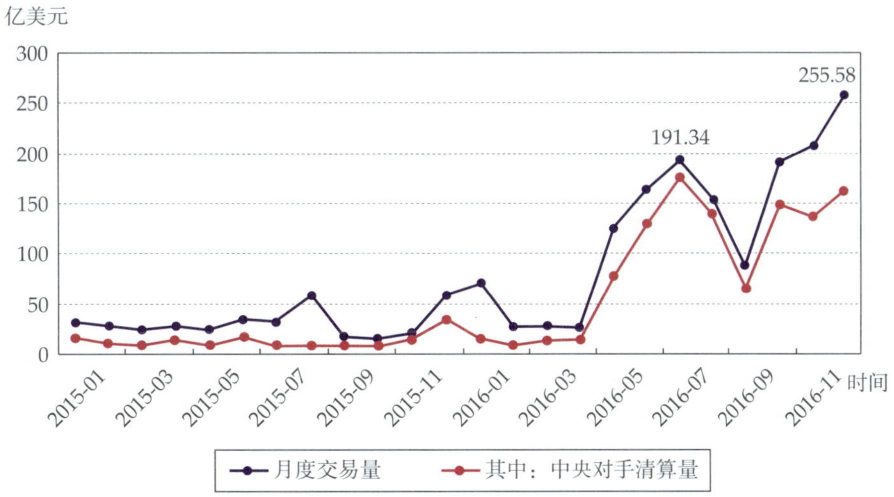

数据来源：国家外汇管理局、上海清算所。

图8-5　2015—2016年银行间市场外汇远期衍生品交易量

中中央对手清算量为1 038.83亿美元，同比增长627%。特别是2016年5月后，外汇远期交易量由月均不足40亿美元跃升至月均逾160亿美元。

3. 远期外汇市场价格波动较大

受本外币利差、外汇供求、市场预期等因素影响，2016年境内外远期市场价格呈现震荡走势。年初市场看空人民币预期、外币债务去杠杆等因素刺激企业大量远期净购汇，推动人民币远期汇率走弱。此后，随着人民币汇率预期趋稳，企业远期净购汇大幅回落，加之本外币利差逐步收窄，人民币远期汇率明显回升，但下半年以来再度走弱。2016年，境内可交割、境外可交割和境外无本金交割远期市场1年期人民币兑美元汇率累计分别下跌5.6%、6.6%和6.9%。

（三）市场创新与制度建设

1. 推出人民币外汇远期标准化交易C-Forward

继2015年推出标准化人民币外汇掉期交易C-Swap之后，2016年5月，银行间外汇市场推出了人民币外汇远期标准化交易C-Forward。C-Forward是在双边授信额度内，按照价格优先、时间优先的原则进行订单自动化匹配和点击成交，与既有的OTC询价交易模式互利互补。一方面，C-Forward降低了参与者风险管理压力、操作风险，保证了市场交易效率和透明度；另一方面，由于交易系统、成交数据流、交易确认、清算路径等都和原来保持一致，C-Forward不会增加市场会员的交易成本。2016年全年远期交易量为1 572亿美元，同比增长近三倍，C-Forward在其中的份额接近60%。与此同时，2016年C-Swap继续保持稳步增长，全年通过C-Swap成交的掉期交易量为4.6万亿美元，占掉期市场总成交量的46%。

2. 推出人民币外汇期权组合产品

2016年，银行间外汇市场在现有期权业务的基础上，推出6个期权组合产品，分别是看涨期权价差组合、看跌期权价差组合、风险逆转期权组合、跨式期权组合、异价跨式期权组合和蝶式期权组合。期权组合交易业务的推出大大丰富了银行间外汇期权市场交易种类，提供了更多的风险管理手段和交易模式，有利于银行更好地实现自身交易策略，符合国际市场发展趋势。期权组合业务自上线以来便得到广泛应用，组合交易在期权活跃会员中的普及率达到100%。2016年，期权组合交易量约4 653.8亿美元，占期权市场总成交量的62%。

3. 将人民币外汇期权交易纳入中央对手清算业务

2016年8月15日，上海清算所将期限在1年以内（含）的美元对人民币普通欧式期权交易纳入中央对手清算业务，成为全球首家为场外市场外汇期权交易提供中央对手清算服务的清算机构，也是我国金融创新又一个重要里程碑。

四、外币对衍生品市场

2016年，外币对衍生品市场共交易354.94亿美元，同比下降27.0%。其中，外币对掉期交易是外币对衍生品市场中的主力品种，全年该品种成交311.65亿美元，同比下降28%。外币对远期成交43.29亿美元，同比下降15.1%。

从交易币种来看，EUR/USD、USD/JPY、USD/CHF为交易最活跃的币种，分别成交128亿美元、79.6亿美元和63.4亿美元，三者合计在外币对衍生品交易中占比76%。其中，USD/CHF衍生品交易量比上年增长了4倍。

五、场外大宗商品衍生品市场

（一）场外大宗商品衍生品市场运行情况

2016年，场外大宗商品衍生品市场创新推出了人民币电解铜掉期（以下简称CUS）[①]一只新产品，上海碳配额远期（以下简称SHEAF）也于11月投入试运行，并于2017年1月12日正式上线。至此，场外衍生品市场已实现了对能源、化工、黑色金属、有色金属、航运和碳金融六大行业的覆盖，产品数量增加到了14只。

在供给侧改革、英国“脱欧”、美联储加息、美国大选等国内外大事件的叠加作用下，经济基本面的不确定性大大增加，2016年场外大宗商品衍生品清算业务继续保持高速增长。全年场外大宗商品衍生品清算金额累计达到2 888.85亿元，较上年增长328.4%；清算合约数（按月拆、单边）达到426.59万张，较上年增长133.5%。分月份来看，1~6月的清算金额达到567.16亿元，7~12月的清算金额达到2 321.70亿元，下半年的清算金额较上半年有309.4%的增长。市场参与客户数继续稳步上升，12月末达到482家，较上年新增97家。

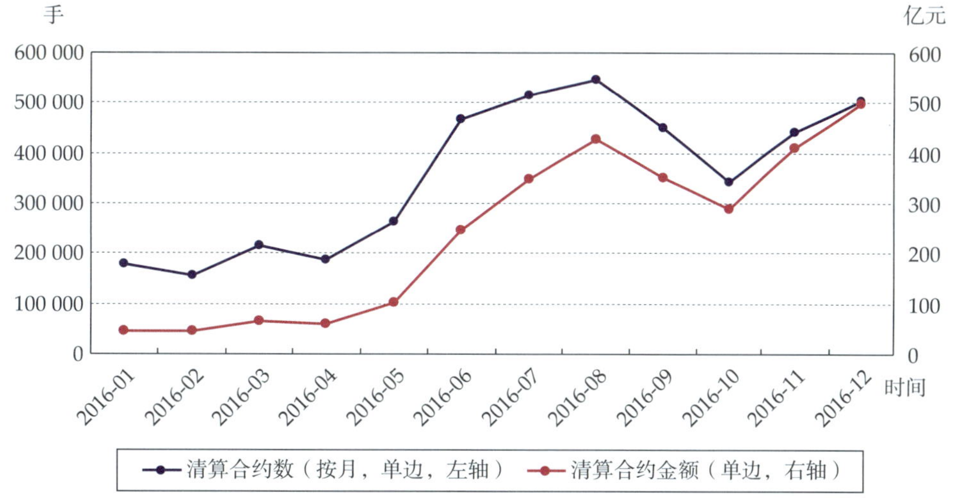

数据来源：上海清算所。

图8-6　2016年场外大宗商品衍生品市场总体情况

① 产品名称：人民币FFA：人民币远期运费协议；CIS：人民币铁矿石掉期；CSS：人民币动力煤掉期；FCP：自贸区铜溢价掉期；CSM：人民币苯乙烯掉期；FMEG：自贸区乙二醇进口掉期；CS：人民币集装箱掉期；CFFA：中国沿海煤炭远期运费协议；CUS：人民币电解铜掉期。

（二）场外大宗商品衍生品市场运行的特点

1. 航运类金融衍生品触底反弹

目前上海清算所已推出了三个航运类金融衍生品，分别是人民币FFA、CS和CFFA。近年来国际航运市场持续低迷，波罗的海干散货指数于2015年触底反弹，2016年有所回升，但仍处于低位。受此影响，2016年航运类金融衍生品业务量有所回升，清算金额为3.92亿元，同比增长112.5%。

2. 供给侧改革推动能源类金融衍生品需求大涨

2016年全年，在供给侧改革的大背景下，动力煤价格大幅上涨，CSS对应的基础资产——环渤海动力煤（Q5500K）价格指数于2016年初达到2013年来的最低点，2016年一路上扬，尤其是下半年实现大幅增长，年末较年初价格上涨近60%。动力煤场外衍生品市

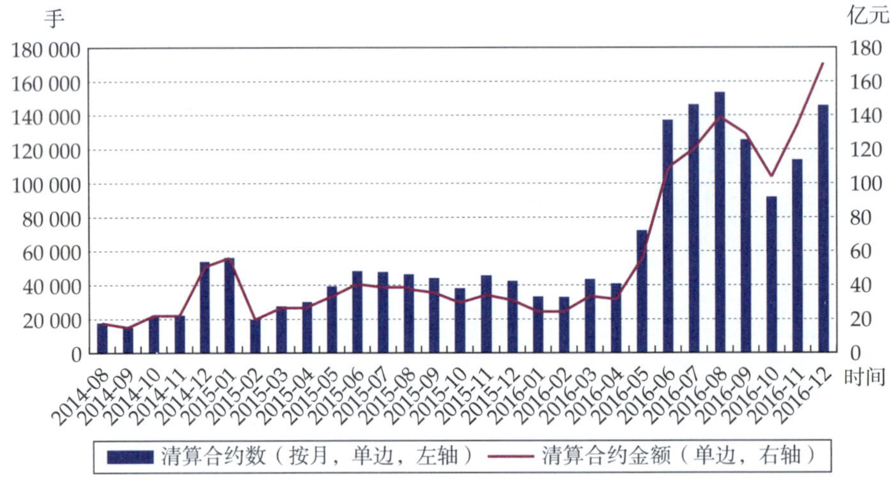

数据来源：上海清算所。

图8-7　CSS上市以来运行情况

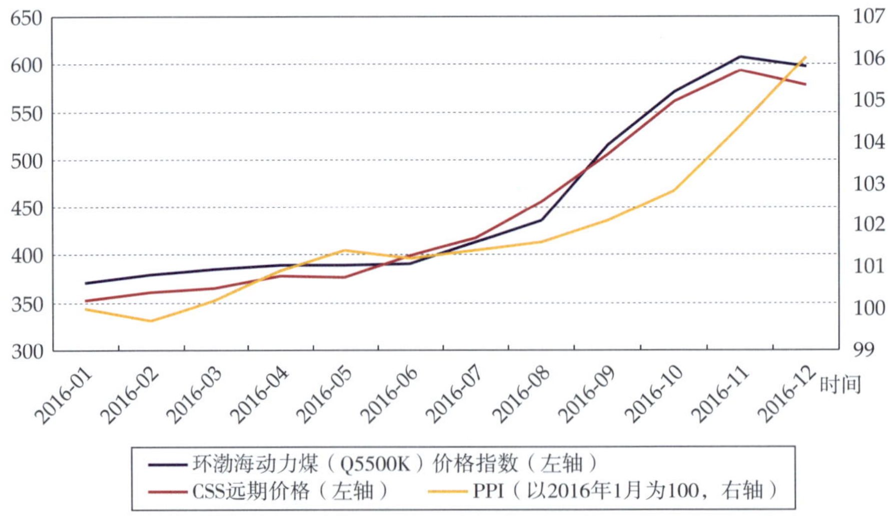

数据来源：上海清算所、Wind资讯。

图8-8　动力煤现货、衍生品价格及PPI变化

场呈现量价齐升的格局。1~12月，CSS清算总额达到1 702.10亿元，同比增长164.2%。从价格上看，CSS合约价格与现货价格指数保持良好的联动。

3. 中美政策影响工业金属类金融衍生品走势

2016年11月因特朗普当选后提出万亿美元基建计划，全球大宗商品价格普涨。1~10月铜现货价格震荡上行，11月、12月两个月铜价上涨幅度超过10%。2016年7月，上海清算所创新推出了全价铜金融衍生品CUS。该产品的适时上线为相关企业提供了有效对冲铜现货价格波动的风险管理工具，丰富了铜衍生品种类的多样性，是对场内铜期货产品的有力补充。CUS自推出到12月末清算金额达到778.27亿元。2015年推出的铜溢价产品FCP受到美元升值的影响，全年清算总额达到21.2亿元，同比减少12.0%。

2016年下半年，去产能带动焦煤、焦炭价格上涨，钢厂对高品矿石需求猛增，62%

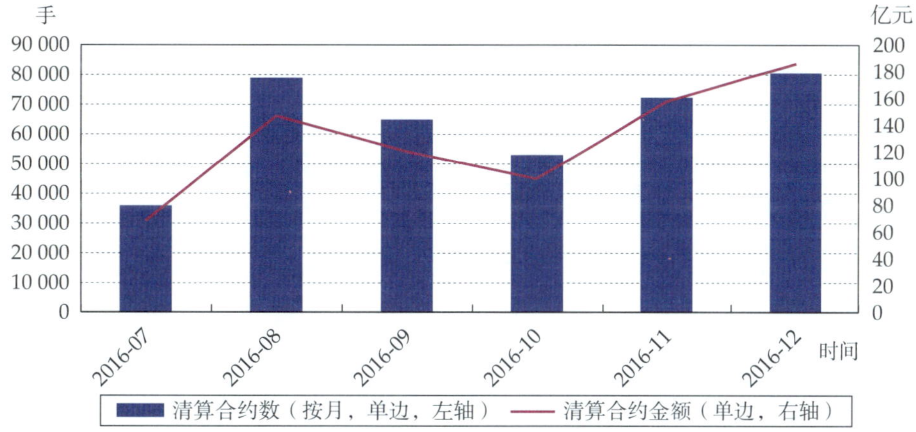

数据来源：上海清算所。

图8-9 CUS上市以来运行情况

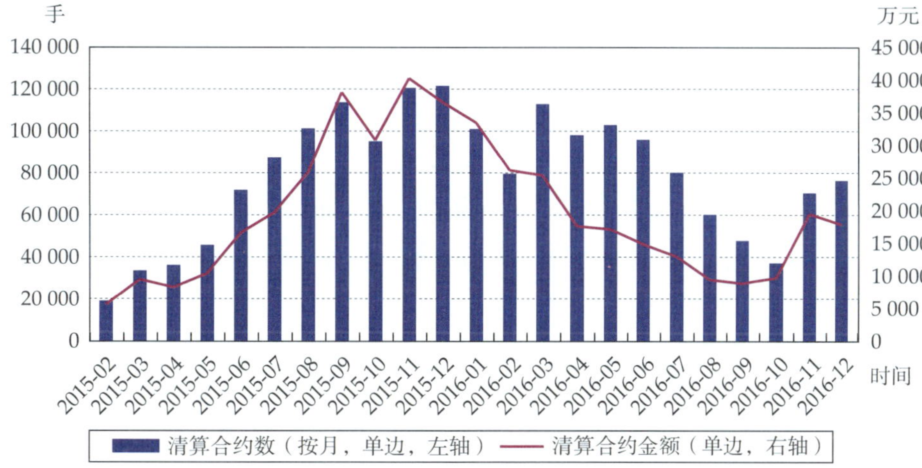

数据来源：上海清算所。

图8-10 FCP上市以来运行情况

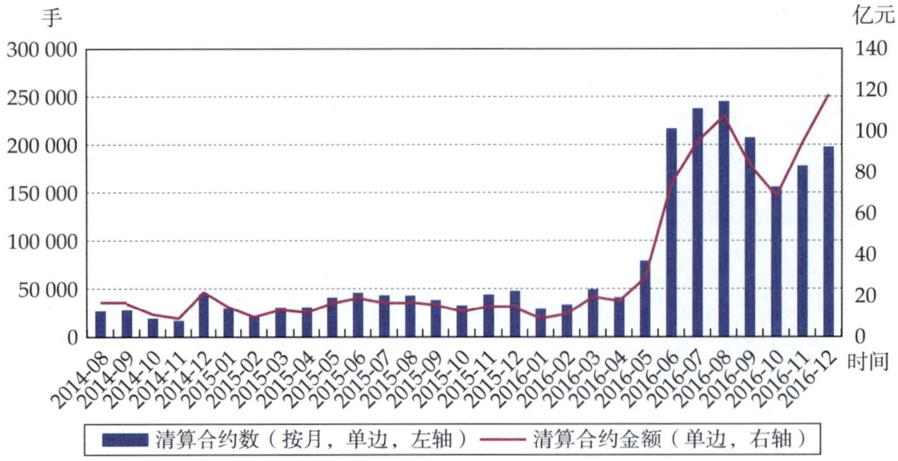

数据来源：上海清算所。

图8-11 CIS上市以来运行情况

品位以上铁矿石现货价格大幅上涨，对高品位铁矿石衍生品需求也大幅增加，铁矿石掉期CIS清算量总额达到727.49亿元，同比增长314.0%。

4. 化工类金融衍生品清算额稳步上升

上海清算所目前推出了两只化工类金融衍生品——人民币苯乙烯掉期（CSM）和自贸区乙二醇进口掉期（FMEG）。苯乙烯和乙二醇均为塑料制品行业的重要原料。与能源行业和工业金属行业不同，塑料制品行业不是2016年去产能的重点，因此受此政策影响相对较小，受原油价格传导影响较大。2016年全年CSM与FMEG的价格走势与原油价格类似，呈震荡上行的趋势，尤其是11月底OPEC限产协议达成后，价格出现了大幅上扬。2016年，CSM清算金额同比增加353.1%，FMEG清算金额同比增加124.7%。

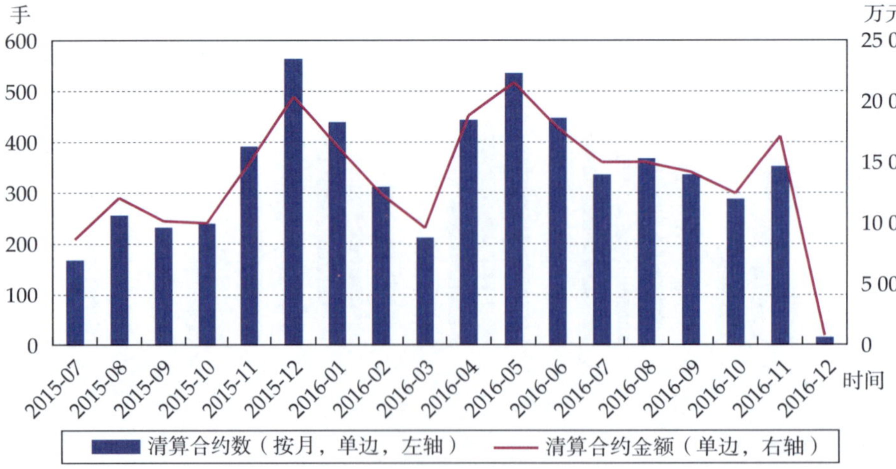

数据来源：上海清算所。

图8-12 FMEG上市以来运行情况

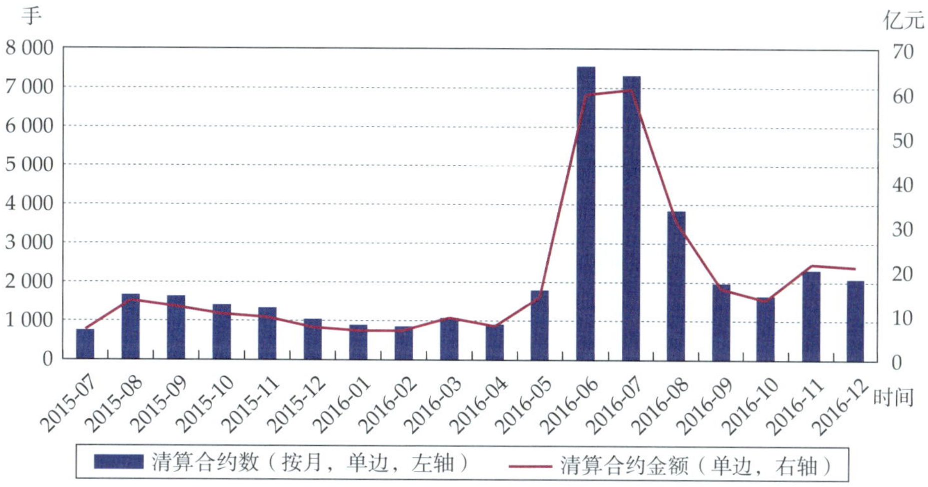

数据来源：上海清算所。

图8-13　CSM上市以来运行情况

（三）碳金融衍生品中央对手清算业务将推出

2016年，中国人民银行联合相关部委发布了《关于构建绿色金融体系的指导意见》，旨在构建完整的绿色金融政策体系和多层次的绿色金融市场体系。在中国人民银行的指导下，上海清算所认真研究推动建立碳排放市场统一的清算和托管体制，深入研究碳交易金融衍生产品的创新和风险控制，围绕人民币碳排放金融衍生品开展中央对手清算业务的研发工作，并拟于2017年初正式推出上海碳配额远期交易中央对手清算业务。该业务的成功推出不仅可以弥补我国绿色金融的市场空白，满足实体经济多样化需求，也将进一步推动绿色发展理念的落实及碳排放交易市场的创新和发展。

六、金融衍生品市场发展展望

（一）产品创新和市场建设将加大推进力度

2017年，衍生品市场产品创新力度将继续加大，现有产品序列将得以完善，市场机构开展风险对冲操作将更为便利。研究推出利率互换期权、利率上下限期权以及长期限的利率互换合约品种。同时将继续标准化人民币外汇期权、集中清算的标准利率互换等业务的可行性研究。市场建设方面，不断优化包括X-Swap在内的电子交易平台功能和交易机制，双边匿名撮合交易模式在银行间外汇衍生品市场的应用将进一步开展。进一步健全外汇衍生品市场的基准价格体系，根据市场需要适时引入部分期权交易活跃的人民币外汇远期掉期做市商对期权关键期限波动率进行报价，进一步构建期权市场统一定价机制。

（二）市场风险管理和法制建设将更加凸显

2017年，将继续推动培育场外金融衍生品市场的发展环境，不断优化金融衍生品市场的制度建设、风险防范机制建设和法制建设。一是研究构建人民币利率衍生品监管框架。二是进一步完善包括各类场外金融衍生品在内的监测机制，加强自律管理，并要求强化，有效防范风险。三是进一步加强投资者培育，随着不同风险承担能力的市场参与者更多地参与金融衍生品市场，投资者类型将进一步优化丰富。市场法制建设方面，将场外金融衍生品市场法律制度建设放在更为重要的位置，进一步推动解决终止净额结算等机制安排的法律不确定性问题，继续推广和应用履约保障机制，进一步降低金融机构对非法人产品授信难度，进一步优化市场参与者风险管理成本。

（三）支持实体经济作用将得到充分发挥

一是随着人民币汇率、利率市场化改革进程稳步推进，实体企业对汇率风险和利率风险的避险需求将不断提高，场外金融衍生工具主动管理和分散风险的重要作用将进一步显现。二是随着我国信用债市场规模逐渐扩大和信用风险事件增加，市场参与者将更多地运用信用衍生品来提高主动管理信用风险的水平，信用衍生品市场的深入发展将进一步完善债务市场信用定价机制，促进债券市场健康稳健发展。金融衍生品市场进一步满足参与主体经济业务发展、风险管理需求的功能将充分发挥，以实现场外金融衍生品市场服务实体经济的目的。

专题八　场外金融衍生品履约保障机制

一、我国场外金融衍生产品市场履约保障机制现状

在国际市场上，运用较为广泛的履约保障机制是国际互换与衍生工具协会（ISDA）于1994年推出的《信用支持附件》（CSA）。CSA具有灵活性，并且明确了风险敞口管理和对风险敞口的估值，通常境外机构普遍使用最大潜在风险敞口（Maximum Potential Exposure，MPE）来确定交易对手方的可交易的规模以及风险暴露规模，并且普遍参考三大评级机构的评级对担保品进行估值，为担保品和保证金收取留出了灵活空间。我国场外金融衍生产品市场的履约保障机制包括履约保障文件和主体授信两种方式。2009年，在中国人民银行的统一部署下，交易商协会发布了《中国银行间市场金融衍生产品交易主协议》，并配套发布了《中国银行间市场金融衍生产品交易质押式履约保障文件》和《中国银行间市场金融衍生产品交易转让式履约保障文件》。前期，银行间市场开展场外金融衍生产品交易的机构以银行等金融机构为主，主体信用情况较好，履约保障机制以主体授信为主。近年来，随着非法人产品入市开展交易，金融机构对非法人产品授信面临较大困难，推广应用履约保障文件迎来良好的契机。

二、履约保障机制的原理和估值类型

（一）机制原理

履约保障协议本质上是建立在一揽子被交易的金融衍生产品之上的用于管理风险敞口的资产组合。当被交易的金融衍生产品发生价值变动或者交易方发生违约时，履约担保品就可能进入处置或交易环节。其中被交易的产品受到金融衍生产品交易主协议、补充协议、交易确认书等法律文件的管辖制约，而履约担保品则受到履约保障文件的管辖制约。

因此，对于履约担保品组合管理，实际上是对一揽子资产或者金融衍生产品进行组合管理。而履约保障文件则是履约担保品相应的交易协议，管理的内容至少包括估值、现金流、账户管理、权责、法律管辖等。由于市场参与者的复杂性，通常履约担保品也会存在较大的差异性，因此履约担保品管理的核心内容就是对履约担保品组合的价值和价值波动进行估值。现金、国债等高流动性和价值稳定的担保品的估值较为简单，而公司信用类债券做担保品的估值则相对复杂。同时履约保障协议对于应当收取多少履约担保品还会和对手方的信用等级高度相关。

（二）估值类型

履约担保品的估值通常有市场法和模型法。市场法即以担保品的市场价格作为担保品的价值，然后按照其价格的预期波动情况赋予一定折扣率，最后得到担保品可以担保的交易敞口额度和交易规模额度。模型法则是利用理论模型对担保品的价值和预期波动范围进行估计。模型法存在模型参数选取的随意性，不同参与方对模型理解存在差异而会选取不同的模型对同一担保品估值，且模型的维护成本非常高，因此模型法的操作性相对较差。并且

市场法得到的担保品价值更容易保证透明公正，通常更加容易获得各方广泛认可。但是在极端风险条件下，例如金融危机期间，恐慌情绪和市场挤兑会对价格造成非正常的不利影响，而在金融膨胀时，则会加剧金融泡沫的增长。因此在2008年全球金融金融危机后，学术界、监管者和市场进行了广泛的讨论，模型法也开始重新被广泛使用。例如在2009年之后，美联储开始使用模型法估值对银行的资本充足率进行压力测试。

在实际交易中，由于经营范围、监管等原因，许多机构通过关联公司开展金融衍生产品交易，出现交易主体的资产规模实际比需求主体的资产规模小，难以开展足够额度交易的问题。因此，允许母公司、第三方进行履约担保对交易正常开展至关重要，需要在现有履约保障机制中增加第三方作为履约担保方的设定。

三、履约保障机制未来展望

（一）推广应用履约保障文件

推广应用履约保障文件有助于降低市场参与者交易成本。多数场外金融衍生品交易都依赖于双方信用，或者双方单独拟定的履约保障文件，这可能增加双方的谈判成本和法律风险。履约保障文件对风险敞口和收付金额的计算方式作了标准化定义，可帮助机构实现有效的担保品估值和管理，降低成本，提高效率。此外，推广应用履约保障文件还有助于金融管理部门实现宏观审慎监管，掌握市场整体风险，实现风险的准确评估和定位，为制定相关政策提供支持。

（二）扩大履约担保品范围

目前履约担保品多用现金或者高等级债券，一方面是其价值稳定，另一方面是市场对价值或者价值的波动有比较一致的预期。尤其是有权威的第三方机构对债券质押率划定了标准，债券就成了除现金之外最方便的履约担保品。而参与场外金融衍生产品市场的机构中，许多可能并不持有足够的债券做担保品，或者难以参与到债券市场中。因此，能对其他类别的可作为担保品的资产进行标准化就对建设灵活高效的履约保障机制非常重要。

（三）推动履约担保品估值的标准化

履约担保品的估值存在市场法和模型法两种估值方式。市场法对于股票、债券等有集中交易市场的担保品起到有效估值的作用。但是对于没有集中交易市场，或者流动性比较差的担保品，则需要采用模型法进行估值。而模型估值则存在参数随意性和模型多样性的问题，如果没有统一的标准，就不能实现良好的市场流动，无法提供金融衍生产品交易过程中需要的灵活有效担保。因此，对于模型法估值，需要考虑由监管机构或权威的第三方机构提供一套合理的基准供市场参考使用。

专题九 外汇期权的中央对手清算

2016年8月15日，经国家外汇管理局批准，外汇期权中央对手清算业务在上海清算所正式开展，上海清算所成为全球第一个向场外市场外汇期权交易提供中央对手清算服务的机构。这是中国金融市场体制改革和业务创新的又一个具有国际影响的里程碑。外汇期权产品是银行间市场继即期、远期、掉期之后第四类纳入中央对手清算的外汇产品，将外汇期权纳入中央对手清算业务有利于进一步完善银行间外汇市场的清算体系，实现外汇市场系统性风险防范覆盖所有活跃交易品种。2016年，纳入中央对手清算的外汇期权共1 299笔，清算金额434.64亿美元，发展外汇期权清算会员20家。

一、业务基本情况

外汇期权的中央对手清算业务，是指清算参与者之间达成的符合一定条件的外汇期权交易，提交至上海清算所并通过相应的合规和风控检查后，由中央对手方进行合约替代，对期权交易进行存续期管理，并对期权费以及期权行权生成的交易或现金流进行轧差和担保交收的业务。

（一）产品要素

1.交易货币对：美元/人民币（USD/CNY）。

2.期权类型：普通欧式期权。

3.期权费类型：基点（Pips）。

4.关键时间节点：期权合约的近端结算日为T+2日，远端结算日为T+F日（F≤1Y+2，即一年以内），期权费交割日为T+2日，期权到期日不限（其中，T日表示交易日）。

5.保证金：期权清算相关的变动保证金包括超限保证金、盯市保证金和特殊保证金。超限保证金指会员因超过风险敞口限额而产生的保证金。期权盯市实施双向盯市制度，盯市损益金额的结算币种为人民币。特殊保证金指特殊事件触发的保证金，特殊事件包括外汇市场汇率异常波动、连续假期和会员违约三类。

（二）交易、交割方式

外汇期权通过中国外汇交易中心外汇交易系统交易，采用由做市商向系统发送各货币对的买卖报价，系统自动筛选其最优买卖报价并向市场发布，会员自行选择有授信关系的对手方进行询价的询价交易模式。这种交易方式支持期权及即期、远期、掉期交易，适合多种类型客户，并方便跨品种操作。

外汇期权通过外汇交易系统达成交易后，合约信息传送至上海清算所，由上海清算所作为中央对手方对期权合约进行合约替代、担保交收及后续清算。上海清算所对同一会员的外汇期权的期权费与期权差额行权生成的人民币现金流合并轧差，外汇即期、远期和掉期交易与期权全额行权生成的即期交易合并轧差。目前外汇期权实行全额交割制度，待后期条件成熟后推出差额交割。

二、业务研发过程

自2011年银行间市场推出外汇期权交易以来，上海清算所高度重视期权清算业务的研究。为满足市场需求，上海清算所组织完成了大量工作。从产品设计到试运行、正式交易，上海清算所开展了多方面工作保障期权清算业务的顺利、平稳、安全运行和快速、健康发展。

市场建设方面，上海清算所开展十余轮市场调研并召开研讨会，就外汇期权清算的业务方案征询市场机构意见。产品设计完成后，上海清算所组织完成会员单位清算业务相关人员的业务培训，并与首批申请外汇期权清算会员单位完成系统联调测试。

制度建设方面，在国家外汇管理局的指导和批准下，上海清算所完成外汇中央对手清算业务规则和指南的修订，为外汇期权中央对手清算夯实了制度基础。此外，上海清算所邀请参与外汇期权交易的市场机构进行历时3个多月的风险管理模型验证，分三个阶段分别对波动率曲面的构建方法、报价数据的处理方法和交易估值及希腊字母的计算结果等处理方法进行验证，确保外汇期权的估值准确。

系统平台建设方面，上海清算所与中国外汇交易中心密切合作，历时10个月完成了内部的系统开发和改造工作。在中国外汇交易中心的大力支持下，上海清算所完成了外汇期权交易提交清算的接口开发，实现了外汇期权交易、清算前后台电子化直通式处理。双方适时开展了市场联调测试，提高了市场机构参与交易和中央对手清算的可行性、安全性及效率。

外汇期权中央对手清算业务开展后，上海清算所严格按照《金融市场基础设施原则》的要求，保障外汇中央对手清算业务的平稳运行，并持续提升清算服务水平：一是对外汇清算业务参与者的风险敞口进行实时监控，定期对风险模型进行回归测试和压力测试，保证业务平稳运行；二是根据市场需求，继续研究拓展清算产品品种、期限，如外汇期权组合交易等；三是大力发展外汇代理清算业务，扩大清算参与者范围，为金融市场对外开放和人民币国际化做好基础设施服务工作。

三、运行概况

截至2016年底，14家清算会员共计提

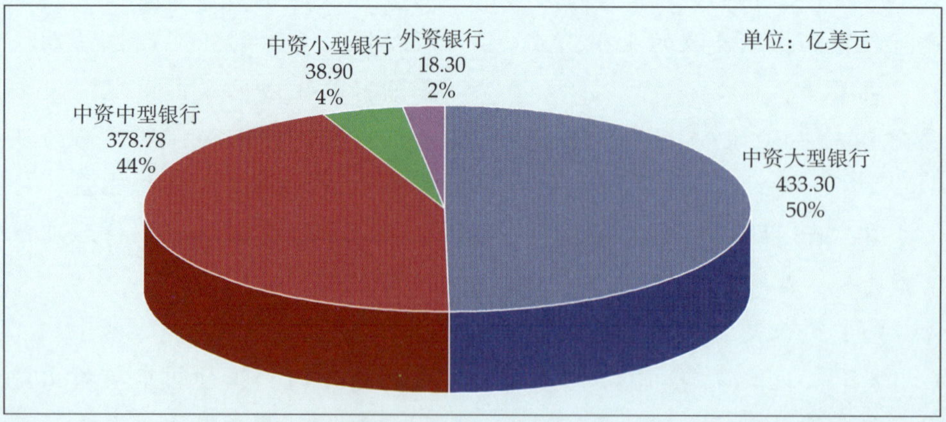

数据来源：上海清算所。

图8-14 外汇期权中央对手清算业务参与者分布

交1 299笔外汇期权交易纳入中央对手清算，合计清算金额434.64亿美元。中资银行贡献了清算量的98%，其中工商银行和平安银行参与活跃度最高。

从纳入中央对手清算的外汇期权交易期限来看，以一周及以内的交易（特别是期限为一周的）为主，清算金额占比达62%，其中，期限为一周的金额占比36%。期限为一周以上一月以下及一月以上一年以下的清算金额各占总清算金额的18%和20%。与纳入中央对手清算的外汇远期及掉期交易的期限比较，外汇期权长期限合约比例明显提升，体现了外汇期权产品在长期限风险对冲中的成本效率优势。

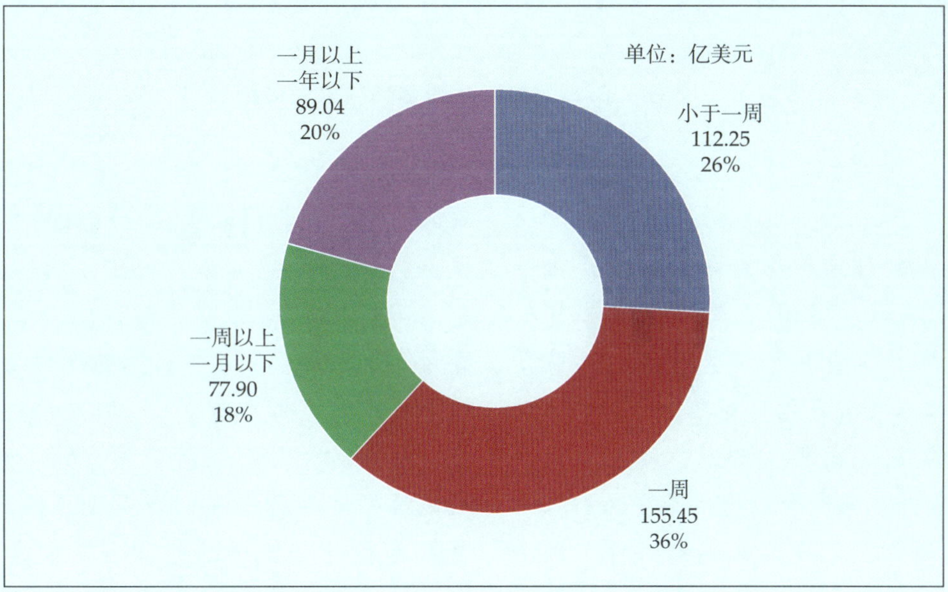

数据来源：上海清算所。

图8-15　外汇期权中央对手清算业务合约期限分布

从合约价格来看，不同期限的合约价格能够反映期限越长合约价值越高的欧式期权价值特征。而从期限相近的合约价格比较而言，存在1D-1W、2W-3W、1M-3M、6M-9M、1Y五级价格台阶。同台阶的合约价格相近，其合约价格有受合约流动性制约的迹象，可能存在套利空间，表明中央对手清算场外期权业务规模仍有很大的增长潜力。

四、市场意义

外汇期权纳入中央对手清算业务具有多方面的重要意义：

一是全球首家推出场外外汇期权中央对手清算业务，标志着中国的金融市场基础设施建设迈入国际领先行列。

二是顺应国际场外衍生品清算发展趋势，提高衍生品的透明度，保障银行间外汇市场健康发展。

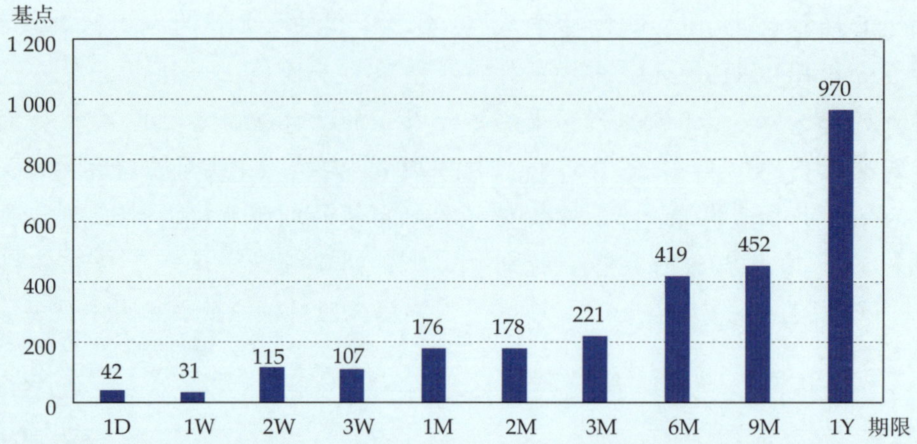

数据来源：上海清算所。

图8-16　纳入中央对手清算业务的外汇期权价格

2008年全球金融危机以后，各国监管机构开始认识到对场外衍生品的监管严重不足。二十国集团（G20）2009年在匹兹堡峰会提出将实施中央对手清算作为场外金融衍生品市场监管改革的目标之一。

目前，美国、欧盟、日本、印度等大多数G20国家针对场外金融衍生品交易引入强制清算机制作出了规定或规划。外汇期权、货币掉期、无本金交割远期（NDF）等场外外汇衍生品被明确纳入强制清算范围。

此次将外汇期权纳入中央对手清算业务，是继2014年11月推出外汇询价中央对手清算业务后的又一重大创新里程碑，顺应了国际场外衍生品清算市场的发展趋势。

三是有效降低清算参与者成本。外汇期权交易与外汇即期、远期、掉期交易合并计算风险敞口，实现风险对冲，还能根据相关监管要求按照合格中央对手方作为交易对手计提风险资本要求，而且能够有效提高保证金使用效率、降低清算参与成本。

四是进一步完善了银行间外汇市场清算体系。目前纳入银行间外汇市场中央对手清算的产品包括涉及12种外币对人民币或外币对的外汇竞价交易，6种外币对人民币的即期询价交易以及期限在1年以内的美元对人民币的远期和掉期询价交易。纳入中央对手清算的期限在1年以内的美元对人民币外汇期权交易，可覆盖银行间市场约95%的人民币外汇期权交易量。

随着人民币国际化进程的加快及汇率形成机制改革的深入，外汇市场的波动性加大，外汇期权越来越受到市场参与者的欢迎，银行间市场人民币外汇期权交易量显著提升。将外汇期权纳入中央对手清算业务有利于进一步完善银行间外汇市场的清算体系，实现外汇市场系统性风险防范覆盖所有活跃交易品种。

附录一　2016年中国金融市场发展大事记

1月，上海黄金交易所发布《上海黄金交易所银行间黄金询价市场做市商管理办法》，会同中国外汇交易中心启动银行间黄金询价市场做市业务。

1月18日，中国人民银行决定，自2016年1月25日起，对境外金融机构在境内金融机构存放执行正常存款准备金率政策。

1月20日，中国人民银行办公厅印发《关于调整境外机构人民币银行结算账户资金使用有关事宜的通知》。

1月29日，中国外汇交易中心发布《关于人民币购售业务境外参加行进入银行间外汇市场有关事项的公告》。

2月4日，国家外汇管理局发布《合格境外机构投资者境内证券投资外汇管理规定》，对合格境外机构投资者（QFII）外汇管理制度进行改革。

2月14日，中国人民银行发布施行《全国银行间债券市场柜台业务管理办法》。

2月17日，中国人民银行发布公告〔2016〕第3号，进一步放开境外机构投资者投资银行间债券市场，引入更多符合条件的境外机构投资者，取消额度限制，简化管理流程。

2月18日，中国人民银行发布公告，决定从即日起正式建立公开市场每日操作常态化机制，根据货币政策调控需要，原则上每个工作日均开展公开市场操作。

2月19日，银行间市场交易商协会正式发布实施2016年版《非金融企业债务融资工具注册发行规则》、《非金融企业债务融资工具公开发行注册工作规程》和《非金融企业债务融资工具公开发行注册文件表格体系》。

2月29日，中国人民银行决定，自2016年3月1日起，普遍下调金融机构人民币存款准备金率0.5个百分点。

3月4日，中国人民银行、民政部、银监会、证监会、保监会联合印发《关于金融支持养老服务业加快发展的指导意见》，大力推动金融组织、产品和服务创新，改进完善养老领域金融服务，支持养老服务业加快发展。

3月7日，中国人民银行与新加坡金管局续签了规模为3 000亿元人民币/640亿新加坡元的双边本币互换协议。

4月19日，"上海金"人民币集中定价交易业务正式启动。

4月26日，中国人民银行、海关总署联合发布公告〔2016〕第9号，自2016年6月1日起，决定开展《中国人民银行黄金及黄金制品进出口准许证》"非一批一证"管理试点工作。

4月27日，中国人民银行发布公告〔2016〕第8号及配套实施细则，明确机构投资者的合格性标准，拓宽投资者范围，优化备案、开户、联网流程，明确依法对相关业务开展进行检查，强调中介机构与自律组织监测与自律管理职责。

4月27日，中国人民银行和银监会共同发布了《关于加强票据业务监管　促进票据市场健康发展的通知》。

4月29日，中国人民银行发布《关于在全国范围内实施全口径跨境融资宏观审慎管理的通知》，决定自2016年5月3日起，将全口径跨境融资宏观审慎管理政策推广至全国范围。

5月9日，上海清算所发布《中国（上海）自由贸易试验区跨境债券业务登记托管、清算结算实施细则》、《上海自贸区跨境债券业务登记托管、清算结算业务指南》，上海清算所开始为上海自贸区跨境人民币债券业务提供登记托管、清算结算服务。

5月11日，中国人民银行与摩洛哥中央银行签署了规模为100亿元人民币/150亿迪拉姆的双边本币互换协议。

5月27日，国家外汇管理局发布《关于境外机构投资者投资银行间债券市场有关外汇管理问题的通知》。

5月27日，中国人民银行、国务院扶贫办、银监会、证监会、保监会等五部门联合印发《关于加强金融精准扶贫信息对接共享工作的指导意见》，推动建立金融扶贫信息与扶贫基础信息对接共享机制，夯实金融精准扶贫工作基础。

6月6日，中国人民银行发布公告〔2016〕第13号，将个人投资人认购大额存单起点金额由不低于30万元调整为不低于20万元。

6月7日，中国人民银行与美国联邦储备委员会签署了在美国建立人民币清算安排的合作备忘录，并给予美国2 500亿元人民币合格境外机构投资者（RQFII）额度。

6月14日，中央国债登记结算有限责任公司发布实施《债券充抵上海国际黄金交易中心交易保证金担保品管理服务指引》。

6月15日起，中国人民银行发布中国国债及其他债券收益率曲线，其中 3 个月期国债收益率是用于计算国际货币基金组织特别提款权（SDR）利率的人民币代表性利率。

6月17日，中国外汇交易中心宣布自6月20日起在银行间外汇市场正式开展人民币对南非兰特直接交易。

6月17日，中国人民银行与塞尔维亚中央银行签署了规模为15亿元人民币/270亿塞尔维亚第纳尔的双边本币互换协议。

6月24日，中国外汇交易中心宣布自6月27日起在银行间外汇市场正式开展人民币对韩元直接交易。

6月24日，全国外汇市场自律机制在上海成立。

7月15日，中国人民银行决定进一步改革存款准备金考核制度，将人民币存款准备金的交存基数由旬末一般存款余额时点数调整为旬内一般存款余额的算术平均值。同时，按季交纳存款准备金的境外人民币业务参加行存放境内代理行人民币存款，其交存基数也调整为上季度境外参加行人民币存放日终余额的算术平均值。

8月4日，银行间市场交易商协会发布实施《银行间债券市场做市业务指引》及《银行间债券市场做市业务评价指标体系》。

8月9日，中国外汇交易中心发布实施《全国银行间同业拆借市场业务操作细则》。

8月15日，上海清算所将期限在1年以内（含）的美元对人民币普通欧式期权交易纳入中央对手清算业务。

8月25日，波兰共和国在中国银行间债券市场成功发行3年期人民币主权债券30亿元。

8月30日，中国人民银行、国家外汇管理局发布《关于人民币合格境外机构投资者境内证券投资管理有关问题的通知》，规范人民币合格境外机构投资者境内证券投资管理。

8月31日，中国人民银行、财政部、国家发展和改革委员会、环境保护部、中国银行业监督管理委员会、中国证券监督管理委员会、中国保险监督管理委员会联合印发《关于构建绿色金融体系的指导意见》。

8月31日，世界银行（国际复兴开发银行）首期特别提款权（SDR）计价债券在中国银行间债券市场成功发行，发行规模为5亿SDR，期限为3年，结算货币为人民币。

9月7日，中央国债登记结算有限责任公司发布《中央国债登记结算有限责任公司中国（上海）自由贸易试验区债券业务指引》，自2016年9月8日起实施。

9月8日，中国保监会发布《关于保险资金参与沪港通试点的监管口径》。

9月8日，银行间市场交易商协会发布《投资人保护条款范例》。

9月12日，中国人民银行与匈牙利央行续签双边本币互换协议，协议规模为100亿元人民币/4 160亿匈牙利福林，有效期为3年。

9月20日，中国人民银行授权中国银行纽约分行担任美国人民币业务清算行。

9月23日，中国外汇交易中心发布公告，自2016年9月26日起在银行间外汇市场开展人民币对阿联酋迪拉姆、人民币对沙特里亚尔直接交易。

9月23日，中国人民银行授权中国工商银行（莫斯科）股份有限公司担任俄罗斯人民币业务清算行。

9月23日，加拿大国民银行获准在中国银行间债券市场发行规模不超过50亿元的人民币债券。

9月23日，上海清算所推出自贸区债券柜台业务。

9月23日，银行间市场交易商协会发布实施《银行间市场信用风险缓释工具试点业务规则》。

9月27日，中国人民银行与欧洲中央银行签署补充协议，决定将双边本币互换协议有效期延长三年至2019年10月8日。互换规模仍为3 500亿元人民币/450亿欧元。

9月30日，国际货币基金组织（IMF）宣布纳入人民币的特别提款权（SDR）新货币篮子于10月1日正式生效。

9月30日，中国证监会发布施行《内地与香港股票市场交易互联互通机制若干规定》。

9月30日，中国证监会批复上海证券交易所和深圳证券交易所发布实施《上海证券交易所公司债券簿记建档发行业务指引》、《深圳证券交易所公司债券簿记建档发行业务指引》。

9月30日，财政部、中国人民银行联合印发《国债做市支持操作规则》。

10月10日，国务院发布《关于积极稳妥降低企业杠杆率的意见》、《关于市场化银行债权转股权的指导意见》。

10月13日，国务院办公厅印发《互联网金融风险专项整治工作实施方案》。

10月13日，中国人民银行等17部门联合发布《通过互联网开展资产管理及跨界从事金融业务风险专项整治工作实施方案》。

10月20日，中国外汇交易中心发布通知，将大额存单发行主体范围进一步扩大至2016年9月底以前发行过同业存单的自律机制核心成员与基础成员。

10月21日，中国证监会发布《公司债券发行人现场检查工作指引》。

11月11日，中国外汇交易中心发布公告，自2016年11月14日起银行间外汇市场完善人民币对加拿大元的交易方式，发展人民币对加拿大元直接交易。

11月14日，国务院办公厅印发《地方政府性债务风险应急处置预案》。

11月25日，中国证监会批复上海、深圳证券交易所发布分级基金业务管理指引。

12月5日，深港股票市场交易互联互通机制正式启动。

12月6日，中国人民银行与埃及中央银行签署了双边本币互换协议，规模为180亿元人民币/470亿埃及镑，互换协议有效期3年，经双方同意可以展期。

12月6日，中国人民银行公布施行《票据交易管理办法》。

12月7日，中国人民银行决定授权中国农业银行迪拜分行担任阿联酋人民币业务清算行。

12月8日，上海票据交易所正式开业。

12月9日，中国外汇交易中心发布公告，自2016年12月12日起银行间外汇市场开展人民币对波兰兹罗提、人民币对匈牙利福林、人民币对丹麦克朗、人民币对瑞典克朗、人民币对挪威克朗、人民币对土耳其里拉、人民币对墨西哥比索直接交易。

12月9日，中国证券登记结算有限责任公司、上海证券交易所、深圳证券交易所发布实施《债券质押式回购交易结算风险控制指引》。

12月12日，中国外汇交易中心发布施行《全国银行间债券市场债券预发行交易规则》和《全国银行间债券市场债券预发行交易标准条款》。

12月12日，银行间市场交易商协会发布实施《非金融企业资产支持票据指引（修订稿）》和配套表格体系。

12月12日，中国证监会发布《证券期货投资者适当性管理办法》，自2017年7月1日起施行。

12月13日，中央国债登记结算有限责任公司发布实施《中央国债登记结算有限责任公司债券预发行业务结算规则》。

12月16日，中国证监会批准郑州商品交易所和大连商品交易所分别开展白糖和豆粕期权交易。

12月21日，中国人民银行与冰岛中央银行续签了双边本币互换协议，互换规模保持35亿元人民币/660亿冰岛克朗，有效期3年，经双方同意可以展期。

12月21日，经国务院批准，人民币合格境外机构投资者（RQFII）试点地区扩大到爱尔兰，投资额度为500亿元人民币。

12月23日，经银行间市场交易商协会接受注册的首单扶贫社会效应债券成功发行。

12月28日，中国人民银行发布经修订的《金融机构大额交易和可疑交易报告管理办法》，自2017年7月1日起施行。

12月30日，上海票据交易所、银行间市场交易商协会联合发布《票据交易主协议（2016年版）》。

附录二 中国金融市场统计

表1 1998—2016年主要宏观经济金融指标(年末余额)

单位：亿元、%

项目 \ 年份	1998	1999	2000	2001	2002	2003	2004	2005	2006	2007	2008	2009	2010	2011	2012	2013	2014	2015	2016
国内生产总值(GDP)	84 402	89 677	99 215	109 655	120 333	135 823	159 878	184 937	216 314	265 810	314 045	340 903	408 903	484 124	534 123	588 019	635 910	676 708	744 127
增长率	7.8	7.6	8.4	8.3	9.1	10.0	10.1	10.4	12.7	14.2	9.6	9.2	10.6	9.5	7.7	7.7	7.3	6.9	6.7
进出口总额(亿美元、亿元)	3 239.3	3 607	4 743	5 097.7	6 208	8 512	11 547	14 221	17 607	21 738	25 616	22 073	201 723	236 402	244 160	258 168	264 335	245 741	243 386
增长率	-0.4	11.3	31.5	7.5	21.8	37.1	35.7	23.2	23.8	23.5	17.8	-13.9	34.7	17.2	3.2	5.7	2.4	-7.0	-0.9
出口(亿美元、亿元)	1 837.6	1 949	2 492	2 661	3 256	4 384	5 934	7 620	9 690	12 205	14 307	12 016	107 023	123 241	129 359	137 131	143 912	141 255	138 455
进口(亿美元、亿元)	1 401.7	1 658	2 251	2 436.1	2 952	4 128	5 614	6 601	7 915	9 561	11 326	10 059	94 700	113 161	114 801	121 037	120 423	104 485	104 932
外汇储备(亿美元)	1 450	1 546.8	1 655.7	2 121.7	2 864	4 033	6 099	8 189	10 663	15 282	19 460	23 992	28 473	31 811	33 116	38 213	38 430	33 304	30 105
外商直接投资(亿美元)	454.6	404	408	468.5	527	535	606	603	694.7	747.7	924	900	1 057	1 160	1 117	1 176	1 196	1 263	1 260
财政收入	9 876	11 444.1	13 380.1	16 371	18 914	21 691	26 355.9	31 628	38 760	51 304	61 330	68 518	83 102	103 874	117 254	129 210	140 350	152 217	159 552
财政支出	107 98.2	13 187.7	15 879.4	18 844	22 012	24 607	28 360.8	33 708.1	40 222.7	49 565.4	62 593	76 300	89 874	109 248	125 953	140 213	151 662	175 768	187 841
赤字或盈余	-922.2	-1 743.6	-2 499.3	-2 473	-3 098	-2 916	-2 004.9	-2 080.1	-1 462.5	1 738.6	-1 263	-7 782	-6 772	-5 374	-8 699	-11 003	-11 312	-23 551	-28 289
货币供应量(M2)	104 499	119 898	134 610.3	158 301.9	185 007	221 222.8	254 107	296 040.1	345 577.9	403 401.3	475 166.6	606 223.6	725851.79	851 590.9	974 148.8	1 106 524.98	1 228 374.81	1 392 278.11	1 550 066.67
增长率	15.3	14.7	12.3	17.6	16.9	19.6	14.9	16.5	16.7	16.7	17.8	27.6	19.7	13.5	14.4	13.6	11.0	13.3	11.4
货币供应量(M1)	38 953.7	45 837.2	53 147.2	59 871.6	70 822	84 118.6	95 969.7	107 279.9	126 028.1	152 519.2	166 217.1	220 004.5	266 621.54	28 9847.7	308 664.2	337291.05	348056.41	400 953.44	486 557.24
增长率	11.9	17.7	15.9	12.7	18.3	18.8	14.1	11.8	17.5	21.0	9.0	32.4	21.2	7.9	6.5	9.3	3.2	15.2	21.4

（续）

项目 \ 年份	1998	1999	2000	2001	2002	2003	2004	2005	2006	2007	2008	2009	2010	2011	2012	2013	2014	2015	2016
货币供应量(M0)	11 204.2	13 455.5	14 652.7	15 688.8	17 278	19 746	21 468.3	24 032.8	27 072.6	30 334.3	34 218.96	38 245.97	44 628.17	50748.46	54 659.77	58 574.44	6 0259.53	63 216.58	68 303.87
增长率	10.1	20.1	8.9	7.1	10.1	14.3	8.7	11.9	12.6	12.0	12.8	11.8	16.7	13.8	7.7	7.1	2.9	4.9	8.1
城镇居民人均可支配收入(元)	5 245	5 854	6 280	6 859.6	7 703	8 500	9 422	10 493	11 759	13 786	15 781	17 175	19 109	21 810	24 565	26 955	28 844	31 195	33 616
实际增长率	5.8	9.3	6.4	8.5	13.4	9.0	7.7	9.6	10.4	12.2	8.4	9.8	7.8	8.4	12.6	9.7	6.8	6.6	5.6
农村居民人均纯收入(元)	2 163.6	210	2 253	2 366	2 475.6	2 622	2 936	3 255	3 587	4 140	4 761	5 153	5 919	6 977	7 917	8 896	9 892	11 422	12 363
实际增长率	4.3	3.8	2.1	4.2	4.8	4.3	6.8	6.2	7.4	9.5	8.0	8.5	10.9	11.4	13.5	9.3	11.2	7.5	6.2
金融机构各项存款	95 697.9	108 779	123 804.4	143 617.2	170 917.4	208 055.6	241 424.3	300 208.6	348 015.6	401 051.4	478 444.2	612 005.1	733 382.03	826 701.35	943 102.27	1 070 587.72	1 173 734.59	1 397 752.11	1 555 247.07
增长率	16.1	13.7	13.8	16.0	19.0	21.7	16.0	24.3	15.9	15.2	19.3	27.9	19.8	12.7	14.1	13.5	9.6	19.1	11.3
金融机构各项贷款	86 524.1	93 734.3	99 371.1	112 314.7	131 293.9	158 996.2	178 197.8	206 838.5	238 279.8	277 746.5	320 048.7	425 622.6	509 225.95	581 892.5	672 874.61	766 326.64	867 867.89	993 459.69	1 120 551.79
增长率	15.5	8.3	6.0	13.0	16.9	21.1	12.1	16.1	15.2	16.6	15.2	33.0	19.6	14.3	15.6	13.9	13.3	14.5	12.8
居民消费价格指数 (CPI)	-0.8	-1.4	0.4	0.7	-0.8	1.2	3.9	1.8	1.5	4.8	5.9	-0.7	3.3	5.4	2.6	2.6	2.0	1.4	2.0

注：1. 根据最新公布数据有所调整往年数据。

2. 2009年以后的进出口总额、进口、出口数据以人民币计。

数据来源:国家统计局、中国人民银行、中国财政部。

表2 1998—2016年新增本外币存贷款构成及增长率(年末余额)

单位：亿元、%

项目 \ 年份	1998	1999	2000	2001	2002	2003	2004	2005	2006	2007	2008	2009	2010	2011	2012	2013	2014	2015	2016
金融机构各项存款	95 697.9	108 778.9	123 804	143 617.2	170 917.4	208 055.6	241 424.3	300 208.6	348 015.6	401 051.4	478 444.21	612 005.1	733 382.03	826 701.35	943 102.27	1 070 587.72	1 173 734.59	1397752.11	1 555 247.07
比上年末增长	16.1	13.7	13.8	16	19	21.7	16	24.3	15.9	15.2	19.3	27.9	19.8	12.7	14.1	13.5	9.6	19.1	11.3
其中:城乡居民储蓄	53 407.5	59 621.8	64 332.4	73 762.4	86 910.7	103 617.7	119 555.4	147 053.7	166 616.2	176 213.3	221 503.47	264 756.9	307 166.39	357 901.58	415 549.87	471 090.18	512 790.14	551 928.92	606 522.23
比上年末增长	17.1	11.6	7.9	14.7	17.8	19.2	15.4	23	13.3	5.8	25.7	19.5	16	16.5	16.1	13.4	8.9	7.6	9.9
企业存款	32 486.6	37 182.4	44 093.7	51 546.6	60 028.6	72 487.1	84 669.5	101 750.6	118 851.7	144 814.1	164 385.79	224 360.0	252 960.27	423 086.61	478 730.2	541 793.87	591 069.28	455 208.83	530 895.41
比上年末增长	13.4	14.5	18.6	16.9	16.5	20.8	16.8	20.2	16.8	21.8	13.5	36.5	12.7	67.3	13.2	13.2	9.1	-22.9	16.6
金融机构各项贷款	86 524.1	93 734.3	99 371.1	112 314.7	131 293.9	158 996.2	178 197.8	206 838.5	238 279.8	277 746.5	320 048.68	425 622.6	509 225.95	581 892.5	672 874.61	766 326.64	867 867.89	993 459.69	1 120 551.79
比上年末增长	15.5	8.3	6	13	16.9	21.1	12.1	16.1	15.2	16.6	15.2	33	19.6	14.3	15.6	13.9	13.3	14.5	12.8
其中:短期贷款	60 613.2	63 887.6	65 748.1	67 327.2	76 822.4	87 397.9	90 808.3	91 157.5	101 698.2	118 898	128 571.47	151 390.7	171 236.64	217 480.1	268 152.19	311 771.97	336 371.27	359 190.66	371 286.36
比上年末增长	9.4	5.4	2.9	2.4	14.1	13.8	3.9	0.4	11.6	16.9	8.1	17.7	13.1	27.0	23.3	16.3	7.9	6.8	3.4
中长期贷款	20 717.8	23 968.3	27 931.2	39 238.1	51 731.6	67 251.7	81 010.1	92 940.5	113 009.8	138 581	164 160.42	235 591.3	305 127.55	333 746.51	363 894.22	410 345.5	471 818.36	537 832.55	634 209.87
比上年末增长	33.9	15.7	16.5	40.5	31.8	30	20.5	14.7	21.6	22.6	18.5	43.5	29.5	9.4	9.0	12.8	15.0	14.0	17.9

数据来源:中国人民银行。

表3　2006—2016年贷款余额、债券存量、股票市值与GDP的比例

单位：亿元、%

年份	GDP	贷款余额	贷款余额/GDP	债券存量	债券存量/GDP	股票总市值	股票总市值/GDP
2006	216 314	238 280	110.2	92 740	42.9	89 404	41.3
2007	265 810	277 747	104.5	124 470	46.8	327 140.9	123.1
2008	314 045	320 049	101.9	151 648	48.3	121 366.4	38.6
2009	340 903	425 623	124.9	176 430	51.8	243 939.12	71.6
2010	397 983	509 226	128	205 481	51.6	265 422.59	66.7
2011	471 564	581 893	123	223 786	47.5	214 758.1	45.5
2012	519 470	672 875	130	262 058	50.4	230 357.6	44.3
2013	568 845	766 327	135	296 165	52.1	239 077.2	42
2014	636 463	867 868	136	355 778	55.9	372 546.92	59
2015	676 708	993 460	147	478 978	70.8	531 304.2	78.5
2016	744 127	1 120 552	151	636 614	85.6	508 245.11	68.3

注：1. 贷款余额指金融机构本外币各类贷款。

2. 债券存量指包括银行间债券托管数和交易所债券托管数在内的总托管量。

数据来源：中国人民银行、中国证监会。

表4　2010—2016年社会融资增量结构情况

单位：万亿元

年份	融资增量总额	人民币贷款	外币贷款	委托贷款	信托贷款	未贴现银行承兑汇票	企业债券净融资	非金融企业境内股票融资	其他
2010	13.94	7.86	0.49	0.88	0.39	2.34	1.11	0.58	0.29
2011	12.83	7.47	0.57	1.30	0.20	1.03	1.37	0.44	0.45
2012	15.76	8.20	0.92	1.28	1.28	1.05	2.26	0.25	0.00
2013	17.29	8.89	0.58	2.54	1.84	0.78	1.80	0.22	0.00
2014	16.41	9.78	0.36	2.51	0.52	-0.13	2.43	0.44	0.00
2015	15.29	11.27	-0.64	1.59	0.04	-1.06	2.82	0.76	0.00
2016	17.80	12.40	-0.56	2.18	0.86	-1.95	3.00	1.24	0.60

数据来源：中国人民银行。

表5 1997—2016年银行间同业拆借与债券回购成交情况

单位：亿元

年份	同业拆借	质押式回购交易额	买断式回购交易额
1997	8 298	310	—
1998	1 978	1 021	—
1999	3 291	3 957	—
2000	6 728	15 785	—
2001	8 082	40 133	—
2002	12 107	101 885	—
2003	24 113	117 203	—
2004	14 556	93 105	1 263
2005	12 783	156 784	2 223
2006	21 503	263 021	2 892
2007	106 466	440 672	7 253
2008	150 492	563 830	17 376
2009	193 505	677 007	25 891
2010	278 684	846 533	29 402
2011	334 412	966 650	27 885
2012	467 044	1 366 174	50 966
2013	355 190	1 519 757	61 882
2014	376 626	2 124 191	120 035
2015	642 135	4 324 109	253 528
2016	959 131	5 682 693	330 335

数据来源：中国外汇交易中心。

表6 1997—2016年银行间同业拆借成员变化情况

单位：家

年份	银行	证券公司	保险公司	信托公司	财务公司	租赁公司	农村信用联社	城市信用社	资产管理公司	汽车金融公司	其他	总计
1997	59	—	—	—	—	—	—	—	—	—	37	96
1998	165	—	—	—	—	—	—	—	—	—	2	167
1999	187	7	—	—	—	—	99	—	—	—	3	296
2000	232	14	—	—	20	—	148	—	—	—	3	417
2001	246	18	—	—	25	—	198	—	—	—	3	490
2002	261	41	—	—	25	—	202	4	—	—	3	536
2003	289	56	—	—	32	—	229	10	—	—	1	617
2004	309	64	—	—	35	—	236	11	—	—	1	656
2005	323	66	—	—	38	—	239	12	—	—	1	679
2006	339	53	—	—	46	—	250	15	—	—	0	703
2007	326	56	—	3	49	—	267	16	—	—	0	717
2008	340	58	—	16	55	4	298	13	2	2	0	788
2009	348	65	6	26	68	6	320	9	3	3	0	854
2010	347	68	6	30	72	11	338	8	3	5	0	888
2011	347	70	7	38	77	11	369	7	4	6	1	937
2012	359	77	7	39	81	16	422	7	5	8	1	1 022
2013	368	82	9	45	98	16	482	7	5	9	1	1 122
2014	349	87	10	54	129	17	547	7	5	13	1	1 219
2015	355	90	15	57	154	20	661	7	5	16	2	1 382
2016	390	95	31	62	180	24	916	0	8	17	2	1 725

数据来源：全国银行间同业拆借中心。

表7 1998—2016年票据市场情况

单位：万亿元

年份	累计签发商业票据发生额	累计贴现发生额
1998	0.38	0.27
1999	0.51	0.25
2000	0.74	0.64
2001	1.28	1.55
2002	1.61	2.31
2003	2.77	4.44
2004	3.42	4.71
2005	4.45	6.75
2006	5.43	8.49
2007	5.87	10.11
2008	7.09	13.51
2009	10.27	23.16
2010	12.2	48.6
2011	15.1	25.0
2012	17.9	31.6
2013	20.3	45.7
2014	22.1	60.7
2015	22.4	102.1
2016	18.1	84.5

数据来源：中国人民银行。

表8 2006—2016年债券市场现券与期货交易情况

单位：亿元、%

年份	银行间市场				交易所市场			
	现券交易额	同比增长	柜台交易额	同比增长	现券交易额	同比增长	国债期货交易额	同比增长
2006	102 558.6	70.55	42.8	-34.86	1 977.83	—	—	—
2007	156 038.21	52.15	35.7	-16.59	2 051.75	3.74	—	—
2008	371 082.7	137.82	30.4	-14.85	4 294.73	109.32	—	—
2009	472 646.43	27.37	62.8	106.58	4 659.86	8.5	—	—
2010	640 418.98	35.5	41.7	-33.6	5 832.26	25.16	—	—
2011	636 422.9	-0.62	27.89	-33.12	6 839.9	17.28	—	—
2012	751 952.83	18.15	14.99	-46.25	9 852.7	44.05	—	—
2013	416 106.44	-44.66	18.72	24.88	17 387.6	76.48	3 063.89	—
2014	403 565.2	-3	71.7	283.01	27 874.4	60.31	8 785.17	186.73
2015	867 370.1	114.9	109.3	52.4	33 994.6	22	60 106.8	584.18
2016	1 270 918.3	46.5	87.6	-19.8	51 269.9	50.8	89 013.6	48.09

数据来源：中国人民银行。

表9 2016年债券市场现券交易情况

单位：亿元、%

时间	银行间债券市场					交易所债券市场		
	现券交易额	同比增长	银行间债券总指数	柜台市场交易额	同比增长	现券交易额	同比增长	上证国债指数
2016年1月	93 098.0	115.0	120.25	2.0	-96.4	2 857.2	-17.9	155.20
2016年2月	60 441.2	99.5	120.17	3.3	-83.2	2 216.4	21.3	155.72
2016年3月	113 409.3	114.7	120.47	5.3	163.5	3 835.5	58.3	156.63
2016年4月	96 314.7	55.9	119.25	1.1	-80.2	3 290.4	30.0	156.68
2016年5月	99 387.7	39.4	119.32	7.3	139.1	4 142.0	59.3	157.18
2016年6月	108 212.6	53.8	119.73	9.3	397.3	3 774.2	48.8	157.67
2016年7月	115 309.6	27.8	120.34	5.6	188.6	4 315.5	12.5	158.44
2016年8月	137 376.5	68.3	120.49	16.5	1 084.2	6 206.4	88.3	159.22
2016年9月	111 870.1	45.9	120.59	10.0	204.6	4 292.7	42.5	159.73
2016年10月	97 599.0	26.5	120.69	7.3	600.0	4 017.0	103.0	160.72
2016年11月	122 806.1	19.6	119.30	9.5	-21.7	5 588.6	90.5	160.36
2016年12月	115 093.4	4.8	117.56	10.6	381.0	6 734.1	89.5	159.79
合计	1 270 918.3	46.5	—	87.6	-19.8	51 269.9	50.8	—

注：银行间债券总指数指中债银行间债券总指数净价指数。

数据来源：中国人民银行、中央国债登记结算有限责任公司、上海证券交易所、中国外汇交易中心。

表10 2004—2016年债券市场发行基本情况

单位：亿元

年份	政府信用债			政府支持机构债	央行票据	金融债券				同业存单	公司信用类债券				资产支持证券	国际机构债券	总计
	国债	地方政府债	小计			政策性银行债	券商短融	其他金融债	小计		非金融企业债券融资工具	企业债券	公司债券	合计			
2004	7 318.8	0	7 318.8	0	17 037	4 348 .0	0	748.8	5 096.8	—	0	326.0	209.0	535.0	—	—	29 988.0
2005	7 042 0	0	7 042.0	0	27 882	6 051.7	29.0	1 036.3	7 117 .0	—	1 424 .0	654.0	0	2 078.0	172.7	—	44 160.8
2006	8 883.3	0	8 883.3	0	36 574	8 980 .0	0	525.0	9 505.0	—	2 919.5	995.0	142.9	4 057.4	280.0	—	59 135.3
2007	23 483.4	0	23 483.4	0	40 721	10 931.9	0	972.7	11 904.6	—	3 349.1	1 720 .0	407.3	5 476.4	178.1	—	81 763.8
2008	8 546.3	0	8 546.3	0	42 960	10 809.3	0	974.0	11 783.3	—	6 075.5	2 367 .0	976.5	9 419.0	302.0	—	73 010.6
2009	16 213.6	2 000	18 213.6	0	39 740	11 678.1	0	3 071.0	14 749.1	—	11 509.7	4 252.0	715.0	16 476.7	0	—	89 179.4
2010	17 778.2	2 000	19 778.2	1 090	46 608	13 192.7	0	979.5	14 172.2	—	11 863.0	3 627.0	1 320.3	16 810.3	0	—	98 458.6
2011	15 397.9	2 000	17 397.9	1 000	14 140	19 972.7	0	3 528.5	23 501.2	—	18 503.2	2 473.5	1 707.4	22 684.1	12.8	—	78 723.2
2012	14 360.4	2 500	16 860.4	1 500	0	21 399.0	561.0	4 233.7	26 193.7	—	26 547.2	6 499.3	2 722.8	35 769.3	224.4	—	80 515.9
2013	16 945.0	3 500	20 445.0	1 900	5 362	20 760.3	2 995.9	1 321 .0	25 077.2	340.0	28 357.9	4 752.3	4 081.4	37 191.6	231.7	—	90 133.5
2014	17 047.3	4 000	21 047.3	2 100	0	22 900.5	4 246.9	5 459.5	32 606.9	8 985.6	41 217.6	6 952.0	3 483.8	51 653.4	3 220.6	—	110 201.1
2015	19 875.4	38 350.6	58 226 .0	2 400	0	25 790.2	3 515.6	14 794.9	44 100.7	52 975.9	53 660.6	3 431.0	13 292.4	70 384.1	6 157.2	115.0	234 358.9
2016	29 457.7	60 428.4	89 886.1	2 250	0	33 529.7	1 178.6	12 717.9	47 426.2	129 931.0	50 297.9	5 917.7	25 770.0	81 985.5	8 647.0	1 266.40	361 392.0

注：1. 国债包含记账式国债、电子式储蓄国债。
2. 其他金融债从2015年起包括银行间市场金融债券、交易所市场金融债券，资产支持证券包含银行间信贷资产支持证券、交易所资产支持证券。
3. 国际机构债券指境外机构法人在境内发行的债券，发行主体包含主权机构、准主权机构、境外金融和非金融机构。

数据来源:中国人民银行。

表11　2006—2016年债券市场债券托管情况

单位：亿元

年份	政府信用债			政府支持机构债及其他	央行票据	金融债券				同业存单	公司信用类债券				信贷资产支持证券	国际机构债券	银行间托管总量	交易所托管总量	总托管量
	国债	地方政府债	合计			政策性银行债	券商短融	其他金融债	合计		非金融企业债券融资工具	企业债券	公司债券	合计					
2006	29 048	0	29 048	30	32 300	22 836	0	2 552	25 388	0	2 667	2 832	288	5 786	188	—	88 910	3 830	92 740
2007	46 503	0	46 503	30	36 587	28 784	0	3 486	32 270	0	3 203	4 422	1 131	8 756	324	—	120 102	4 368	124 470
2008	48 753	0	48 753	30	48 121	36 720	0	4 255	40 975	0	5 875	6 803	539	13 218	551	—	148 100	3 548	151 648
2009	55 411	2 000	57 411	40	42 326	44 498	0	6 454	50 952	0	13 196	10 971	1 135	25 301	399	—	172 476	3 954	176 430
2010	62 628	4 000	66 628	1 130	40 909	51 604	0	6 662	58 266	0	20 271	14 511	3 584	38 366	182	—	199 019	6 462	205 481
2011	67 839	6 000	73 839	2 130	21 290	64 778	0	9 785	74 563	0	29 047	16 799	6 023	51 869	95	—	214 260	9 526	223 786
2012	74 236	6 500	80 736	8 532	13 440	78 582	295	13 126	92 003	0	40 327	19 310	7 441	67 078	269	—	250 014	12 044	262 058
2013	83 165	8 615	91 780	10 067	5 522	88 720	810	13 535	103 064	340	51 483	23 359	10 553	85 394	354	—	277 128	19 377	296 505
2014	91 450	11 624	103 073	11 706	4 282	99 874	1134	17 213	118 221	5 995	67 901	29 513	12 335	109 749	2 751	—	329 803	25 975	355 778
2015	101 503	48 255	149 757	13 275	4 282	110 069	436	32 174	142 678	3 0274	85 910	31 632	15 582	133 123	5 463	125	440 640	38 337	478 978
2016	114 663	106 250	220 913	14 605	60	124 070	82	42 026	166 178	62 761	87 771	35 305	42 312	165 387	6174	537	563 298	73 316	636 614

注：1. 国债包含记账式国债、电子式储蓄国债。
　　2. 其他金融债券包括银行间市场金融债券、交易所市场金融债券。
数据来源:中国人民银行。

表12 2006—2016年记账式国债发行与兑付情况

单位：亿元

年份	发行额	兑付额	期末余额
2006	6 533.3	4 162.55	28 648.17
2007	21 849.5	3 951.60	46 202.05
2008	6 665.0	4 903.30	47 891.05
2009	12 718.1	7 271.51	53 327.45
2010	14 581.9	8 262.48	59 627.85
2011	12 446.5	7 493.37	64 533.45
2012	12 032.8	5 637.83	70 674.35
2013	13 374.4	5 909.80	78 122.85
2014	14 363.3	6 935.97	85 529.55
2015	18 016.2	8 630.90	94 889.55
2016	27 465.8	14 380.58	107 863.7

注：1.兑付额不含提前兑付和利息支付。
　　2.期末余额指托管量。

数据来源：中央国债登记结算有限责任公司。

表13　银行间债券市场参与机构数

单位：家

机构		年份	2014	2015	2016
境内参与机构	法人类产品	存款类金融机构	1 088	1 302	1 501
		其他银行业金融机构	158	182	208
		证券类金融机构	169	171	180
		保险类金融机构	148	152	154
		非金融机构	278	280	279
		其他	7	7	7
		合计	1 848	2 094	2 329
	非法人类产品	证券投资基金	1 556	2 151	3 058
		企业年金	1 275	1 431	1 521
		社保基金	105	105	104
		保险产品	145	311	629
		信托产品	569	666	680
		基金公司特定客户资管组合	176	1 140	2 720
		证券公司资管计划	560	1 388	2 631
		银行理财产品	48	48	48
		其他	0	0	0
		合计	4 434	7 240	11 391
境外参与机构			180	302	407
合计			6 462	9 636	14 127

数据来源：中国人民银行。

表14　银行间债券市场结算代理人名单

序号	机构名称	序号	机构名称
1	中国工商银行	25	长沙银行
2	中国农业银行	26	大连银行
3	中国银行	27	青岛银行
4	中国建设银行	28	成都银行
5	交通银行	29	重庆银行
6	招商银行	30	河北银行
7	中国民生银行	31	厦门银行
8	中国光大银行	32	富滇银行
9	中信银行	33	晋商银行
10	华夏银行	34	福建海峡银行
11	兴业银行	35	贵阳银行
12	上海浦东发展银行	36	西安银行
13	广发银行	37	东莞银行
14	北京银行	38	哈尔滨银行
15	恒丰银行	39	广东顺德农村商业银行
16	南京银行	40	宁波银行
17	上海银行	41	常熟农村商业银行
18	杭州银行	42	包商银行
19	上海市农村商业银行	43	汉口银行
20	天津银行	44	汇丰银行（中国）有限公司
21	齐商银行	45	渣打银行（中国）有限公司
22	平安银行	46	法国巴黎银行（中国）有限公司
23	齐鲁银行	47	德意志银行（中国）有限公司
24	乌鲁木齐市商业银行	48	花旗银行（中国）有限公司

注：名单截至2017年2月21日。
资料来源：中央国债登记结算有限责任公司。

表15 2016年度公开市场业务一级交易商名单

交通银行股份有限公司	中国建设银行股份有限公司
中国银行股份有限公司	中国工商银行股份有限公司
中国农业银行股份有限公司	国家开发银行股份有限公司
招商银行股份有限公司	中国邮政储蓄银行股份有限公司
兴业银行股份有限公司	中国光大银行股份有限公司
广发银行股份有限公司	中国民生银行股份有限公司
平安银行股份有限公司	上海浦东发展银行股份有限公司
中信银行股份有限公司	恒丰银行股份有限公司
浙商银行股份有限公司	华夏银行股份有限公司
上海银行股份有限公司	宁波银行股份有限公司
南京银行股份有限公司	江苏银行股份有限公司
郑州银行股份有限公司	杭州银行股份有限公司
福建海峡银行股份有限公司	北京银行股份有限公司
洛阳银行股份有限公司	广州银行股份有限公司
徽商银行股份有限公司	厦门银行股份有限公司
大连银行股份有限公司	天津银行股份有限公司
富滇银行股份有限公司	河北银行股份有限公司
西安银行股份有限公司	盛京银行股份有限公司
贵阳银行股份有限公司	齐商银行股份有限公司
广州农村商业银行股份有限公司	北京农村商业银行股份有限公司
上海农村商业银行股份有限公司	汇丰银行（中国）有限公司
花旗银行（中国）有限公司	渣打银行（中国）有限公司
中信证券股份有限公司	第一创业证券股份有限公司
国泰君安证券股份有限公司	中国国际金融股份有限公司

资料来源：中国人民银行。

表16 1997—2016年股票市场统计表

年份	上市公司数（家）	上市总股本（亿股）	市价总值（亿元）	流通市值（亿元）	A股筹资总额（亿元）	成交金额（亿元）	平均换手率（%）		平均市盈率（%）		投资者账户（万户）
							上海	深圳	上海	深圳	
1997	745	1 942.7	17 529.2	5 204.4	—	30 721.8	701.8	817.4	39.9	39.9	3 480.3
1998	851	2 526.8	19 505.6	5 745.6	—	23 527.3	453.6	406.6	34.4	30.6	4 259.9
1999	949	3 089.0	26 471.2	8 214.0	—	31 319.6	471.5	424.5	38.1	36.3	4 810.6
2000	1 088	3 791.7	48 090.9	16 087.5	—	60 826.6	492.9	509.1	58.2	56.0	6 123.2
2001	1 160	5 218.0	43 522.2	15 228.8	—	38 305.2	269.3	227.9	37.7	39.8	6 898.7
2002	1 224	5 875.5	38 329.1	12 484.6	737.23	27 990.5	214.0	198.8	34.4	37.0	6 841.8
2003	1 287	6 428.5	42 457.7	13 178.5	665.07	32 115.3	250.8	214.2	36.5	36.2	6 981.2
2004	1 377	7 149.4	37 055.6	11 688.6	642.78	42 333.9	288.7	288.3	24.2	24.6	7 215.7
2005	1 381	7 629.5	32 430.3	10 630.5	339.03	31 663.1	274.4	320.6	16.3	16.4	7 336.1
2006	1 434	14 897.6	89 403.9	25 003.6	2 335.22	90 468.7	541.1	671.3	33.4	33.6	7 854.0
2007	1 550	22 416.9	327 140.9	93 064.4	7 791.57	460 556.2	927.2	1 062.1	59.2	72.1	9 280.6
2008	1 625	24 522.85	121 366.44	45 213.90	2 619.71	267 113.00	392.5	—	14.86	17.13	10 449.70
2009	1 718	26 162.85	243 939.1	151 258.70	3 894.53	535 986.70	—	—	28.73	46.01	12 037.70
2010	2 063	33 184.35	265 422.59	193 110.41	8 954.99	545 633.54	—	—	21.61	44.69	13 391.04
2011	2 342	36 095.52	214 758.10	164 921.30	5 073.07	421 649.72	—	—	13.40	23.11	14 050.37
2012	2 494	38 295.00	230 357.62	181 658.26	1 380.42	314 667.41	—	—	12.30	22.01	14 054.91
2013	2 489	40 569.08	239 077.19	199 579.54	2 802.76	468 728.60	—	—	10.99	27.76	13 247.15
2014	2 613	43 610.13	372 546.96	315 624.31	4 856.43	743 912.98	—	—	15.99	34.05	14 214.68
2015	2 827	49 997.26	531 304.20	417 925.40	8 329.89	2 550 538.29	—	—	17.63	52.75	21 477.57
2016	3 052	55 820.50	508 245.11	393 266.27	18 910.35	1 267 262.64	—	—	18.94	62.36	—

数据来源：中国证监会、上海证券交易所、深圳证券交易所。

表17 1997—2016年股票市场成交量和股票指数变化情况

单位：亿元

年份	成交金额	日均成交	上证综数				深证综指			
			开盘	最高	最低	收盘	开盘	最高	最低	收盘
1997	30 721.8	126.4	914.06	1 510.18	870.18	1 194.10	326.33	517.91	305.81	381.29
1998	23 527.3	97.1	1 200.95	1 422.98	1 043.02	1146.70	382.85	441.04	317.10	343.85
1999	31 319.6	131.0	1 144.89	1 756.18	1 047.83	1 366.58	343.29	525.14	310.65	402.18
2000	60 826.6	254.5	1 368.69	2 125.72	1 361.21	2 073.48	402.71	654.37	414.69	635.73
2001	38 305.2	159.6	2 077.08	2 245.00	1 515.00	1 645.97	636.62	664.85	439.36	475.94
2002	27 990.5	118.1	1 643.49	1 748.89	1 339.20	1 357.65	475.14	512.38	371.79	388.76
2003	32 115.3	133.3	1 347.43	1 649.60	1 307.40	1 497.04	386.61	449.42	350.74	378.63
2004	42 333.9	174.2	1 492.72	1 783.01	1 259.43	1 266.50	377.93	470.55	315.17	315.81
2005	31 663.1	130.8	1 260.78	1 328.53	998.23	1 161.06	313.81	333.27	237.18	278.75
2006	90 468.7	375.4	1 163.88	2 698.90	1 161.91	2 675.47	278.99	710.14	278.99	706.01
2007	460 556.2	1 903.1	2 728.19	6 092.06	2 612.54	5 261.56	555.26	1 567.74	547.89	1 447.02
2008	267 113	1 085.8	5 265 .00	5 497.90	1 706.70	1 820.81	1 450.33	1 584.39	452.33	553.08
2009	535 986.7	2 196.7	1 849.02	3 478.01	1 844.09	3 277.14	560.09	1 234.12	560.10	1 201.34
2010	545 633.5	2 254.7	3 289.75	3 306.75	2 319.74	2 808.08	1 207.33	1 412.64	890.24	1 290.87
2011	421 649.7	1 728.1	2 825.33	3 067.46	2 134.02	2 199.42	1 298.59	1 316.19	828.83	866.65
2012	314 667.4	1 295.0	2 212 .00	2 460.69	1 959.77	2 269.13	871.93	1 020.29	724.97	881.17
2013	468 728.6	1 969.5	2 289.51	2 434.48	1 950.01	2 115.98	887.37	1 106.27	815.89	1 057.67
2014	743 913	3 036.4	2 112.13	3 239.36	1 974.38	3 234.68	1 055.88	1 504.48	1 004.93	1 415.19
2015	2 550 538.3	10 453.0	3 258.63	5 178.19	2 850.71	3 539.18	1 419.44	3 156.96	1 408.99	2 308.91
2016	1 267 262.6	5 193.7	3 536.59	3 538.69	2 638.30	3 103.64	2 304.48	2 304.49	1 618.12	1 969.11

数据来源：中国证监会、上海证券交易所、深圳证券交易所。

表18　银行间市场人民币外汇即期交易做市商名单

序号	机构	序号	机构
1	中国工商银行股份有限公司	2	中国农业银行股份有限公司
3	中国银行股份有限公司	4	中国建设银行股份有限公司
5	交通银行股份有限公司	6	中信银行股份有限公司
7	招商银行股份有限公司	8	中国光大银行股份有限公司
9	华夏银行股份有限公司	10	广发银行股份有限公司
11	平安银行股份有限公司	12	兴业银行股份有限公司
13	中国民生银行股份有限公司	14	国家开发银行
15	中国邮政储蓄银行股份有限公司	16	上海银行股份有限公司
17	南京银行股份有限公司	18	宁波银行股份有限公司
19	法国巴黎银行（中国）有限公司	20	上海浦东发展银行
21	星展银行（中国）有限公司	22	美国银行有限公司上海分行
23	汇丰银行（中国）有限公司	24	蒙特利尔银行（中国）有限公司
25	花旗银行（中国）有限公司	26	渣打银行（中国）有限公司
27	三井住友银行（中国）有限公司	28	德意志银行（中国）有限公司
29	瑞穗银行（中国）有限公司	30	三菱东京日联银行（中国）有限公司

资料来源：中国外汇交易中心。

表19 1994—2016年人民币兑外币中间价

年份	美元	欧元	日元	港元	英镑	林吉特	卢布	兰特	韩元	迪拉姆	里亚尔	福林	兹罗提	丹麦克朗	瑞典克朗	挪威克朗	里拉	比索	澳元	加元	新西兰元	新加坡元	瑞士法郎
1994	844.91	—	7.78	112.66	—	—	—	—	—	—	—	—	—	—	—	—	—	—	—	—	—	—	—
1995	831.79	—	8.0703	107.6	—	—	—	—	—	—	—	—	—	—	—	—	—	—	—	—	—	—	—
1996	829.92	—	7.1613	107.19	—	—	—	—	—	—	—	—	—	—	—	—	—	—	—	—	—	—	—
1997	827.98	—	6.3627	106.81	—	—	—	—	—	—	—	—	—	—	—	—	—	—	—	—	—	—	—
1998	827.87	—	7.1719	106.78	—	—	—	—	—	—	—	—	—	—	—	—	—	—	—	—	—	—	—
1999	827.93	—	8.0933	106.51	—	—	—	—	—	—	—	—	—	—	—	—	—	—	—	—	—	—	—
2000	827.81	—	7.2422	106.06	—	—	—	—	—	—	—	—	—	—	—	—	—	—	—	—	—	—	—
2001	827.66	—	6.3005	106.06	—	—	—	—	—	—	—	—	—	—	—	—	—	—	—	—	—	—	—
2002	827.73	863.6	6.9035	106.11	—	—	—	—	—	—	—	—	—	—	—	—	—	—	—	—	—	—	—
2003	827.69	1033.8	7.7263	106.57	—	—	—	—	—	—	—	—	—	—	—	—	—	—	—	—	—	—	—
2004	827.65	1126.3	7.9701	106.37	—	—	—	—	—	—	—	—	—	—	—	—	—	—	—	—	—	—	—
2005	807.02	957.97	6.8716	104.03	—	—	—	—	—	—	—	—	—	—	—	—	—	—	—	—	—	—	—
2006	780.87	1026.7	6.563	100.47	1 532.3	—	—	—	—	—	—	—	—	—	—	—	—	—	—	—	—	—	—
2007	730.46	1066.7	6.4064	93.638	1 458.1	—	—	—	—	—	—	—	—	—	—	—	—	—	—	—	—	—	—
2008	683.46	965.9	7.565	88.189	987.98	—	—	—	—	—	—	—	—	—	—	—	—	—	—	—	—	—	—
2009	682.82	979.71	7.3782	88.048	1 097.8	—	—	—	—	—	—	—	—	—	—	—	—	—	—	—	—	—	—
2010	662.27	880.65	8.126	85.093	1 021.8	46.649	462.05	—	—	—	—	—	—	—	—	—	—	—	—	—	—	—	—
2011	630.09	816.25	8.1103	81.07	971.16	50.279	508.6	—	—	—	—	—	—	—	—	—	—	—	640.93	617.77	—	—	—
2012	628.55	831.76	7.3049	81.085	1 016.1	48.865	485.28	—	—	—	—	—	—	—	—	—	—	—	653.63	631.84	—	—	—
2013	609.69	841.89	5.7771	78.623	1 005.6	54.141	539.85	—	—	—	—	—	—	—	—	—	—	—	543.01	572.59	—	—	—
2014	611.9	745.56	5.1371	78.887	954.37	56.737	905.36	—	—	—	—	—	—	—	—	—	—	—	501.74	527.55	480.34	463.96	—
2015	649.36	709.52	5.3875	83.778	961.5	66.051	1131	—	—	—	—	—	—	—	—	—	—	—	472.76	468.14	444.26	458.75	640.18
2016	693.7	730.68	5.9591	89.451	850.94	64.406	869.06	196.75	17371.0	52.938	54.062	4247.68	60.355	101.71	131.16	124.27	50.757	298.64	501.57	514.06	483.08	479.95	679.89

注：1. 外币兑人民币中间价取当年最后一个交易日的中间价。

2. 人民币兑马来西亚林吉特、俄罗斯卢布、南非兰特、韩国韩元、阿联酋迪拉姆、沙特里亚尔、匈牙利福林、波兰兹罗提、丹麦克朗、瑞典克朗、挪威克朗、土耳其里拉、墨西哥比索汇率中间价采取间接标价法，人民币兑其他10种货币汇率中间价仍采取直接标价法。

数据来源：中国外汇交易中心。

表20　1993—2016年期货市场成交情况

单位：亿元、万手

年份	商品期货市场		金融期货市场	
	成交额	成交量	成交额	成交量
1993	5 521.99	890.69	—	—
1994	31 601.41	12 110.72	—	—
1995	100 565.30	63 612.07	—	—
1996	84 119.16	34 256.77	—	—
1997	61 170.66	15 876.32	—	—
1998	36 967.24	10 445.57	—	—
1999	22 343.01	7 363.91	—	—
2000	16 082.29	5 461.07	—	—
2001	30 144.98	12 046.35	—	—
2002	39 490.16	13 943.26	—	—
2003	108 389.03	27 986.42	—	—
2004	146 935.31	30 569.76	—	—
2005	134 448.38	32 284.75	—	—
2006	210 046.34	44 947.41	—	—
2007	409 722.43	72 842.68	—	—
2008	719 141.94	136 388.71	—	—
2009	1 305 107.20	215 742.98	—	—
2010	2 269 852.69	304 194.19	821 397.94	9 147.66
2011	937 503.93	100 372.53	437 659.55	5 041.62
2012	952 862.59	134 546.42	758 406.878	10 506.18
2013	1 264 695.80	186 827.38	1 410 066.21	19 354.93
2014	1 279 712.50	228 343.25	1 640 169.73	21 758.10
2015	1 356 307.36	323 715.31	4 173 852.33	34 052.95
2016	1 774 124.99	411 943.24	182 191.10	1 833.59

注：2011年起成交量以单边计算；表中数据均不含期转现交易。

数据来源：中国期货业协会。

表21　2003—2016年黄金市场成交情况

单位：亿元、吨

年份	成交金额	成交量
2003	459.2	470.7
2004	731 .0	665.3
2005	1 069.8	906.4
2006	1 947.5	1 249.6
2007	3 164.9	1 828.1
2008	8 683.9	4 457.6
2009	10 288.8	4 710.8
2010	16 157.8	6 051.5
2011	24 772.2	7 438.5
2012	21 506.3	6 350.2
2013	32 133.8	11 614.5
2014	45 891.6	18 486.7
2015	80 083.9	34 067.3
2016	130 240.6	48 676.6

数据来源：上海黄金交易所。

表22 2007—2016年商业银行OTC黄金业务统计表

业务类别		账户金		实物金			其他业务								
产品（单位）		美元账户金（万盎司、亿美元）	人民币账户金（吨、亿元）	自营（吨、亿元）	代理（吨、亿元）	黄金积存、定投（吨、亿元）	黄金租赁（吨、亿元）	黄金拆借（吨、亿元）	黄金质押（吨、亿元）	境内美元报价黄金远期（万盎司、亿美元）	境内美元报价黄金期权（万盎司、亿美元）	境内美元报价黄金掉期（万盎司、亿美元）	境内人民币报价黄金远期（吨、亿元）	境内人民币报价黄金掉期（吨、亿元）	境内人民币报价黄金期权（吨、亿元）
2007年	成交量	157.68	352.71	6.09	3.96	—	33.11	1.20	—	204.93	8.48	—	—	—	—
	成交金额	11.08	607.05	11.20	7.16	—	56.40	2.31	—	11.84	0.60	—	—	—	—
2008年	成交量	293.09	1 332.55	33.12	4.13	—	73.99	11.40	—	574.85	6.28	—	—	—	—
	成交金额	25.37	2 546.30	66.68	8.18	—	141.50	20.16	—	54.44	0.58	—	—	—	—
2009年	成交量	579.96	1 381.16	40.73	3.43	0.54	91.29	7.56	—	162.06	2.29	—	—	—	—
	成交金额	57.34	2 923.48	89.90	7.64	1.30	191.98	15.09	—	15.98	0.22	—	—	—	—
2010年	成交量	418.67	1 205.15	80.40	3.06	12.27	155.80	10.63	0.27	257.82	1.74	—	3.09	—	—
	成交金额	51.47	3 227.49	222.90	8.53	35.29	413.25	28.85	—	32.75	0.21	—	8.78	—	—
2011年	成交量	447.20	1 864.40	129.50	6.16	30.30	301.30	31.99	4.56	407.04	6.06	17.99	5.09	—	—
	成交金额	72.21	6 271.71	428.50	21.49	102.18	970.55	104.92	—	64.69	0.90	2.74	17.59	—	—
2012年	成交量	424.35	1 458.89	126.20	10.55	59.85	465.01	54.80	7.43	1 331.50	61.46	49.93	20.95	—	—
	成交金额	70.71	4 947.18	443.70	41.20	205.82	1 583.70	187.23	—	222.01	10.17	8.35	70.91	—	—
2013年	成交量	497.26	1 864.54	198.63	24.89	298.24	947.65	407.23	39.85	991.99	146.88	524.56	29.76	18.63	—
	成交金额	70.39	5 159.69	618.25	87.76	838.09	2 656.29	1 094.43	78.96	136.48	20.39	75.63	79.86	60.86	—
2014年	成交量	250.37	910.78	91.36	25.16	594.24	1 370.69	474.80	17.14	1 735.95	40.87	341.08	197.29	10.35	0.03
	成交金额	31.59	2 289.79	250.76	94.19	1 483.77	3 438.19	1 180.97	32.83	218.64	5.18	43.68	496.33	26.01	0.07
2015年	成交量	377.34	1 109.83	128.18	27.54	535.02	1 582.71	849.22	27.47	2 414.39	28.74	1 314.93	737.86	309.82	0.31
	成交金额	43.95	2 609.08	321.01	100.54	1 252.41	3 739.06	2 009.87	74.63	281.36	3.37	151.75	1 767.57	7 101.86	0.74
2016年	成交量	685.04	1 889.54	143.47	34.40	463.96	1 827.78	1 242.59	3.42	1 359.40	50.53	1 814.90	799.26	32.01	0.08
	成交金额	86.47	5 064.28	396.04	135.83	1 239.66	4 855.60	3319.76	6.00	168.84	6.34	217.35	2 134.97	85.47	0.21

注：自营、代理品牌金的成交量统计销售量和回购量；黄金积存（黄金定投）成交量统计销售量和赎回量；2007—2013年黄金租赁业务成交量统计黄金租出量和归还量，自2014年起，仅统计黄金租出量；2007—2013年黄金拆借业务统计黄金拆出量和黄金拆入量，自2014年起，仅统计黄金拆出量；黄金质押统计接收质押黄金的重量。

数据来源：中国人民银行上海总部黄金市场监测分析系统。

表23 2006—2016年利率衍生产品交易情况

单位：笔、亿元

年份	普通利率互换		标准利率互换		债券远期		标准债券远期		远期利率协议	
	交易笔数	名义本金额	交易笔数	名义本金额	交易笔数	交易量	交易笔数	交易量	交易笔数	名义本金额
2006	103	355.7	—	—	398	664.5	—	—	—	—
2007	1 978	2 186.9	—	—	1 238	2 518.1	—	—	14	10.5
2008	4 040	4 121.5	—	—	1 327	5 005.5	—	—	137	113.6
2009	4 044	4 616.4	—	—	1 599	6 556.4	—	—	27	60.0
2010	11 643	15 003.4	—	—	967	3 183.4	—	—	20	33.5
2011	20 202	26 759.6	—	—	436	1 030.1	—	—	3	3.0
2012	20 945	29 021.4	—	—	56	166.1	—	—	3	2.0
2013	24 409	27 277.8	—	—	1	1.0	—	—	1	0.5
2014	43 071	40 384.5	207	393	—	—	—	—	—	—
2015	64 812	82 587.3	996	5 024	83	19.6	59	17.2	—	—
2016	87 882	99 307.0	8	8	7	14.9	8	1.0	1	1.0

数据来源：中国外汇交易中心。